Innovation of Food Production Systems
Product Quality and Consumer Acceptance

Prof. dr. P. **van Beek**, professor of operational research at Wageningen Agricultural University, The Netherlands

Prof. ir. A.J.M. **Beulens**, professor of Applied Computer Science at Wageningen Agricultural University, The Netherlands

Dr. ir. M.A.J.S. **van Boekel**, associate professor of Integrated Food Science at Wageningen Agricultural University, The Netherlands

Dr. ir. M. **Dekker**, senior researcher/lecturer of Integrated Food Science at Wageningen Agricultural University, The Netherlands

Dr. J.P. **Hoogland**, Senior researcher at the Agency for the registration veterinary medical products, Wageningen, The Netherlands

Ir. A. **Jellema**, quality management lecturer of Integrated Food Science at Wageningen Agricultural University, The Netherlands

Prof. dr. W.M.F. **Jongen**, professor of Integrated Food Science at Wageningen Agricultural University, The Netherlands

Dr. ir. A.R. **Linnemann**, senior researcher/lecturer of Integrated Food Science at Wageningen Agricultural University, The Netherlands

Dr. H.F.Th. **Meffert**, retired food technologist at the former Sprenger Institute, Wageningen, The Netherlands

Prof. dr. ir. M.T.G. **Meulenberg**, professor of marketing and consumer behaviour at Wageningen Agricultural University, The Netherlands

Dr. H. **de Sitter**, inspector at the Inspectorate for Health Protection, The Hague, The Netherlands

Prof. dr. J.E.B.M. **Steenkamp**, professor of marketing at the Catholic University of Leuven, Belgium and the GfK professor of international marketing research at Wageningen Agricultural University, The Netherlands

Dr. ir. J.C.M. **van Trijp**, consumer behaviour scientist at Unilever Research Laboratory, Vlaardingen, The Netherlands

Prof. dr. J. **Viaene**, professor of agricultural marketing at the University of Gent, Belgium

Innovation of Food Production Systems

Product Quality and Consumer Acceptance

W.M.F. Jongen and M.T.G. Meulenberg (editors)

 *Wageningen* Pers

CIP-data Koninklijke Bibliotheek Den Haag

ISBN 90-74134-51-3 paperback

Subject headings:
Food
Product innovation

First published, 1998

Cover design:
Voorheen De Toekomst

© Wageningen Pers, Wageningen
The Netherlands, 1998

Printed in The Netherlands

Contents

Contents

Contents

1 Introduction.

Innovation of products and services is of paramount importance to food production systems for various reasons. At the global level product innovation is indispensable in order to produce sufficient food for a steadily increasing world population. By contrast in Western countries product innovation has become an important competitive tool of food productions systems in order to maintain or increase market share in a - in terms of volume - saturated market. Product innovation can also contribute to the sustainability of the food system.

The Western food industry seems well aware of the need for product innovation as a continuous process. However, translating this awareness into a systematic strategy and a coherent set of innovation programmes is not yet common practice in this sector. In order to be innovative a food production system depends on a host of factors, both exogenous and endogenous to the company.

The following *exogenous* factors seem to influence food innovation a great deal at present. Sophisticated suppliers, highly demanding food retailers and fierce competition between food companies stimulate innovation as a marketing strategy. Changing consumer demands and needs create market opportunities for new products and services. A continuous stream of scientific and technological inventions offers new opportunities for product development. The abolition of trade barriers and market protection within the European Union and by the World Trade Organization enlarge the market potential of a specific food innovation.

Endogenous characteristics of food production systems determine whether available market opportunities for new products are actually utilised. Crucial to this matter are company characteristics such as market orientation, technological skills and willingness to invest in R&D and new markets. Effective planning and implementation of innovation processes, both within and between companies of a food production system, are also important in this respect.

A great many interesting books have been published recently on innovation in food production systems and on related issues, such as market orientation. Most of these contributions take an economic or a managerial approach to the innovation process (e.g. Dodgson, M., and R. Rothwell (ed.),1994; Traill, B. and K.G.Grunert (ed.), 1997). Many studies have also been made of technological and scientific elements of the innovation process (e.g. Fito et al. (ed), 1997; Heldman, D.R. and D.B.Lund (ed.),1992; Larsson, K. and S.E. Friberg (ed.), 1990). To our knowledge, studies which integrate the economic, managerial and technological elements of the innovation process are still scarce. By adopting a techno-managerial approach to food product innovation, this book is intended as a first step towards filling this gap. It covers the main issues of product innovation, devoting ample attention to both technological and managerial aspects of the innovation process. Important elements of this process are discussed in separate chapters.

The book starts with a chapter on the food production system as a marketing system. It discusses developments in the environment and in the structure of food marketing systems and related strategies. Market orientation, and in particular consumer orientation, is recognized as a basic feature of food marketing systems. Consumer perception of food products and its translation into desirable product characteristics is covered thoroughly in the chapter on the principles and practice of consumer orientation in new product development. The determination of product quality, in particular quality deployment and the house of quality concept receive special attention in a separate chapter. Food product innovation is not simply a one-sided operation, translating consumer wants and needs into a new product. Such a process might occur where innovation consists of slight modification of existing products. However, the extent to which new products can be tailored to consumer needs will usually be constrained by the available technological skills. For that reason a chapter on current developments in food technology is included in the book. Effective control of both production and logistical processes is essential for the maintenance of product quality. This is all the more important since food security has become vital to food marketing, in particular to the image of a brand or company. As a result, one chapter of the book is devoted to an in-depth description of hazard analysis critical control points (HACCP) and risk management in food production systems. Product and service innovation in food production systems profit a great deal from dynamic developments in information and communication technology (ICT). Advances in logistical processes and logistical planning also contribute to food product innovation. In keeping with a broad view of the food innovation process, this book also contains a chapter on basic notions of and important developments in logistics and ICT. Product innovation has to abide by government regulations on production and marketing of food. In this respect not only food and drug laws, but also agreements between the food industry and government, such as on packaging waste and other environmental issues are important. These issues are covered in a chapter on legal aspects of food production and marketing, which pays particular attention to the impact of the EU and Codex on the national food law system.

The outline above indicates the techno-managerial approach to food product innovation which we have adopted in this book. We have structured the main issues into separate chapters and provide the reader with detailed information about new developments in the respective areas. We hope that the book will thus serve as a guide to students of food product innovation, both those studying food technology and those specialising in management of the food industry. The non-technical treatment of the various topics is intended to help in the achievement of this objective.

The Editors.

References

Dodgson, M. and R. Rothwell (ed.), 1994, The Handbook of Industrial Innovation, Edgar Elgar, Publishing Limited, Gower House, Croft Road, Aldershot, Hampshire, England.

Fito, P., E. Ortega-Rodriguez and G.V. Barbosa-Cánovas (ed), 1997, Food Engineering 2000, Chapman and Hall, pp. 416.

Heldman, D.R. and D.B. Lund (ed.), 1992, Handbook of Food Engineering, Marcel Dekker Inc., New York, pp. 756.

Larsson, K. and S. Friberg (ed.), 1990, Food Emulsions, Marcel Dekker Inc., New York, pp. 510.

Traill, B. and K.G. Grunert (ed.), 1997, Product and Process Innovation in the Food Industry, Blackie Academic & Professional, London.

2 Changing food marketing systems in western countries

M.T.G. Meulenberg and J. Viaene

2.1 Introduction

Agricultural and food products have traditionally been marketed through institutionalized markets, such as commodity exchanges, auctions and wholesale markets. Prices are the central coordination mechanisms in such markets. However, agricultural and food markets have changed drastically in the last few decades. Perhaps the most fundamental change is the shift from production to market orientation. In order to establish a strong competitive position in their market, agricultural and food companies have to produce goods and services which match the wants and needs of consumers. In this context the coordination of company decisions in the food marketing system has become extremely important. Consumer orientation, competitive strength and marketing efficiency are key words in agricultural and food marketing. In conjunction with this development, food marketing systems have become more diverse and more sophisticated.

This chapter is concerned with changes in the food marketing system, in particular in the European Union (EU). First, a framework of the marketing system is proposed in order to analyse marketing and markets of agricultural and food products. Afterwards developments in the environment of the food marketing system are reviewed. Subsequently structural developments in food marketing systems are analysed. Attention will be paid to actors in the marketing channel, such as farmers, wholesalers, the food industry and retailers. Marketing strategies which have become important in the European food marketing systems are reviewed. The chapter ends with some conclusions.

2.2 The food marketing system: a framework

Direct marketing from farmer to consumer is the exception rather than the rule in Western countries. Agricultural marketing channels have evolved into food marketing systems consisting of different actors, such as farmer, wholesaler, the food industry and retailer.

Farmer	Farmer	Farmer	Farmer	Industry
Consumer	Middleman	Wholesaler	Wholesaler	Farmer
	Consumer	Retailer	Industry	Industry
		Consumer	Retailer	Retailer
			Consumer	Consumer

Figure 2.1 Basic patterns of food marketing channels

These actors, sometimes organized in a specific way, such as cooperatives, have emerged in the food marketing channel for reasons of effectiveness, efficiency or equity. For instance, dairy cooperatives have been set up in the past in order to: (a) increase marketing *effectiveness*, e.g. by product innovation and better product quality; (b) improve marketing *efficiency* e.g. by economies of scale in processing and logistics, and (c) enlarge *equity* by strengthening farmers' bargaining power vis-à-vis other actors in the marketing channel.

The exchange process for food and agricultural products can take place through institutionalized markets, such as commodity exchanges, auctions and wholesale markets. Other types of exchange processes, such as a direct relationship between producer and retailer, are becoming more popular. The structure of markets and marketing channels has become more diverse and depends on the marketing strategy pursued by the actors of the food marketing system. In some cases food marketing systems need specific inputs within the context of their product policy, and for that reason agribusiness companies, such as mixed feed or seed companies, are becoming a part of the system. In other cases food marketing systems shrink by excluding or integrating companies, e.g. the exclusion or integration of a wholesale company in the exchange process between producer and retailer.

The analysis of food marketing and markets should cover the system of actors involved in the marketing of a food product. In real life there is a great variety of food marketing systems ranging from *conventional marketing channels*, where actors are connected by markets and coordinated by market prices, to *vertical marketing systems*, where actors operate on the basis of a coordinated marketing plan.

Essentially an analysis of food marketing systems is based on the following questions: Which marketing functions are performed? How is the performance of these functions institutionalised? What kind of relationship exists between these institutions? This framework can structure the analysis of current dynamic food marketing systems.

2.2.1 Functions

The performance of marketing functions should be based on a thorough knowledge of the environment of the marketing system. Various aspects of the environment can be differentiated: the *general environment*, which influences medium and long term marketing policies of a company, and the *task environment*, which is relevant in a specific product-market combination. Within the *general environment* a distinction can be made between the economic, demographic, social, political, physical and technological environments. On the demand side, trends in the general environment cause changes in consumer wants and needs with respect to food products and services, and, on the supply side, new systems of production and information. For instance, many agricultural and food companies are interested in future developments in biotechnology and in their acceptance by consumers. These environmental trends determine the opportunities for and threats to food marketing systems in the medium and/or long run.

The *task environment* of a food marketing system consists of: (a) consumers or customers, as well as consumer groups and lobby groups representing societal interests, (b) competitors who operate in the same target market; (c) a government, which both stimulates and regulates agricultural and food marketing. Every product/market combination has a specific task environment. However, task environments of many product-market combinations have developments in common since they result from the same general environment. These common changes in the task environment will be included in our discussion of the general environment.

2.2.2 Institutions

How should the fulfilment of marketing functions be institutionalized, in order to best serve the chosen target group? Should companies differentiate or integrate specific marketing functions and which criteria should be applied for that purpose? In general, such decisions are based on the criteria of *effectiveness, efficiency and equity*. Theories about marketing channel structure use specific criteria which essentially are related to these three basic criteria. For instance, marketing theories about the length of marketing channels, use efficiency/costs criteria (Stigler, 1951; Bucklin, 1965; Mallen, 1977). Effectiveness criteria, such as sales volume and margins, have also been used in theories about channel length (Aspinwall, 1962). Equity criteria, in particular channel power, have been applied in the behavioural analysis of marketing channels (Stern, 1969; Brown et al., 1995).

2.2.3 Relationships

The relationship between actors in the food marketing system is a correlate of the marketing strategy and marketing functions to be performed. In spot markets relationships between actors are weak. They are close in food marketing systems when marketing policies have to be coordinated precisely, such as in the case of marketing private brand names. These relationships between actors in the food marketing system can be informal or legally binding. Consequently, an analysis of food marketing systems has to consider the implications of changing marketing strategies for the relationship between actors in the system.

In summary, the proposed framework for analysing changing food marketing systems perceives the actors involved in the marketing of food products as members of a *marketing system* which has to respond to changes in its environment with an effective marketing strategy. Also, autonomous developments within companies of the system, such as the development of new retail concepts, new processing technologies and breeding methods, will have a strong impact on food marketing. Good *relationships* between the actors of a food marketing system are crucial for good performance.

Figure 2.2

A framework for food marketing systems

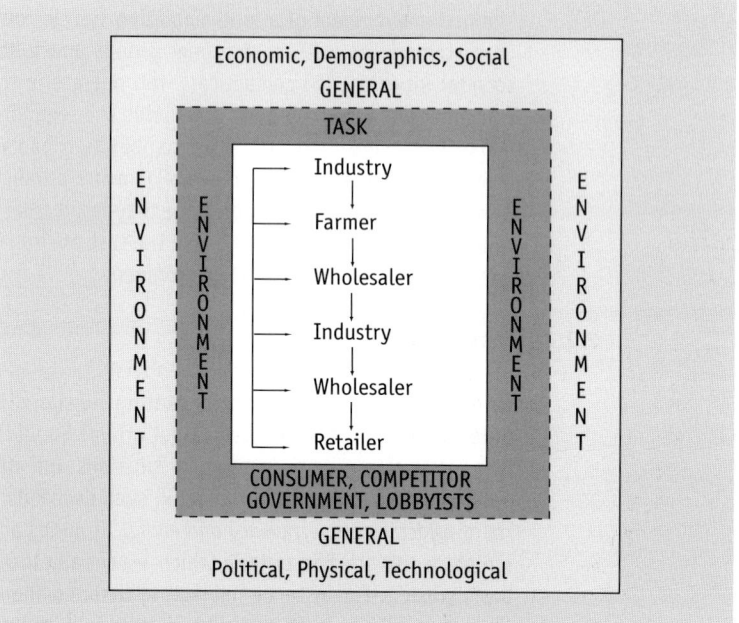

2.3 Developments in the environment of the food marketing system

Changes in the environment of the food marketing system are opportunities and threats for marketing strategies. We will discuss these changes concisely and elaborate some topics. In our exposition we follow the classification outlined in Section 2.2, of economic, demographic, social, political, physical and technological environments.

2.3.1 Economic environment

The economic environment influences marketing strategies of the food system in various ways. Per capita disposable income is a basic determinant of food consumption. Its quantitative impact can be expressed in the income elasticity of food demand. Income elasticities of the demand for generic food products are small in Western countries. This is one of the reasons for saturation in food consumption: the well-known Engel's law states that with increasing income the percentage of consumers' disposable income spent on food decreases (see table 2.1). However, it should be kept in mind that consumer demand for built-in services and for quality is more sensitive to income changes than the demand for food in terms of volume.

Year	Food, drink and tobacco (ECU)	Total consumption (ECU)	Food, drink and tobacco as a % of total consumption
1982 [1]	1137	5059	22,47%
1985 [2]	1169	5613	20,83%
1989 [2]	1661	8227	20,19%
1993 [3]	1852	9924	18,66%

[1] EUR10 [2] EUR12 [3] EUR15 *Source: Eurostat*

Table 2.1 Per capita consumption of food, drink and tobacco in EU (EEC), expressed in ECU and as a % of the total consumption in EEC

The volume of gross domestic product in the EU increased by 2.75% in 1994, and by 3.0% in both 1995 and 1996 (Centraal Planbureau, 1995, p. 38). It is expected that per capita income in Western countries and in many other parts of the world will still increase substantially yet. Some middle and east European countries also realized substantial increases in gross national product, e.g. the gross domestic product of the Visegrad countries (Czech Republic, Hungary, Poland and Slovak Republic) increased by 4.0% in both 1994 and 1995 %, and by 4.5% in 1996 (Centraal Planbureau, 1995, p. 44). The expected future income growth in Western countries creates only modest opportunities for a volume increase of per capita food demand, because of low income elasticities of demand. The Dutch Planning Bureau (Centraal Planbureau, 1992, p. 160) projected an annual increase in food consumption in the Netherlands of between 1.6-2.6% for the period 1991-2015.

Food sales in a country not only depend on average per capita disposable income, but also on income distribution. In fact, it is argued that income distribution in many Western countries is becoming more skewed. While there is a large number of consumers who earn substantial incomes in booming Western economies, the number of low income consumers, such as unemployed people, immigrants and single mothers, is increasing. Greater income inequality increases opportunities for market segmentation in food marketing, such as by providing price conscious consumers with low prices or by providing quality conscious consumers with high quality products.

Another change in the economic environment of food marketing systems is the shift away from government intervention towards the primacy of the market. This is reflected in changing agricultural policies. This point will be elaborated further in our discussion of the political environment.

2.3.2 Demographic environment

The EU population is expected to increase only slightly in the period 1995 to 2000, from 371.5 million to 375.0 million, and is projected to decrease in the first half of the next century, to 337.3 million by 2050 (Euromonitor, 1997, p. 128). This stability (albeit with a slight decrease in population size), reinforces the tendency towards saturation in EU food markets. However, the total world population is expected to grow substantially from 5.7 billion in 1995 to 8.1 billion by 2025 (Bos et al., 1994), which will stimulate global food demand considerably.

Another important demographic development is a greying population: while in the period 1990 - 1995 the EU population increased from 365.7 million to 371.5 million, the number of persons aged 65 years and over increased from 52.7 million to 56.0 million (Euromonitor, 1997, p. 123, 128).

Studies in the United States suggest that there is no fundamental difference between the food consumption pattern of elderly people and of other consumers, except that they normally have a lower and less nutritious food intake and that they need less energy (Senauer, 1991). In the Netherlands the intake of calcium and phosphate by elderly people has been lower than the recommended quantities (Westenbrink, et al., 1989). The greater need of elderly people for food products accompanied by services, both in the stage of purchasing and of preparation, is also important.

Other demographic developments in the EU which are relevant to food marketing systems include smaller families, better education and an increasingly multiracial society.

The trend towards smaller families, where both partners have a job, stimulates the demand for convenience and 'away from home' consumption. In 1991 expenditure on 'away from home' consumption in the EU was highest in Mediterranean countries: per capita expenditure on 'away from home' consumption in 1991 amounted to $760 in Spain, $600 in France and Italy and $460 in Germany and United Kingdom (quoted from Euromonitor by Gaasbeek, 1996, p. 9,10). However, it appears that expenditure on snacks and fast food is higher in Germany and the UK than in Mediterranean countries. The Mediterranean consumers owe their leading position in 'away from home' consumption to frequent visits to restaurants and hotels. European markets for fast food and takeaway meals are expanding.

It has also been observed that per capita consumption of fresh products such as milk, eggs, and potatoes, is negatively correlated with household size. Whether this is the consequence of a higher consumption level or the consequence of more waste is not yet clear (De Hoog, 1992). Food marketing systems respond to the trend toward smaller households, where both partners have a job, by providing better services such as smaller packages and more attractive opening hours of shops. The mushrooming of fast food restaurants in Western countries is also related to demographic developments.

People are becoming better educated. For instance, while 22.7 % of the bread winners of Dutch households had at least high school education in 1983, this figure increased to 31.4% in 1996 (AGB, 1992; GFK, 1996). As a result, consumers are better equipped to understand and integrate information from commercial and non-commercial sources. However, there is not necessarily a strong correlation between education and food consumption behaviour. For instance, no consistent relationship was found between the level of education and quality consciousness with respect to meat consumption (Steenkamp, 1989).

An important demographic development in Western Europe is that society is becoming increasingly multiracial, at least in the big cities. This development stimulates variety in food supply. It increases opportunities for ethnic food marketing.

2.3.3   Social environment

Socio-cultural changes in the EU which are relevant for food consumption are substantial. Heilig (1993, p. 81) draws attention to three major trends in food preferences, which are related to changing values and life styles: the replacement of simple traditional dishes prepared from raw products in the household with refined, industrially produced food; the disappearing seasonal cycle in food consumption and a trend towards 'exotic' food. Future changes in values and lifestyles will have a great impact on food consumption. Popcorn (1992) suggested social trends for the US economy, which seem relevant for the Western food consumer too: cashing out, cocooning, down-ageing, economics, fantasy adventure, 99 lives, save our society (S.O.S.), small indulgences, staying alive, and the vigilante consumer. 'Fantasy adventure' refers to opportunities for emotional values in food products (exotic food, regional products), '99 lives' refers to the fact that consumers like to have a range of foods available which fit specific consumption situations. The 'S.O.S.' trend stimulates the need for sustainably produced food, 'small indulgences' offer opportunities for delicatessen and speciality foods, 'staying alive' fosters consumer interest in healthy food, and the 'vigilante consumer' requires good quality and safe food.

We will discuss two elements of the changing social environment of food marketing systems, namely changes in values and changes in life styles. These seem particularly relevant to innovation in food marketing systems.

Changes in values

Values are the mental representations of important life goals that consumers are trying to achieve. Rokeach (1973) makes a distinction between terminal values, the preferred end state of being (e.g. freedom, self-respect, happiness) and instrumental values, cognitive representations of preferred modes of conduct or behaviour (e.g. competent, courteous, self-reliant) (see Table 2.2).

Various studies have been made of the value systems of European consumers. One study observed much similarity in the ranking of terminal values: happiness, nice family, a world of peace and true friendship ranked highest in the Netherlands, Great Britain, Germany and Italy. Interestingly there was a substantial difference in the ranking of the value 'a beautiful world': 9th in the Netherlands, 6th in Germany, 9th in Italy and lower than 10th in Great Britain (De Waard, 1990, as quoted by Steenkamp, 1992, p. 14).

Discussing changing values in Western civilization, Plummer argues that the self-fulfilment ethic, better quality of life, and 'work to live' are of increasing

Table 2.2	Instrumental Values	Terminal Values
Instrumental and Terminal Values according to Rokeach	**(Preferred modes of behavior)**	**(Preferred end states of being)**
	Competence	Social Harmony
	Compassion	Personal Gratification
	Sociality	Self-actualization
	Integrity	Security
		Love and Affection
		Personal contentedness

Source: Rokeach (1973) as quoted by Peter and Olson (1993, p. 98)

importance (Plummer, as quoted by Engel et al. 1995, p. 627). Increasing importance of these values influences consumers' perception and evaluation of product and production systems, in particular the importance of sustainability (animal welfare, food safety, package waste and manure problems) in product evaluation. Consumers do not only demonstrate their environmental concern by their food consumption behaviour, but also articulate their concern by joining consumers' groups and environmental lobbies (e.g. Rifkin, 1992). The impact of these groups on environmentally friendly food production and marketing is substantial.

Understanding the impact of values on food consumption is important for marketing strategy. A model which centres on the relationship between values and product characteristics is the means-end chain model. According to Peter and Olson (1993, p. 100): 'Researchers have developed several means-end chain models of consumers' knowledge structure. Despite different terminology, each model includes the three levels of product meaning discussed above - knowledge about attributes, consequences (benefits or risks), and values. Each means-end model proposes that consumers form meaningful associations that link product attributes with consequences and values.'

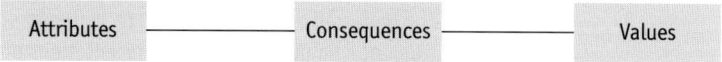

Many means-end chain analyses have been made for food products (e.g. van den Abeele, 1992).

Changes in life styles

Life styles, a summary construct defined as *'patterns in which people live and spend time and money'* (Engel, et al., 1995, p. 449), are related to consumption patterns. While values are relatively enduring, life styles change more rapidly (Engel, et al., 1995, p. 449). They are measured on the basis of activities, interests and opinions of people. Food-related life styles have been analysed in some detail. For instance, it has been reported that the company General Foods identified a segment of health-conscious consumers and repositioned its Sanka brand of decaffeinated coffee towards that group of consumers (Engel, et al., 1995, p. 454). Recently research has been done by Grunert et al. on food related life styles, defined as: '...non-product specific traits of people's purchasing motives, quality aspects, shopping habits, cooking methods, and consumption situations with regard to food.' (Grunert, et al. 1996, p. 49). On the basis of data from France, Germany and Great Britain these authors differentiated seven food-related life styles: the uninvolved food consumer, the careless food consumer, the moderate food consumer, the conservative food consumer, the rational food consumer, the hedonistic food consumer, the adventurous food consumer. The French consumer appeared to be a more hedonistic, and uninvolved or careless consumer, and the adventurous consumer was more important in Germany and Great Britain (Grunert, et al., op. cit.).

Fischler (1993, p. 58) summarized socio-cultural trends in food consumption: 'The socio-cultural context of culinary systems ...which traditionally determined what should be eaten, by whom, and when, has rapidly changed. Social norms are eroding or loosening. In all developed countries, market research shows the existence of a trend towards apparently unstructured food intake. In France, for instance, in a growing part of the population, the structure of the traditional food pattern tends to become less constraining (length of meals, number of dishes, snacking, skipping courses or meals, etc.).'

These socio-cultural changes create opportunities for and threats to the food marketing system. They stimulate new product development, repositioning of products and the addition of services with the product.

2.3.4 Political environment

The following changes in the political environment of the food marketing system seem important for marketing strategies: (a) more open international markets; (b) decreasing government support to agriculture; and (c) increasing concern of government about environment and health issues.

a) The rules to which member countries of the GATT are committed by the Uruguay Round, concluded in December 1993, lead to more open world markets. The main commitments are (see Anania, 1997, p. 162):
   - reduction of market intervention (measured by an Aggregate Measure of Support) by 20% over the six-year implementation period;
   - improved market access through replacement of non-tariff barriers by 'equivalent' tariffs, and through reduction of the tariff's unweighted average by at least 36% within a period of six years;
   - reduction of subsidised exports by 21% and reduction of the subsidy expenditure by 36% over a period of six years up till 2001.
b) Total Common Agricultural Policy (CAP)-related expenditure amounted to about 40 billion ECU in 1995, within an overall budget of about 75 billion ECU. The agricultural expenditure of the EU is criticized by some

member states because of the excessive costs of the CAP.

The CAP reform of 1992, the 'MacSharry' reform, consisted of three parts: a reduction of the market intervention price for cereals by approximately 30 %, combined with compensatory income support payments per ha; a 15 % reduction in the market intervention price for beef within three years; a number of accompanying measures related to environmentally friendly production, afforestation of farm land and early retirement schemes (SER, 1996).

The costs of CAP will, *other things remaining equal*, increase as a result of the forthcoming EU membership of some middle and east European states. As a result, more changes are in the offing and the CAP will probably shift further from market intervention to income support. Total agricultural expenditures of the CAP are projected by the European Commission to increase from 43.3 million ECU in 1990, to 50.0 billion ECU in 2005 (Commissie van de Europese Gemeenschappen, 1997, p. 95).

c) Governments are becoming increasingly concerned about the sustainability of the physical environment and the viability of rural areas. Agricultural policies are complemented by rural and environmental policies. Environmental policies of governments comprise constraints to production and marketing (environmental rights), eco-taxes, environmental covenants, and eco-labelling programmes. There is no one way solution for environmental problems. Many governments combine different types of policies: 'push strategies' which stimulate businesses to pursue environmentally friendly methods of production and marketing; 'pull strategies' which stimulate consumers to search for environmentally friendly products and 'interface strategies' which try to make market supply more transparent with respect to environmental friendliness.

2.3.5 Physical environment

The degradation of the ecological environment is a societal problem, which is relevant to agriculture, the food industry and society at large. Many consumers are aware of environmental problems, but are not knowledgeable in this respect, let alone behave in an environmentally friendly way. Consumers cannot distinguish the environmental friendliness of a product as such. It is a 'credence' attribute which has to be differentiated in the market by information provided with the product (such as by a label or a type of shop). Since environmental friendliness offers no hedonistic utility, but satisfaction from socially responsible behaviour, this attribute is difficult to market. However, consumers appreciate environmental friendliness also, since this product attribute is perceived to be associated with animal friendliness and health (Oude Ophuis, 1992, p. 37) Limited consumer awareness and appreciation of environmental friendliness of food products makes the promotion of environmentally friendly behaviour by consumer groups and by environmental lobbies important.

In this context it should be noted that environmental friendliness is not only difficult to evaluate for consumers but also for experts. Experts sometimes have different opinions about the urgency of environmental problems, such as global warming, and about the methodology of measuring environmental problems, e.g. life cycle analysis (e.g. Guinée, et al., 1993, as quoted in Simmons, p.254). Simmons (1996, p 252) argues: '..environmental problems cannot be defined exclusively in terms of objective physical processes. Just as they have their origins in particular patterns of social activity, so their significance and meaning for us is socially negotiated. The 'environment' is no longer something external to society but is, in a very real sense, implicated in the complex patterns of social and economic activity in which we engage.'

Ecological aspects are particularly important for specific food marketing systems, such as the production and marketing of pigs and poultry. The wave of biotechnological inventions has also triggered discussion about the sustainability of food marketing systems.

2.3.6   Technological environment

During the past fifty years food marketing systems have experienced a great many innovations, both process and product innovations. Technological developments are expected to change future food marketing systems a great deal. New findings in the fields of information technology (IT), computer science, biotechnology, and transportation methods will be introduced into the food marketing system. Key areas in food preservation and processing include irradiation, micro filtration, microwave pasteurisation, extrusion cooking and high-pressure processing. In addition, biotechnology offers a new spectrum of opportunities. A major packaging trend is packaging under modified and controlled atmosphere, preferably using recyclable or biodegradable materials.

These technological developments create opportunities for new products and services, and are instrumental in decreasing marketing and production costs. Advances in information technology will also improve the speed and precision of exchange processes. New exchange methods, such as marketing through the Internet, will emerge. Computerization of production and logistical processes will further reduce production and marketing costs and increase the flexibility of food marketing systems. Advances in biotechnology enlarge opportunities for new products which fit specific needs, e.g. with respect to health and environment. However, many European consumers (or at least consumer groups) seem to be suspicious about the health characteristics of food produced by modern biotechnological methods. The enormous potential of new technologies in food preservation, processing and packaging have to be analysed, taking into account relations with the consumer and the market structure (Viaene & Gellynck, 1996). It is of major importance to the food industry that consumer resistance and prejudice concerning innovation be overcome. It is vital to know whether a technologically new food product or packaging responds to consumers' needs or will be accepted by the consumer in order to determine its economic feasibility. A major task lies in closing the communication gap between the scientist, technologist, and the consumer. The technological know-how has to be translated in understandable and acceptable terms for the consumer. The consumer has to be able to make choices based on credible and widely available information.

2.4 Changing actors in the food marketing system

Changes of actors in food marketing systems are to a large extent a response to a changing environment. Food marketing systems are also changing because of autonomous developments of actors themselves: companies invent new technologies and concepts which are transformed into product/process innovations in the food marketing system.

There is a great diversity of actors in Western food marketing systems. Nevertheless many actors show similar developments. An important one is the move towards consumer orientation. Therefore we start our discussion of actors in the food marketing system with the food retailer, being nearest to the consumer.

2.4.1 Food retailers

Trends in European food retailing since World War II basically concern the effectiveness and efficiency of policies, processes and organizations.

Effectiveness of food retailers: marketing policies

Food retail companies have become more market oriented. They are increasingly concerned with how to serve customers best through specific marketing policies. The width and depth of the product assortment are the cornerstone of the marketing policy of a food retailer. This marketing policy is reflected in the type of store, such as supermarket, hypermarket, speciality shop or discount store (see Figure 2.3).

Figure 2.3
Store type as a function of Width and Depth of assortment

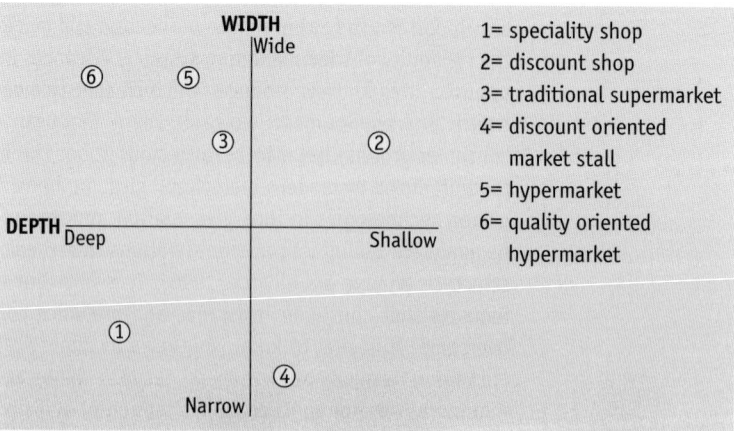

1= speciality shop
2= discount shop
3= traditional supermarket
4= discount oriented market stall
5= hypermarket
6= quality oriented hypermarket

Decisions with respect to the assortment, and its 'width and depth', have implications for other marketing instruments, such as price, promotion, location and opening hours. For instance, the wide and shallow assortment of discount stores goes along with a low retail price. The policy of a narrow and deep assortment by speciality shops leads to high retail prices.

Targeting of specific market segments, such as 'hurried consumers' or 'price-conscious consumers', is a core element of many retailers' strategies. Positioning vis-à-vis competitors in the target market has become a strategic issue too.

Food retailers are constantly searching for new products and services, and adapt to changing markets. Options include longer opening hours, delivery at home, selling prepared meals and a location at convenient spots (e.g. petrol stations).

While mass distribution by supermarkets has become the dominant type of food retailing, the speciality shop has expanded to complement mass distribution by supermarkets. The increasing attention paid by food retailers to fresh produce is often implemented by setting up shops within the shop, which carry wide and sometimes even deep assortments. In this way retailers respond to consumer demand for the convenience of one-stop shopping and to the need for quality and variety.

Retailers benefit from new opportunities by introducing innovative retail formulas. Recent developments include home-delivery, drive-ins, automatic food dispensers, food shops in petrol and railway stations. These new distribution formulas offer a wide variety of choices and respond to the demand for availability of food wherever and whenever the consumer wishes.

Although retailing through the Internet is still at a very early stage in Europe, it is expected to have potential for the future. The consumer is also becoming increasingly familiar with technology, which offers new opportunities for technology-based in-store promotions and advertising.

Efficiency of food retailing; efficient logistics

Retail costs per unit of product will (other things remaining equal) increase when assortments are broadened and services are increased. Consequently the shift towards larger supermarkets is reinforcing the efficiency drive of supermarkets. Low price strategies, such as discounting, also stimulate efficiency and the search for low purchase prices by food retailers.

Efficiency improvements in food retailing are in particular pursued by logistical planning. The paramount importance of logistical efficiency is obvious in view of the large number of items per store and the number of outlets per food chain. Aldi have about 600 lines, Warehouse clubs typically about 3500, Carrefour about 5000 grocery lines, Casino about 9000, Sainsbury and Tesco stores between 10,000 and 20,000 lines (Corstjens and Corstjens, 1995, p. 197). Albert Heijn, a food chain of the Dutch holding Ahold, had 665 stores in 1997. Minimizing inventory costs, e.g. by converting storage floor space in supermarkets to sales floor space, by efficient transport routing, standardization of pallets and package size are devices to improve logistical efficiency. Technological innovations are helpful in this respect. For instance, advances in Information Technology, such as the use of bar-codes, scanning at check-outs and electronic data interchange have contributed to efficient sales monitoring and ordering processes.

In logistical planning, concepts and models such as Just in Time (JIT), and route planning models contribute to higher efficiency. Logistical efforts of food retailers have decreased the lead time from supplier to food store substantially. (Table 2.3)

Table 2.3
Lead-time from supplier to distribution centre (DC) and from distribution centre (DC) to store in the Dutch food chain Albert Heijn

Leadtime	Supplier/DC	DC/Store
Past	120-48 hours	48-36 hours
Present	48-24 hours	18-12 hours
Future	12- 4 hours	18- 4 hours

Source: Willemse, J.N. (1996)

Logistical costs have also decreased through contracting-out of logistical functions. This is particularly the case in the UK, where already in 1989 specialist contractors were responsible for about 44% of retail logistics for grocery multiples (Cooper, et al., 1994, p.114).

Low purchase prices are an important ingredient of a low-cost retail strategy. The strong bargaining power of retail chains vis-à-vis suppliers is important in this respect. In fact, food retail chains have substantial bargaining power because:

Table 2.4
European food retailing groups: top 10 by turnover

Company	Listing	Turnover billion US $	Net income million US $	Mkt. cap. billion US $
Metro [1]	Germany	31.19	235.72	4.97
Carrefour	France	27.82	680.17	13.13
Promodès	France	19.24	192.74	4.76
Karstadt	Germany	17.51	123.01	3.09
J. Sainsbury	UK	17.15	808.61	10.47
Ahold	Netherlands	16.86	238.27	6.22
Tesco	UK	15.25	573.8	9.11
P'Printemps	France	14.97	290.46	6.81
Casino	France	12.33	121.76	2.41

[1] formerly Asko and Kaufhof
Source: Poole (1997, p. 8) Adapted from Financial Times (1996a)

- food retail chains have become big companies purchasing products in oligopsonistic markets. As a result they are attractive clients for food manufacturers.

  In some cases concentration of purchasing by retail chains has been even extended to international alliances of retail companies, such as the German group Gedelfi, consisting of the chains DAGAB, Spar, Karstadt, Allkauf, Norma and Unigro (Patt, 1993, p. 86).

- there is a surplus of production capacity in Western agriculture and food industry. The CAP of the EU has stimulated production. Notwithstanding the production limitation by quota (milk, sugar), and the recent shift from market support to income support, there is still productive over-capacity. In the discussion paper of the European commission for the year 2000 it is argued that overproduction in agriculture should be further decreased by reducing price support (Commissie van de Europese Gemeenschappen, 1997).

- most food producers supply products to the market which are only to a limited extent unique. Many innovations are modifications of existing products. Competitors imitate successful products before long. As a result food retail chains can select from a great many alternatives.

In view of the strong bargaining power of retail chains it is extremely important for food manufacturers to build a close relationship with food retailers. The Food Marketing Institute argues that this relationship should be guided by the following principles: 'Focus on providing better value to consumers,...Move from win/lose to win/win...Develop accurate and timely information....Maximize value-adding processes....Develop a common and consistent performance and reward system...'. ECR (Efficient Consumer Response) has become an important concept to frame the relationship between supplier and food retailers. The cost and financial savings to be made by ECR are categorized as efficient assortment, efficient replenishment, efficient promotion, and efficient product introduction (Kahn and McAlister, 1997, p. 64, 66).

The market share of own brands is steadily increasing. While own brands in leading UK food chains, such as Sainsbury, Tesco and Marks and Spencer, already accounted for more than 50% of total turnover in 1991, this figure was still substantially lower in other West European countries (quoted by Corstjens and Corstjens, op. cit., p. 146, 149). Own brands increasingly dominate in many generic food and beverage categories. Own brands are lower priced, but nevertheless, because of low purchasing costs, carry attractive margins for retailers. While in the past own brands were introduced as the cheap alternative to many cheap producer brands, there is currently a growing tendency to position these as products of good quality, which are cheaper than national brands.

Figure 2.4 (Datamonitor, 1996) indicates how the market share of retailer brands in the food market increased during the period 1975-1995.

Figure 2.4

Own brand share of
grocery business
1995 vs 1975

*Source: Datamonitor
(1996, p. 40)*

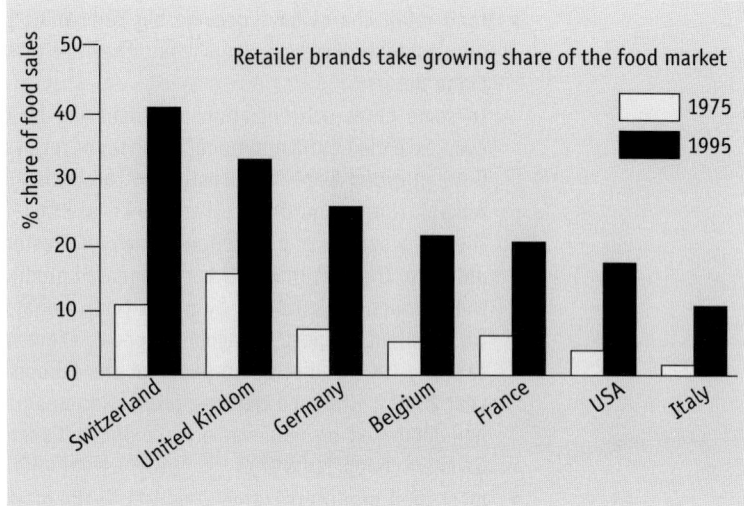

Organisation of food retailing: institutional dynamics

A dynamic organisational structure is also a characteristic of modern food retailing. Food retailing has shifted from small independent outlets, grocery stores, greengrocers, butchers' shops or bakeries to large food chains. During the period 1984 - 1994, large and middle-sized distribution chains (both big retail companies and voluntary chains) continuously increased their market share in many Western countries. This increase in market share is at the expense of the market share of the small independent and traditional shops, whose share in the retail market decreased, e.g. the market share of small independents and traditional shops in Belgium decreased from 19.2% in 1984 to 12.1% in 1994, while the market share of the two largest food retail groups (GIB and Delhaize) increased from 31% in 1982 to about 50% in 1996.

The dominant type of enterprise in food retailing has become the food chain operating in national and international markets. Some food retail chains are in turn a member of a holding company which owns different types of retail chains, sometimes even other types of business. A minor group of small independents remains competitive as speciality shops.

Wholesaler sponsored voluntary chains, such as Spar, have become important in food retailing: independent food retailers often have a contractually binding relationship with a food wholesaler. This relationship between independent retailers and a wholesaler combines the advantages of central planning and purchasing by the wholesaler with the personal motivation of retailers who own their store. In some instances policies of wholesaler and retailers have not been coordinated sufficiently to make voluntary food chains competitive.

Other independent food retailers have joined a *retailer-sponsored volun-*

tary chain, in order to compete with large food chains. In this type of voluntary chain retailers not only cooperate in purchasing but also in marketing strategy and management.

Still other independents have joined a *franchise organization* in order to survive. A franchise organization consists of:

- a *franchiser*, e.g. McDonald's which owns a franchise concept in fast-food selling, or a big retail chain which owns a franchise concept in mass food retailing.
- *franchisees*, independent entrepreneurs who lease the franchise concept. Franchisers select franchisees on the basis of criteria which are related to the sales potential of the franchisee, such as location of the outlet and managerial capacities of the franchisee. Franchise contracts specify marketing and management procedures to be implemented by the franchisee. These include the product assortment, price level, service, store atmosphere and trade name. Franchisees pay an entrance fee and royalties to the franchiser. A precise specification of the relationship is very helpful to position a franchise organization in its target market.

Consumer cooperatives in food retailing, which started in Rochdale UK in 1844, are still important in Scandinavia and in Switzerland and Italy, but are only of minor importance in many other European countries.

Internationalisation, both international expansion of retail companies and international purchasing agreements through buying groups and alliances, is another organisational feature of modern food retailing. Retail chains such as Aldi (Germany), Intermarché (France), Marks & Spencer (U.K.), Delhaize (Belgium) and Ahold (Netherlands) have internationalized substantially. This process reinforces competition in food retailing.

2.4.2 Food manufacturers

The size of the EU food, drink and tobacco industry is substantial. Its growth rate, however, is decreasing (Table 2.5).

Table 2.5
The EU food, drink and tobacco industry (billions of ECUs, current prices)

	1980	1985	1990	1992	1993	annual change (%) 1983-1988	forecast annual (%) 1988-1992	1993-1997
Production	256	338	412	454	456	3.2	3.0	1.5
Exports to outside EU	N.A.	25	25	28	25	2.3	4.2	3.5
Trade balance	1	4	5	7	5			
Apparent consumption	255	334	407	447	452	2.1	3.0	1.5

Source: Heijbroek, et al. 1995, p. 25

In 1988 Linda (1988, p.130) characterized the European food industry as follows: '(a) widely diversified, this process having dramatically accelerated since 1980; (b) diversification may take place in the form of *product extensions*, limited to a single geographical area. ... more frequently the main objective is to enter a spatially distinct market geographic diversification; it is more appropriate to speak of a functional diversification process propelled by multiple interdependent industrial commercial and financial factors; (c) diversification is the only reliable and practical means for increasing the size as well as the global power of the firm; (d) in the present world of *global competition* research and development is the real *engine* of competitive performance and growth. As a matter of fact, R&D is increasingly *converging* and *commonly orientated*, since it is possible and even economically necessary to *split up* the R&D output between a wide and growing number of market sectors and countries; (e) with respect to the performance of food manufacturing firms, it is evident that they are highly connected with the competitiveness of market structures, the retailing and distributive networks.'

Mergers, joint companies and new ventures in the food manufacturing industries represent the means for materializing the diversification process. Linda (1988, p. 143, 144) distinguished different degrees of diversification: (a) *monosectoral firms* dealing either in foods or in drinks only; (b) food and drinks conglomerates; (c) mega firms which are 'distribution and services' orientated; (d) *Polycentric groups*. Their growth is based upon two or more 'poles' of diversified activity, one of which is food and/or drink manufacturing.

About ten years later, in 1997, it looks as if the trend towards diversification is being reversed. Companies are increasingly focusing on *core competencies* and expanding in international markets. For instance, the Anglo-Dutch multinational Unilever shed its chemical activities and is concentrating on food and human-care products. The Dutch company Nutricia is focusing on baby- and health foods in international markets. The UK holding Hillsdown specialises in chilled food production.

It looks as if such developments will lead to further concentration within the food industry but this is not clear yet. The top 100 food companies in Europe had a turnover of 350 billion dollars in 1993, representing 62% of total production in the industry and the 15 largest had a market share of over 31% (Heijbroek, et al., 1995, p. 25). A recent study concludes, '...tales of a structural revolution in the food industry are exaggerated. ...In fact, we have found it in only two countries, Denmark and the Netherlands, and in a small number of subsectors...' (Gilpin, et al., 1997, p. 21).

Internationalisation of the food industry is continuing. Food companies, such as Danone, Nestlé and Unilever have already been operating on an international scale for a long time. Today, companies which have traditionally set up their production plants and management facilities in the domestic market are also steadily internationalizing businesses. A case in point are dairy cooperatives, such as MD foods in Denmark, Sodiaal in France, Campina Melkunie in the Netherlands and Avonmore in Ireland.

A characteristic of today's food industry is the importance of product *innovation*. One indication of this is the fact that the world's twenty leading manufacturers of packaged foods generated 28% of their current annual sales from new products introduced in the previous five years (Datamonitor, 1996).

The relationship of food companies with clients is intensified because of specific customer needs regarding products and services. While food companies in the USA, such as Kraft Food and General Mills relied in the past on their product quality and promotional skills, they now try to base their position in the market on a close relationship with the customer in so-called customer business teams (Kahn, McAlister, 1997, p. 79).

Out-sourcing, on the increase in many sectors, is also gaining importance in food manufacturing. Examples include the out-sourcing of logistical operations and the out-sourcing of food component production by food companies which produce 'ready to eat' meals.

2.4.3 Wholesale companies

Wholesalers traditionally perform important functions in food marketing systems by 'sorting out, accumulation, allocation, and assorting', the elements of the sorting principle of Alderson (1957, p.195). Wholesale companies have adapted themselves to changes in the food marketing system. The need for 'sorting out' and 'accumulation' has decreased because of concentration and standardization in agricultural production. For instance, in egg marketing there is no longer a need for an assembling wholesaler who collects eggs from poultry farms since farm size has increased substantially. In some sectors the wholesale functions of 'allocation' and 'assorting' have been integrated by other channel actors, such as by food retail chains.

While losing business in some food marketing systems, wholesalers remain important actors in many others. In particular, they play an important role in markets for fresh produce and in markets with a heterogeneous product supply, such as cattle markets. They have sometimes even strengthened their market position, by responding appropriately to the market challenges. Types of evolution in wholesaling are:
- big wholesale companies, which buy and sell at an international, sometimes global scale. Their core competencies are market knowledge, international or even global relational networks and logistical capacities. They profit from more open international markets. Globally operating grain merchants are a case in point.
- wholesale companies, which have a special relationship with their suppliers can be an attractive marketing partner because of their market knowledge and their logistical capacities. Food brokers and agents operating on behalf of a foreign food company are examples.
- wholesale companies specialising in specific aspects of the exchange process, such as cash and carry wholesalers. Cash and carry wholesalers operate in the food trade, e.g. Makro, but also in the flower trade.

- wholesale companies which differentiate themselves by superior quality and/or services, sometimes even by own brands. This type of wholesaling is important in the wine and cheese trade.
- wholesale companies with both forward and backward linkages in the food marketing system. Wholesaler sponsored voluntary chains already mentioned before, are an example of forward integration by wholesalers.

2.4.4 Farmers

The trends in West European agriculture are specialisation and concentration. The number of farms is steadily decreasing and farm size is increasing. Farmers specialize in milk production, pig raising, broiler production or flower growing. Specialisation is stimulated by economies of scale in production. This is accompanied by concentration into larger farms. The degree of specialisation and concentration in farming varies between countries and regions. The trend seems important in specific parts of Europe, such as the Benelux countries, some parts of Germany, Italy, and France, whereas other parts of Europe, such as the Alpine regions, are still characterized by small mixed farms.

Since family farms are often too small to develop individual marketing policies, they often join marketing cooperatives or build special relationships with wholesalers, food manufacturers or retailers. At present these relationships are becoming increasingly based on the market orientation of farmers. Societal concern about the viability of rural communities and about ecological problems caused by modern agricultural practices have stimulated interest in organic farming. In view of the limited size of organic farming, marketing of ecological and regional products is still a niche operation in many European countries.

2.4.5 Specific marketing institutions

In some food marketing systems specialised marketing institutions operate which perform specific marketing functions, such as price discovery, or even the total marketing operation for an agricultural/food product on behalf of a group of farmers.

- Auctions contribute to the price discovery process in agricultural markets. Dutch auctions (auction starts at an offer price higher than any bidder is willing to pay and which is lowered until a bidder accepts the offer) are used in markets for fresh horticultural products, flowers, fruits and vegetables and fish. English auctions (auctions start at a low offer price; bids are publicly made; a bidder who makes the highest bid receives the offer) are used for selling other products including cattle. Auctions also fulfil an important logistical function by concentrating physical supply and demand.
  Product differentiation and relationship-marketing diminish opportuni-

ties for selling through auctions since no special relationship between supplier and buyer can be developed. On the other hand, better communication facilities increase the accessibility of the auction process, and therefore the opportunity for auctioning a standardized product at an international scale.

- Futures markets have been popular in the US for a long time as a mechanism for hedging price risks for commodities such as corn, soybeans and wheat. Commodity futures exchanges are, as yet, of limited importance in European food marketing systems. Various developments in European food marketing systems may stimulate the interest in commodity futures trading:
  - larger, more specialized farms whose income depends on one product and which operate in more open markets and receive less price support from the CAP.
  - larger food companies, which are concerned about price risks in purchasing agricultural inputs.

  Futures markets have been started, or will start soon, in many European countries, including Hungary, Germany and Spain.

- Various marketing institutions perform marketing of agricultural products on behalf of producers. Important institutions in this respect are farmers' cooperatives. In some countries the relevant Marketing Boards market (or marketed) the product of a particular agricultural sector.

Cooperatives started out as organizations, which tried to improve farmers' product prices by increasing the bargaining power of farmers, or by introducing better quality and quality maintenance of food products. They are defined as user-owned and user-controlled businesses that distribute benefits on the basis of use (Barton, 1989). Three concepts distinguish cooperatives from other businesses: a) the user-owner principle: persons who own and finance the cooperative are those that use it, b) the user-control principle: control of the cooperative is by those who use the cooperative and c) the user-benefits principle: benefits of the cooperative are distributed to its users on the basis of their use. Cropp and Engelsbe (1989) indicate potential classifications of cooperatives based on functions performed, structural arrangements, organizational or financial structure.

The shift towards market orientation in food marketing requires cooperatives to adopt a customer oriented marketing policy. A cornerstone of such policy is an agricultural supply of farmer-members which coincides with the marketing concept of the cooperative processing or marketing company. Farmers' willingness to invest in the cooperative, in particular in its markets and R&D is also essential for the success of such a policy. Adoption of modern marketing and management procedures by cooperatives influences the cooperative structure. The following organizational changes, due to a number of factors including the shift toward market orientation, can be observed:

- increase in company size,
- quality of management improves and the rights and responsibilities of top management are better defined;
- special financial structures are developed to generate the necessary risk-bearing capital for the cooperative enterprise.
- some cooperatives have transformed their companies into limited companies, whose shares, or at least a majority of shares, are in the hands of the cooperative union/farmer-members.

These developments enhance a more rational and less emotional relationship between farmers, in particular young and modern farmers, and their cooperative.

In various countries *agricultural marketing boards* and *commodity boards* contribute to the marketing of food and agricultural products of a sector. Marketing boards which are responsible for the total marketing operation of an agricultural or food product are the exception rather than the rule in Western countries. However, promotional boards which support the marketing of generic food products have been set up in many European countries. Sopexa in France and CMA in Germany are examples. Product differentiation and large company size stimulate marketing efforts for the individual company brands at the expense of marketing efforts for the generic products of a sector. On the other hand, new marketing problems are emerging for some food products, such as the poor image of meat, and these have to be tackled by marketing activities of the sector.

Table 2.6
Market shares of agricultural cooperatives in the EU

Market shares (%)	dairy	fruit & vegetables	meat	farm inputs	credit	grain
Belgium	50	70-90	20-30			–
Denmark	93	20-25	66-93	64-59		87
Germany	55-60	60	30	50-60	–	–
Greece	20	12-51	5-30			49
Spain	35	15-40	20	–	–	20
France	49	35-50	27-88	50-60	–	75
Ireland	100	–	30-70	70		69
Italy	38	41	10-15	15	–	15
Luxembourg	80	–	25-30	75-95	–	70
Netherlands	82	70-96	35	40-50	84	
Austria	90	–	50	–	–	60
Portugal	83-90	35	–	–	–	–
Finland	94	–	68	40-60	34	–
Sweden	99	60	79-81	75	–	75
U.K.	98	35-45	± 20	20-25	–	20

Source: Bekkum, O.F. van en G. van Dijk Eds., (1997, p. 29)

2.5 Basic strategies of food marketing systems

Changes in the environment of food marketing systems and in major actors of these systems have been discussed above. Many of these changes are related to the shift of food marketing systems from selling commodities to marketing differentiated products which suit the needs of a chosen target group. Conditions which ensure the success of such a shift include market orientation and effective coordination of policies in the food marketing system. In addition to these, some other strategic developments can be observed in food marketing systems. They are briefly reviewed below.

2.5.1 Market orientation

Market orientation, '...the organization wide generation of market intelligence, pertaining to current and future customer needs, dissemination of the intelligence across departments, and organization wide responsiveness to it' (Kohli & Jaworski, 1990, p. 6, Grunert, et al., p.11), has become indispensable in food marketing systems, since food markets have become buyers' markets. A market orientation implies first of all that companies monitor and analyse their target markets in a systematic way. In the past much information on agricultural and food markets was collected and disseminated for the generic product, say butter or cheese. Since many companies in the food marketing system are trying to differentiate their product, information on specific product-market combinations has become a must. Markets are monitored on the basis of factory sales, household panel data and/or retail panel data. Many food companies use taste panels and do 'ad hoc' consumer research. Market orientation of a company does not only imply systematic collection and processing of market data, but also effective dissemination of information to decision makers. In particular, a good balance should be struck between keeping decision makers informed and avoiding information overload.

Companies which are market oriented and have a well-organized market information system (consisting of a data bank, statistical bank, model bank and a retrieval system), are still scarce in food marketing systems (Grunert, et al., 1996, 13-17, 247). Clearly, poor market information systems are not unique to food marketing systems, but are a problem in many other industries too (Campen van, et al., 1991).

An essential element of market orientation is also that a company responds effectively to market changes. Such responsiveness depends both on the attitude of management and on the production and marketing capacities of a company, all of which still require substantial improvement in food marketing systems.

2.5.2 Policy coordination, chain strategies

Market orientation enhances companies' ability to produce and market foods and services which coincide with the needs and wants of specific target groups. In order to serve the needs and wants of targeted consumer groups, the decision making of actors in the food marketing system has to be well-coordinated. Coordination of supply and demand by market prices is often not precise enough in present markets and additional coordination mechanisms are used, such as 'mutual adjustment, direct supervision, standardization of work processes, standardization of outputs, standardization of skills/knowledge, standardization of norms' (Mintzberg, 1989; see for a concise discussion: Douma and Schreuder, 1991, p. 37). The choice of a coordination mechanism depends on the transaction costs involved.

Coordination of policies in food marketing systems may lead to a joint strategy of two or more subsequent companies in the system, say 'farmer plus marketing cooperative' or 'pig farmer plus slaughterhouse plus retailer'. Such coordination can be implemented in different ways, for instance through an informal or a contractual agreement. The distinction in the marketing channel literature between administered, contractual and corporate vertical marketing systems (see e.g. Stern, El-Ansary, 1992) has become relevant for food marketing systems too. Chain marketing, i.e. coordinated marketing policies of two or more subsequent companies in a marketing channel vis-à-vis a third party on the basis of consumer orientation, has become important in food marketing. In this context one should be aware of a potentially too rigid coordination, which might prevent an alert response to market opportunities and threats.

It should also be kept in mind that effective policy coordination does not necessarily include all actors of a food marketing system. Coordination may be restricted to specific stages of the channel, say a compound feed company and a farmer. Coordination may also focus on specific flows in the channel, such as focusing on the physical product flow in logistical planning.

2.5.3 Quality orientation

Increase in food sales has to be achieved in Western countries through increasing added value, such as higher nutritional value, better taste and more convenience. Therefore 'focusing' and 'product differentiation' seem better strategies than 'low cost production'. This message has been understood by many food marketing systems but is not so easily implemented. It requires not only changes in capacities and structure of a company but also in company culture. Marketing strategies of companies should be based on a good knowledge of consumers' quality orientation and quality perception (Steenkamp, 1989; Grunert, et al. 1996; Steenkamp and Van Trijp, 1996). Consumer led product development is a must (see Van Trijp and Steenkamp in this book). Quality control in production and in logistical processes (see De Sitter in this book) has become extremely important. Procedures, such as quality certification, Integral Quality Care Programs, and Hazard Analysis of Critical Control Points (HACCP) are applied to maintain and guarantee product quality (see chapters by Van Trijp and Steenkamp, Hoogland et al. in this book).

Product quality is also pursued by environmentally and animal friendly production methods. At the moment there is only limited demand for environmentally friendly products, but it is steadily increasing. While there is great variation per country and type of product, the market share of organic food is in many Western countries below 5% of total food consumption yet. Differentiation of food products on the basis of region of origin is another way of improving the food quality image. The EU has enhanced marketing of regional products by giving some regions the exclusive right to market their product under a specific regional label, e.g. Parmesan cheese. The hope is that regional labels are instrumental in capitalizing on the unique features of regional products.

Product differentiation by branding has a long tradition in food marketing, such as in marketing groceries, margarine and coffee. Currently there is growing interest in branding fresh produce too. Unfortunately, some basic characteristics of a branded product, such as constant quality and stable prices, are more difficult to implement for fresh produce than for groceries. Quality control and quality maintenance of branded fresh food might be expensive and fluctuating prices might have a negative influence on consumer loyalty to a branded fresh food product.

2.5.4 Innovation

In some food marketing systems, such as those for dairy desserts, innovation has become a basic characteristic of marketing strategy: product assortments are renewed constantly, often by product modification. However, in many food companies, product innovation does not yet seem to be well integrated in marketing strategies. Features of innovative strategies are market orientation, product involvement, R&D quality, but in particular management commitment (Traill and Grunert, 1997). In many Western countries R&D for agricultural products and - to a lesser extent - for food products used to be a sector activity. Examples are government sponsored agricultural research institutes, such as INRA in France, and industry sponsored research institutes, such as the Dutch Dairy Research Institute (NIZO). However, product development in food marketing systems is increasingly becoming an activity of individual companies, while industry research institutes are focusing on basic and pre-competitive research.

2.5.5 Segmentation

Few food companies market products and services to the *average* food consumer. Most companies go for market segmentation, serving groups of consumers with specific but similar wants, needs and behaviour with respect to a product or service: discount stores focus on price conscious consumers; some food companies target health-oriented consumers; fast-food marketing systems serve convenience-oriented consumers. These developments refute the argument of Levitt (1983) that, driven by developments in technology and mass communication, consumers tend to develop homogeneous preferences around the world. Researchers have also expressed their doubts about this argument (Brunso, Grunert and Bredahl, 1996). In this context it must be kept in mind that the same person may belong to different market segments, depending on the situation: someone may be convenience-oriented during the week, but quality-oriented when entertaining guests. Increasing interest is paid to the identification of national or cross-national consumer segments (Grunert et al., 1996, Steenkamp, 1992, 1997).

Small and medium-sized agribusinesses and farmers are also showing an increasing interest in special products and consumer groups, such as ecological food and regional products.

2.5.6   Internationalisation

International trade in food and agricultural products has a very long tradition. It is currently becoming a common feature of food businesses in western countries. Food marketing systems are becoming more concerned about their international competitiveness. Factors which influence international competitiveness are summarized by Porter (1990) as 'Factor conditions, demand conditions, related and supporting industries, firm strategy, structure and rivalry'. The competitiveness of food marketing systems depends in particular on natural conditions (climate, soil, etc.), factor costs, infrastructure, location, production, marketing skills, and quality of entrepreneurship. The potential impact of these factors on international competitiveness is influenced by government measures, such as import duties and agricultural protection. Internationalisation of food marketing systems is increasing for reasons reviewed already, such as the progress being made in the areas of IT, efficiency of logistical systems and free trade. Also changes within the food marketing system itself stimulate internationalization. For instance, as a result of concentration in food retailing, big food retail chains have emerged which have the purchasing power to search for food suppliers in international markets.

2.5.7   Market leadership

In various marketing theories market leadership is advocated as an attractive strategy. Portfolio-analysis carried out by the Boston Consulting Group suggests that a Strategic Business Unit with a relative market share (market share over the market share of the largest competitor) of less than one should either quit the market ('dogs') or should invest in order to arrive at a relative market share greater than one (known as 'question marks' or 'problem children').

It has been argued that market leadership is also a desirable strategy for food marketing systems. The advantages of such a strategy seem obvious. In comparison to the competitors, a market leader has more experience with products and markets and as a result profits more from 'economies of scale' in production, marketing and from customers' feedback. A large production volume may mean that a market leader is better placed to supply large buyers and to develop national or international brands than his competitors.

The feasibility of market leadership as a strategy depends also on the chosen target market: can we do better than our competitors in a target market and is that target substantial and durable? A number of producers often focus on the same market-segment, say the market of fast-food consumers. In that case a clear positioning in the target market is necessary to become a market leader. It can be based on product quality, branding, service and price level. Being the first supplier in a market is also helpful for becoming the market leader.

2.5.8   Re-engineering markets

Changing marketing strategies influence markets of food and agricultural products a great deal. Spot markets, where products are physically handled, lose importance. Many local spot markets disappeared as a result of a decreasing need for assembling products from small farmers. The tendency towards a closer marketing relationship between big food producer and big retailer reduces the importance of spot markets too. However, (inter)national spot markets remain important for standardized agricultural commodities, such as grains and potatoes, and for live animals (pigs, cattle), fish and some horticultural products. Spot markets are still attractive for products if both the uncertainty or complexity and the asset specificity of transactions, and consequently transaction costs, are low.

Spot markets also stay in business by improving the efficiency of the exchange process. It is becoming easier to do business by electronic communication without having the physical product at hand. Many spot markets are acquiring a more international scope because of better communication and logistical facilities.

Downstream in the marketing channel spot markets lose importance since a close relationship between actors in the food marketing system, such as between the food industry and food retailer, will be preferred over coordination by market prices at spot markets.

2.6   Conclusions

- The proposed framework of food marketing systems appears to be a useful instrument for the analysis of such systems.

- Our analysis demonstrates that environmental trends - economic, demographic, social, political, physical and technological - have a substantial impact on food marketing systems. The interaction between different trends, such as between economic and social trends on the one hand and political trends on the other, is important in this context.

- Environmental trends are currently influencing food consumer behaviour a great deal:
  - food consumers place greater stress on value for money because of changes in values, as a result of more product information and better education respectively. Lack of meaningful value to the consumer

leads to low product acceptance.
- the demand for convenience in shopping, cooking and consumption is increasing because of changes in lifestyles and values. Demographic changes, such as a smaller household size and more women working outside the home are also important in this respect.
- consumer concern about health and sustainability is causing a growing interest in safe and sustainably produced food. Consumer groups and environmental lobbies are strengthening this trend.
- consumer appreciation of variety and an increasingly multiracial Western society stimulate consumer demand for variety in the food assortment on offer.

- Trends in the technological and political environments of food marketing systems have created opportunities for new products and new processes. In particular the following trends seem important:
  - developments in IT have created new opportunities for collecting, processing and disseminating information. These will lead to improvements in the efficiency of food marketing systems, but also to higher product quality and better quality maintenance.
  - new processing technologies and breeding methods create opportunities for product innovation. Consumers' distrust of specific technologies, such as biotechnology, have become important aspects in the product innovation process.
  - while food markets in Western countries have become less regulated because of changing EU policies and international trade agreements (GATT/WTO), there is more government intervention in the spheres of food production and marketing as a result of environmental problems.

- The actors in the food marketing system have evolved into bigger companies, which pay more attention to strategic issues, such as their mission and core competencies. Strategies such as market orientation, policy coordination, chain strategies, quality orientation, innovation, segmentation, internationalisation and market leadership, have become important in food marketing systems. Markets are being re-engineered as a result of organisational changes and policy changes among the actors of the food marketing system.

- Changes in food marketing systems and their environment create opportunities for new products and services. Innovation has become a strategic issue of food marketing systems. In this respect it is important that some consumers' needs, such as the need for convenience and the need for sustainably produced food, are not always compatible. It is expected that advances in research methods and technology will diminish this incompatibility of product attributes. However, more effort still needs to be made on informing consumers about the positive features of new technologies, such as biotechnology, which are regarded with suspicion by a great many consumers.

product may be assessed from the data already available. If the changes are more substantial, new consumer measurement may be required to recalibrate the consumer models. The 'what-if' forecasts form the input for the managerial *evaluation*/decision on business opportunity. Based on the consumer information, predictions for individual consumers can be made on how their preference and choice probabilities for the new product relate to those of competitive products. These individual level forecasts will be aggregated into a sales forecast. The final estimates of market performance will include consumer awareness of the new product and availability at point of purchase. These predictions will be in the form of scenarios that not only depend on variables under the firm's control but also on assumptions made concerning competitive actions and reactions.

To summarize, successful NPD is critically important to firms, and success is largely determined by the degree of effectiveness (delivering true added value in the eyes of consumers) and efficiency (doing this fast and at lowest possible costs) of the process (Griffin and Hauser, 1996). To achieve this, it is important to have a structured NPD process and procedures, in which consumer needs form the starting point of analysis, but in terminology which can easily be translated into action to guide technical product development. Also, production and engineering will be involved at an early stage to anticipate future production and to integrate these considerations into the design process.

3.3 Putting consumer-oriented NPD into practice

The Urban and Hauser (1993) model delineates most of the activities required in the consumer-oriented NPD process. However, in practice, the communication between the various functional groups involved has proven to be fairly difficult (Souder, 1987), seriously hampering the process of carrying consumer focus all the way through to technical development. Many factors (e.g. Griffin and Hauser, 1996) contribute to the problem of insufficient interaction and cooperation at the marketing and R&D interface, including different time horizons, mutual negative stereotyping (Kotler, 1994), and differences in terminology being adopted (talk about either the consumer or the product, rather than the consumer - product interaction).

Part of the problem in cross-functional communication is that the input to the process (i.e. what consumers want from products) can be defined at different levels of abstraction (see also Figure 3.1). An important distinction needs to be made between strategic (primary), tactical (secondary) and operational (tertiary) consumer needs (e.g. Griffin and Hauser, 1993). Strategic needs reflect the level at which consumers think about and express their needs. In the context of food products, strategic needs may be 'high quality' and 'stylish appearance'. Although these expressions are the level at which the new product will compete in the consumer's mind, the potential for translating these into action remains limited in terms of product design.

For those reasons, action is taken to find more concrete expressions of the elements which constitute these strategic consumer needs. In the food context these may be 'good taste', 'easy to use' and 'attractive shape'. At an even more specific level tertiary or operational needs are defined as the building blocks for the secondary needs. These tertiary or operational needs are more likely to be highly product specific. Examples would include 'sweetness', 'easy to open lid' and 'red colour'.

Marketing and R& D (the key functions that are linked through consumer-oriented NPD) have different levels of concreteness/abstraction in consumer need identification which are most useful to them. From primary to tertiary, the need expressions become more concrete and also more actionable as guidance to technical product development. On the other hand, from tertiary to primary, the need expressions become more abstract and closer to consumer terminology and therefore to marketing communication of the product's CBP. This illustrates the key challenge in consumer-oriented NPD: 'How to translate delivery on abstract consumer needs into tangible product features'. In this section we summarize this challenge in a set of six key consumer issues that need to be addressed when putting consumer-oriented NPD into practice. Together these issues identify consumer-relevant targets, define priorities and make consumer guidance actionable to technical product development. Anticipating the next chapter, we link these issues to Quality Function Deployment (QFD). For expository purposes we have repro-

Figure 3.3
Simplified represen-
tation of the House
of Quality

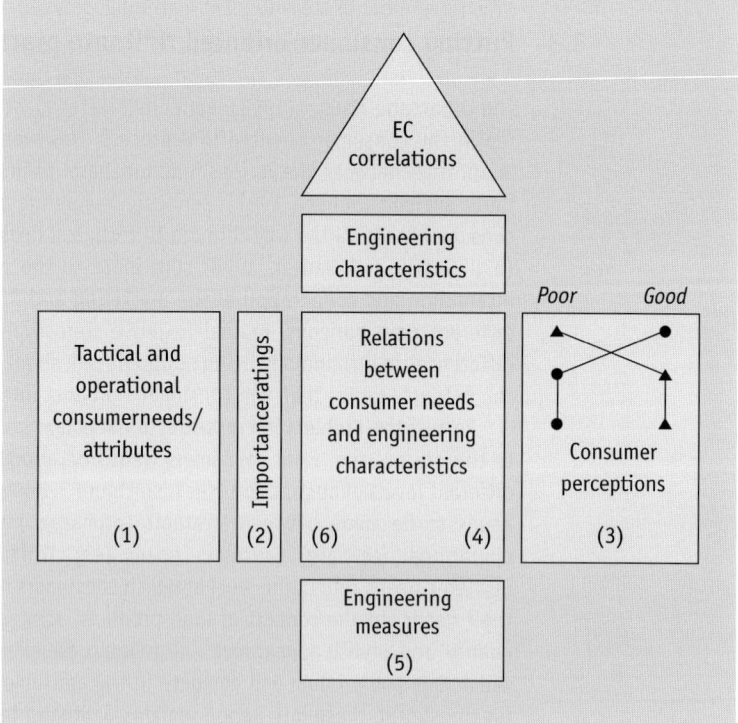

duced a simplified version of QFD's House of Quality (see Chapter 4 for details) in Figure 3.3 and numbered the issues accordingly.

1. *What are the product attributes desired by the consumer?*
This issue constitutes the identification of the key dimensions substantiating the product's Core Benefit Proposition. It includes the product requirements that are necessary to meet and surpass competition and those on which the new product will have improved or provide unique delivery. Marketing and consumer research are the key tools for addressing the consumer needs and their hierarchical nesting (abstract versus concrete). Several qualitative and quantitative research techniques are available for this purpose (see Griffin and Hauser, 1993 for an overview). Examples include exploratory techniques such as in-depth interviews and focus groups as well as more structured approaches such as Kelly's Repertory Grid and Free Elicitation (see Steenkamp and Van Trijp, 1997). A particularly useful technique for revealing the hierarchical nesting of need levels is laddering (Reynolds and Gutman, 1988).

2. *How important are each of these product attributes to the consumer?*
Some needs are more important to consumers than others[2]. Identification of attribute importance is a crucial step in the QFD approach as any company will prefer to spend its limited resources on those attributes that really matter to the consumer in terms of preference and choice probabilities. Attribute importance is a complex and unfortunately not very well-defined concept in the consumer and marketing research literature (Myers and Alpert, 1977), for which a number of measurement methodologies are available (Heeler et al., 1979). An important distinction needs to be made between attributes that are important in an absolute sense and those that are determinant in consumer choice behaviour (Myers and Alpert, 1968). Some attributes are so important that they are a *sine qua non*, whereas other attributes only become important when more urgent needs are satisfied.

3. *Will adjustment of a consumer attribute lead to competitive advantage?*
The ultimate goal of NPD is the development of new products that are differentiated from competition in the marketplace on one or more attributes. Therefore, any intended attribute improvement needs to be evaluated relative to competitor delivery. This is the right hand side of the House of Quality which reflects consumer perceptions of market delivery in terms of attributes. Again, this is a responsibility for marketing and consumer research, and will be conducted in the form of quantitative perceptual mapping research (see Urban and Hauser, 1993 for an overview of methodologies). Perceptual mapping research identifies how the consumer perceives product alternatives for key attributes. Combined with the attribute importances (see above), the analysis of strengths and weaknesses vis-à-vis competitors provides highly diagnostic information. It forms the heart of the definition of the Core Benefit Proposition, in terms of which levels need to be delivered for important attributes to meet and surpass competition as well as which attributes might constitute a 'unique selling point' for the new product.

4. *What are the implications for technical adjustments to the product?*
The previous phases have determined which consumer perceptions will need to be targeted to communicate the desired CBP to the marketplace. In other words, marketing has expressed 'What needs to be done'. Now it is up to R&D to decide 'How this will then be realized'. This is the critical phase of translation of market opportunity (consumer terminology) to technical capabilities (product specification). In the House of Quality representation, this is reflected in the 'relationship' matrix that links perceived consumer attributes to the objective (sensory and instrumental) engineering characteristics of the product. For each combination of consumer attribute and engineering characteristic the matrix will indicate whether there is a relationship and, if so, how strong it is. In many QFD-studies the entries of the relationship matrix are assessed using an informal approach, which can make them sensitive to subjective and erroneous interpretation. In the application section of this chapter we will illustrate Quality Guidance (Steenkamp and Van Trijp, 1996) as an integrated analytical procedure for quantitative assessment of these relations. Quality Guidance recognizes the potentially complex nature of the relationships between engineering characteristics and consumer attributes. Typically, these relationships are not of a one-to-one nature, as multiple engineering characteristics combine into a consumer perception of a product characteristic. Also, the product's engineering characteristics are not orthogonal, implying that they cannot necessarily be manipulated independently of each other. These correlations between the engineering characteristics are depicted in the 'roof' of the House of Quality. A statistical implication of correlations between engineering characteristics is that multivariate statistical methods will be required to account for the intercorrelations among engineering characteristics.

5. *Do the consumer attributes have physico-chemical counterparts?*
It is tempting to think that consumer perceptions have unique counterparts in the physical product and vice versa, but this is only partly true. Variation in some product features may not be perceived by the consumer due to insufficient sensitivity. In other words, it may not exceed the 'Just Noticeable Difference' (JND). Also, some consumer beliefs cannot be unambiguously verified from personal consumption experience. This will typically hold for 'credence' attributes (Darby and Karni, 1973) such as environmental friendliness and health. Rather than performance being assessed on the basis of personal experience, the interpretation depends on accepting communication through third parties (advertising, educational extension etc.), or personal inference making from other characteristics (Fishbein and Ajzen, 1975). In both instances consumer perceptions of attributes may lack strong counterparts in the relationship matrix.

Profiling a selection of product alternatives in terms of their engineering characteristics forms an integral part of the analysis. Together with insight into the 'consumer perceptions', this provides highly diagnostic information, particularly in terms of desired action in the case of poor performance on consumer perception. A situation may occur where two products show up dif-

ferently in consumer perception (3) but not in terms of engineering characteristics (5). In such a case[3], it may be that differences in perception find
their basis in the less tangible, 'image' type of attributes, that can be more
effectively corrected through marketing communication rather than through
technical product development. In the application section of this chapter we
will provide an empirical analysis of this issue.

6. *What is the effect of technical adjustment on other consumer attributes?*
The analysis so far allows for an assessment of which technical parameters
may lead to improvement in consumer attribute perceptions. However,
equally important is the analysis of whether these adjustments may have an
undesirable effect on one or more of the other consumer attributes. This
step is frequently overlooked due to some degree of product myopia. For
example, when developing health foods, it is important to assess at an early
stage whether the lower fat content necessary to substantiate the health
claim affects other consumer benefits such as taste. If this is the case, the
argument should be included in the decision whether or not this trade-off
will justify product introduction.

In summary, the formulation of key consumer issues to be addressed in consumer-oriented NPD provides a useful framework for structuring thinking
about what a new product should be delivering to the consumer and how this
should be done. Its major strength is that it makes a number of key considerations explicit. By doing so, it provides a common basis for the different
functional disciplines involved in the NPD process and makes clear what
agendas and considerations are, how the efforts influence each other, and
what tradeoffs need to be made. Also, as we will see in the next chapter,
these issues constitute the key elements of the first house of Quality
Function Deployment (QFD): the House of Quality. Through the other QFD
houses (see Chapter 4), the consumer orientation may be taken all the way
through to technical product development and supply chain considerations.
In this way the consumer issues provide focus and structure within the QFD
process. This has been found to increase communication within and between
functional disciplines (Griffin, 1992; Griffin and Hauser, 1992). In addition
to these long-term benefits, it has been claimed that QFD reduces design
time and costs considerably (Hauser and Clausing, 1988). These and other
virtues of QFD will be discussed in more detail in Chapter 4.

3.4   Application for Food Quality improvement

Building on Steenkamp's (1989; 1990) work on perceived product quality,
Steenkamp and Van Trijp (1986; 1988; 1996; 1997) refined the basic principles of the delivery of consumer-recognized superior quality of food products. The guiding principle behind this work is illustrated in Figure 3.4.
    The central element in the model is *perceived quality*, a one-dimension-
al overall evaluative judgment about 'the product's fitness for use with

Figure 3.4
The research model guiding food quality improvement: The extended Quality Guidance model (adapted from Steenkamp, 1989)

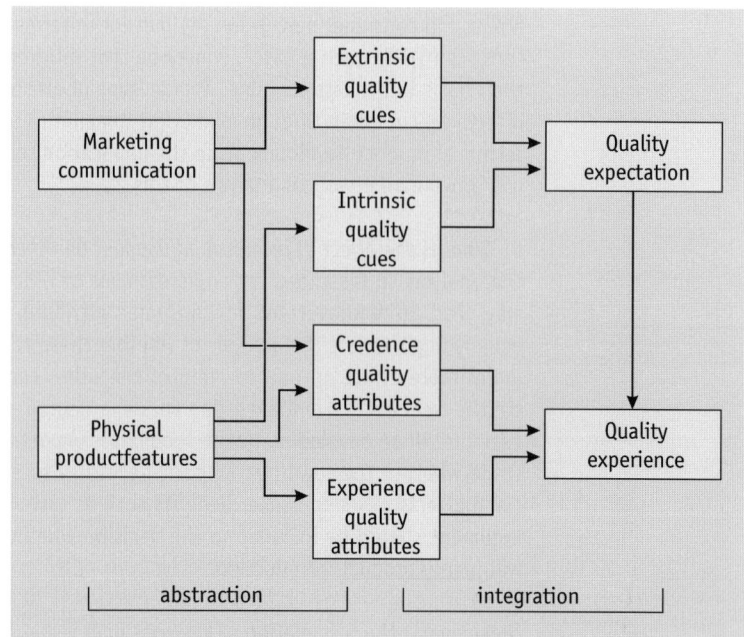

respect to its intended purpose relative to alternatives' (Aaker, 1991; Steenkamp, 1989). For most food products the acts of purchasing and consumption are temporally separated and perceived quality judgments are formed at two different points in time. When the food product is purchased, the consumer forms an impression about the product's expected fitness for consumption. This is the consumer judgment of *'quality expectation'*. The quality expectation of the various product alternatives is an important factor in consumer choice behaviour (Steenkamp, 1989; Narasimhan and Sen, 1992). Upon consumption, the consumer is able to evaluate the product's actual fitness for consumption. This *'quality experience'* judgment may be influenced by the expectations that were formed with respect to the anticipated fitness for consumption (cf. Churchill and Suprenant, 1982).

Expected quality judgments at the point of purchase are based on perceptions of one or more quality cues (e.g. Olson, 1972; Steenkamp, 1990). Quality cues are any informational stimuli that can be ascertained through the senses prior to consumption, and, according to the consumer, have predictive validity for the product's quality performance upon consumption (Monroe and Krishnan, 1985). Perceptions of quality cues are integrated into a more abstract overall judgment of expected quality[4]. An important distinction needs to be made between intrinsic and extrinsic quality cues. *Intrinsic cues* are part of the physical product. They cannot be changed without also changing the physical product itself. Examples of intrinsic cues include colour and texture for salami, and colour, presence of spots, and softness for fruit. *Extrinsic cues* are related to the product, but are physically not part of it. Well-known extrinsic cues are price, brand name, country of origin, and store name. Whereas intrinsic cues are linked to the physical product characteristics, extrinsic cues are predominantly determined by marketing efforts[5]. Quality cues are weighted differently in the formation of quality expectations. It has been found that intrinsic cues are usually weighted more heavily than extrinsic cues (see Steenkamp, 1989 for a review).

It is only upon consumption that the consumer can ascertain the product's true quality performance. The quality experience judgment is based on the integration of product perceptions of quality attributes (Steenkamp, 1990). These quality attributes are the utility-generating functional and socio-psychological benefits provided by the product (Steenkamp, 1990). They represent what the product is perceived as doing or providing to the consumer in relation to the consumer's wants, and form the basis of consumer preferences. Examples of quality attributes of food products include taste, leanness, tenderness and keepability. The integration phase reflects the combinatorial weighting of quality attribute perceptions into an overall quality judgment. The model distinguishes between two types of quality attributes: experience attributes and credence attributes. *Experience quality attributes* are those that can be ascertained by the consumer on the basis of actual consumption experience with the product, as for example with taste, tenderness and ease of preparation. *Credence attribute beliefs*, on the other hand, cannot be unambiguously verified through personal experience even after normal use for a long time, nor without consulting an expert. Examples are the absence of additives, healthiness and environmental friendliness. These two type of attribute beliefs may carry differential weight in the overall quality performance judgment.

Both quality cue and quality attribute perceptions find their basis in product and processing characteristics that are directly or indirectly related to the product. For example, intrinsic cue perceptions will primarily be delivered through product and production technology. Extrinsic cues on the other hand, will be primarily delivered through marketing efforts, such as branding, pricing and labelling[5]. A key issue in consumer-oriented food quality delivery therefore consists of understanding and operationalizing the elements depicted in Figure 3.4 and then using this understanding and measurement to relate it back to product and processing characteristics under the firm's control. This latter step constitutes psychophysics in its broadest sense (Stenson, 1982: 47): the study of relationships among a set of physically defined variables (physical and marketing cues) and a set of variables presumed to be indicators of the psychological counterparts of the physical variables (quality cues and attribute perceptions).

The model thus highlights two key paths along which consumers' quality perception judgments may be influenced, through intrinsic quality cues and through extrinsic quality cues. In the remainder of this chapter we will illustrate this with two case studies that the authors conducted for the Dutch Commodity Board for Livestock, Meat and Eggs. Details of these studies can be found in the original sources (Steenkamp and Van Trijp, 1996; Van Trijp, Steenkamp and Candel, 1997).

3.5   Case studies in food quality improvement

3.5.1   Improving quality perception through the physical product

The first study illustrates how the quality perception model can be used to influence perceived quality through adjustments in the physical product. The focus is purely on the quality of the physical product. The role of marketing communication was not examined in this study.

Background

The study was conducted in the late 1980's when meat quality was seriously under discussion in the Netherlands. In response to concerns expressed by both consumers and retailers, the Dutch Commodity Board for Livestock and Meat initiated an early research project on integrated marketing chains (Meulenberg, 1997; Wierenga, 1997). There was explicit recognition of the fact that product quality as the final consumer encounters it, is affected by all phases of the meat production chain. Quality improvement, therefore, entails a joint effort by all phases of the production chain. The Commodity Board asked the authors, then both at the Department of Marketing and Marketing Research of Wageningen Agricultural University, to conduct a large scale consumer study that should not only unravel how consumers arrive at quality judgments, but should also provide tangible and workable technical product specifications that would substantiate the desired quality image. These findings could subsequently serve as target values for earlier phases of the production chain. The study was designed and carried out in close cooperation with meat experts from the Dutch Commodity Board for Livestock and Meat and the Research Institute for Animal Production 'Schoonoord'.

Design

Stimuli

The study applied the quality guidance model to the formation of quality judgments with respect to blade steak (stewing steak). The basic structure of the quality guidance model is reflected in Figure 3.4. In this application only the effect of physical product features will be considered (see Figure 3.5 for structure). Blade steak was chosen as a representative for a more general class of beef cuts. To obtain a representative set of blade steak samples, 48 carcasses were selected on the basis of the EUROP-classification system by the Research Institute of Animal Production 'Schoonoord'. Most outlets selling fresh meat use this classification for the selection of carcasses.

The meat from random carcasses was evaluated (independently) by four respondents. Nine samples of blade steak were cut from each carcass. Four samples were used for collecting judgments about quality expectations, four samples for evaluation of quality performance, and the centre part of the muscle was used for measurement of the physical characteristics. Meat experts considered the physical characteristics of the centre part to be the best approximation of the other blade steak samples cut from that muscle.

The two meat samples that were judged by a particular respondent came from the same muscle and were situated adjacent to each other.

Meat experts carried out the instrumental analyses and visual judgments on the meat samples. The characteristics measured were colour, fatiness, pH, water-binding capacity, shear force, and sarcomere length. These characteristics are generally used in the field of animal studies to measure the physical quality of beef. Multiple measurements were taken for some physical characteristics using standardized procedures. The reader is referred to Steenkamp and Van Trijp (1996) for further details on the study.

Data collection
Data were collected at the central test facility of a Dutch market research agency in a nationwide sample of 192 respondents. Respondents were the main purchasers of meat in a particular household and used blade steak regularly. Nearly all respondents were female. Age and educational level of the respondent and of her partner, household size and income, and social class varied considerably between respondents. The point of purchase situation was simulated by providing the respondent with a sample of raw blade steak. Respondents rated their perceptions of quality expectation on a seven-point bipolar scale (poles: 1 = poor quality, 7 = good quality), and on a seven-point Likert statement 'is of good quality' (1 = completely disagree, 7 = completely agree). The respondent also rated her quality cue perceptions on eight seven-point bipolar scales: light/dark red, much/little variegation in colour, moist/dry, not fresh/fresh, small/large fat trim, little/much fat, untidy/good appearance, and not freshly cut/freshly cut.

After some other tasks, the respondent was confronted with an identical but cooked sample of blade steak (i.e. a cut from the same muscle of the same carcass, next to the one that was evaluated in the raw condition). This simulated the consumption situation. The preparation of the blade steak samples was carried out by a professional cook following a standard recipe. The respondent ate as much as she wanted of the sample, and rated its quality performance on the bipolar and Likert quality scales described above. She also rated quality attribute perceptions, using the following seven-point bipolar scales: bad/good smell, bad/good taste, tough/tender, not easy/easy to carve, dry/juicy, fat/lean, many/few sinews and tendons.

Methodology
For technical details on the methodology, the reader is referred to the original source (Steenkamp and Van Trijp, 1996). Here it suffices to say that the constructs in the model were operationalized through multiple indicators and that these showed satisfactory measurement reliability. The physical measures were selected by experts in the field as those commonly applied and generally believed to hold predictive validity for blade steak quality as the consumer perceives it. The physical constructs distinguished in the model are: colour, fatiness, pH, water-binding capacity, shear force and sarcomere length of the meat samples. Given the theoretical evidence that consumer's information processing capacity is limited and that they generally use only three or

four more general dimensions in judging products (Engel and Blackwell, 1982), principal components analysis was applied to the quality cue ratings and quality attribute ratings to discover the basic perceptual constructs. The following quality cue dimensions were discovered: *freshness*, with high weighting for the items not fresh/fresh, not freshly cut/freshly cut, much/little variegation in colour, and moist/dry, *visible fat* (small/large fat trim, little/much fat), and *appearance* (light red/dark red, untidy/good appearance). Similarly, the following basic quality attribute dimensions were identified: *tenderness* (tough/tender, not easy to carve/easy to carve, dry/juicy), *non-meat components* (fat/lean, many sinews and tendons/few sinews and tendons), and *flavour* (bad smell/good smell, bad taste/good taste).

The relationships between model constructs were estimated through Partial Least Squares (PLS) analysis. PLS is particularly suited for quality guidance studies as it allows one to estimate fairly complex models (as Figure 3.5) from a relatively small amount of data (48 carcasses as in our case).

Results

Discussion of the results will be restricted to the structural relationships in the model. These are illustrated in a graph in Figure 3.5. For ease of exposition, only the statistically significant ($p<0.10$; two-sided) causal relations are depicted for the physical constructs. Although PLS provides an integral test of the quality guidance model, the stages of quality expectation formation and quality performance assessment will be discussed separately.

Quality expectation of raw blade steaks

All three quality cue dimensions exert a significant influence and together account for 54% of the variation in quality expectation ratings. Expected quality at the point of purchase increases with perceived attractiveness of appearance and perceived freshness, and decreases with the amount of visible fat. The quality guidance model also assesses the predictability of quality cue perceptions on the basis of physical characteristics of the blade steaks. Linear combinations of the six physical constructs incorporated in this study that have maximum predictive validity for the quality cue dimensions are sought. Twenty six percent of the variance in consumers' evaluation of good appearance of raw blade steak can be explained from perceived redness of the blade steak and its pH. Similarly, 41% of consumers' perception of fatiness is based on colour, sarcomere length, water-binding capacity and amount of intramuscular fat. Consumers' perceptions of freshness decrease the darker red the sample and increase with sarcomere length, together accounting for a modest 13% in variation in consumers' perceived freshness ratings.

Quality performance upon consumption

The quality attribute dimensions and quality expectation together account for 67% of the variance in consumers' quality performance ratings. Within the range of meat cuts employed, consumers' quality performance ratings increase with perceived tenderness and decrease with amount of non-meat components, indicating that consumers evaluate fat, sinews and tendons very negatively in the consumption situation. Flavour did not exert a significant effect on quality performance. This was at least partly due to correlations of flavour with other quality attribute dimensions as the bivariate correlation with quality performance was 0.37 (p=0.01). Quality expectation exerts a significant effect (p<0.10; one-sided) on quality performance judgments.

Thirty-nine percent of the variance in consumers' tenderness perceptions can be explained by the physical characteristics of the meat sample. It increases with sarcomere length, and decreases with pH and objective fati-

Figure 3.5
Results of Study 1
(after Steenkamp
and Van Trijp, 1996)

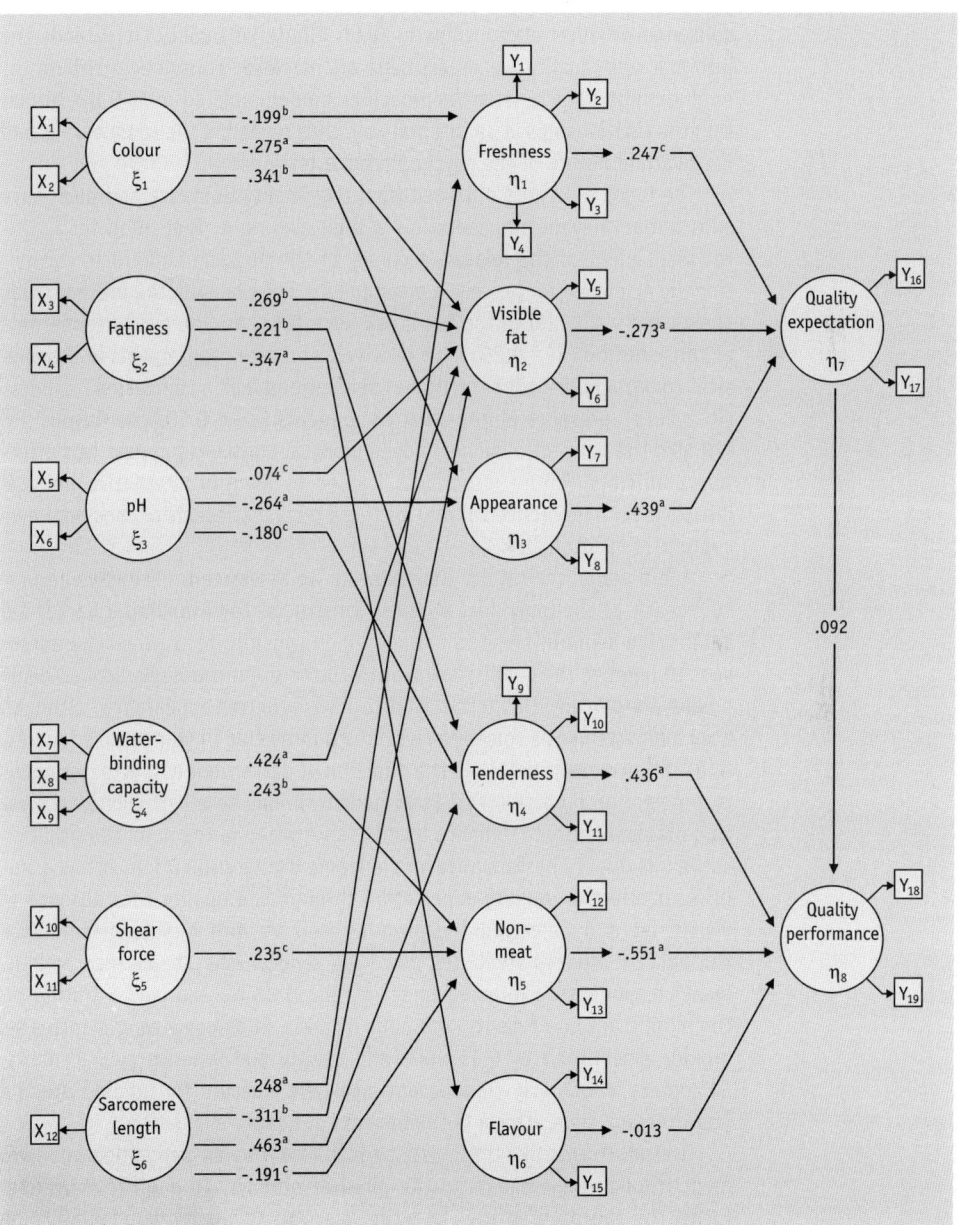

ness. Consumer perceptions of non-meat components in the cooked blade steak increase with water-binding capacity and shear force and decrease with sarcomere length. Together these instrumental measures account for 18% of the variance in perceptions of non-meat components. Only objectively measured fatiness has predictive value for consumers' flavour perceptions, accounting for 19% in the flavour ratings.

Conclusions

The Quality Guidance model provides a quantitative basis for assessing the consumer-product relationships in QFD's House of Quality. It extends the informal and qualitative assessment on pairwise 'consumer attribute-to-engineering characteristics' approach commonly applied in QFD by estimating the relationships in an integral way, thus revealing the complexities and multivariate nature of the psychophysical relationships.

The types of results obtained from the Quality Guidance approach have substantial relevant interpretation in their own right. They allow for a critical assessment of the relative accuracy of the physical constructs conventionally employed for perceived meat quality. For example, the present study shows that visible fat of the raw steak ($R^2 = 0.44$) and perceived tenderness at consumption ($R^2 = 0.39$) have relatively accurate counterparts in the physical constructs. For other consumer perceptions such as perceived freshness ($R^2 = 0.13$), presence of non-meat components ($R^2 = 0.18$) and flavour ($R^2 = 0.19$), the conventionally employed physical constructs appear less effective predictors. Future research is needed to identify alternative physical measures with predictive validity for these relevant aspects of consumer perception of meat quality.

Additionally, the results also allow for an assessment of relative accuracy of each of the individual physical constructs. For example, a darker-red colour may be an interesting measure upon which to focus when the purpose is to improve the quality image at the point of purchase. Darker-red blade steaks are perceived as leaner and to have a better appearance, although they are perceived as somewhat less fresh. Expressed in standardized scores, one unit increase in colour in the direction of darker redness increases quality expectation by 0.18 units. Sarcoma length may be a particularly interesting physical entity to enhance quality expectation in the purchase situation as well as quality performance at the moment of consumption. It has a significant effect on quality expectation through the quality cues absence of visible fat and perceived freshness as well as with quality performance through the quality attributes perceived tenderness and absence of non-meat components. Expressed in standardized units, and concentrating on the significant coefficients, one unit increase in sarcoma length increases quality expectation by 0.15 units and quality performance by 0.31 units. Sarcomere length may thus be an important measure for guiding product improvement, as it affects both moments of quality evaluation.

Overall, results like these assist consumers' quality perception improvement through adjustments in the physical product. Through its consumer focus, the approach ensures that the selection of quality parameters to be adjusted finds its basis in sound empirical research. This is important in order to prevent the situation where the firm might otherwise adjust physical parameters that do not contribute to the quality image as perceived by the consumer. In the next example, we will focus on quality improvement through extrinsic quality cues.

3.5.2 Improving quality perception through extrinsic quality cues

The second study (see Van Trijp, Steenkamp and Candel, 1997 for details) illustrates how consumers' quality perception may be improved through communication by means of extrinsic quality cues (see Figure 3.4).

Background

This study was conducted by the authors in 1993, again commissioned by the Dutch Commodity Board for Livestock, Meat and Eggs which at that time had introduced a system of Integrated Quality Control, known as IKB ('Integrale Keten Beheersing'). IKB certification aims at improved organization of the product chain and providing added value to the consumer through quality guarantees. The IKB scheme for pigs contains a number of basic requirements relating to traceability (by means of the Identification & Registration system), feed, hygiene and the use of veterinary pharmaceuticals.

The Commodity Board approached the authors to investigate whether, and if so, how an IKB label would add value to pork in the eyes of the consumer. A theoretical framework was proposed for analyzing added value from quality labelling, focusing on those elements of consumer behaviour with respect to meat that may be particularly influenced through the availability of a visible IKB label. Such insight is of paramount importance in the understanding of added value and consequently to the decision whether or not to use the IKB label as a vehicle for communicating with consumers, and to increase product differentiation.

Conceptual model of IKB equity

Building on the concept of brand equity (e.g. Aaker, 1991) Figure 3.6 represents the conceptual model for what we call 'IKB equity': the value added to the product by the virtue of it having the IKB label. The IKB added value would come from its guarantees that the pork is produced in accordance with the IKB criteria. More specifically, it is the set of assets linked in the mind of the consumer to the IKB label (cf. Aaker, 1991). The model distinguishes between sources and consequences of IKB equity (see Van Trijp, Steenkamp and Candel, 1997).

Sources of IKB equity

Three categories of assets on which the added value of the IKB label is based, are distinguished: awareness, perceived quality and associations. The IKB value may come from the fact that the label makes the consumer more *aware* of the product. This identification (recognition or recall) will help the consumer in the decision process. After all, a consumer cannot buy IKB pork unless

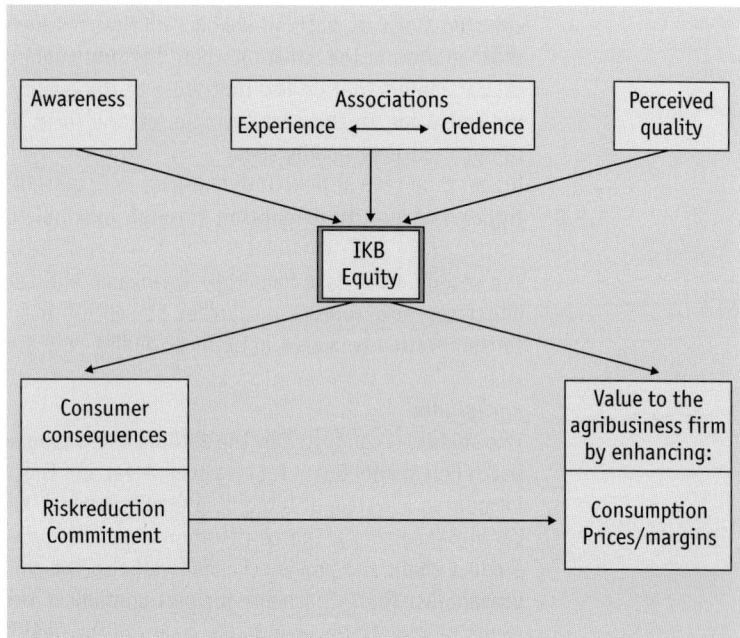

Figure 3.6
Conceptual model for sources and consequences of IKB equity (after Van Trijp, Steenkamp and Candel, 1997)

he or she is first made aware of it, and not surprisingly awareness is strongly correlated with market share (Engel and Blackwell, 1982). Furthermore, awareness provides a sense of familiarity, and familiarity in turn leads to appreciation (Zajonc, 1980, Janiszewski, 1988). People typically buy familiar products rather than unfamiliar products because it is easier, less risky, and it saves time. In low involvement choice situations, awareness may be a frequently used and sufficient choice heuristic (Hoyer and Brown, 1990).

Perceived quality is a second asset underlying IKB equity. Perceived quality itself is a global, summary construct, although it arises from underlying dimensions (see Figure 3.4 and 'associations' below). Superior quality perception has proven an effective product differentiation strategy to create customer loyalty, lower price elasticity, and present barriers to competition (Porter, 1980), positively affecting market share, selling price, and profitability (Buzzell and Gale, 1987). Moreover, consumers are demanding higher quality than ever before, and are willing to pay more for better products (Steenkamp and Van Trijp, 1989). Creating a high quality position through IKB labeling thus may allow pork producers to escape the price competition that rules this market.

Associations include anything that is associated or linked in memory to the IKB concept. For example, is IKB pork seen as tasty, healthy, expensive, etc.? The total set of associations defines the image of IKB, and may form the basis for purchase decisions. Associations can create value to consumers in several ways (Aaker, 1991). First, they help consumers in their decision process. For example, if IKB is strongly associated with 'healthy', a consumer does not have to process various aspects that relate to healthiness each time he or she buys pork. Second, associations form the basis for product differentiation. IKB pork may be differentiated from 'regular' pork on aspects for which regular pork has a bad image. Third, particular key associations provide a reason to buy the product. If a certain consumer cares particularly about animal welfare and he or she is convinced that IKB pork rates higher than regular pork in this respect, this consumer will be more inclined to buy IKB pork. Fourth, some associations are important components of perceived quality, another aspect of IKB equity. Associations may be of the experience and credence type.

In sum, awareness, perceived quality, and associations form the basis of IKB equity. The greater the awareness of IKB pork, the higher its perceived quality, and the more positive the associations consumers have with IKB pork, the greater the value added to the pork by the very fact that it is IKB pork.

Consequences of IKB equity
A first consequence of the IKB quality label is that it is likely to *reduce perceived quality risk*. By perceived quality risk, we mean the amount of risk consumers perceive in the purchase decision because of the uncertainty about the decision and/or the potential consequences of a poor decision (Cunningham, 1967). Since most consumers are risk averse, reduction of quality risk is a valued consequence. Potentially more important, is the fact that IKB can enhance *consumer commitment* to IKB pork. Both perceived quality and brand associations can enhance consumers' satisfaction with the use experience (Aaker, 1991). Many of the quality criteria in the IKB programme are not directly observable to consumers but knowing that the product has guarantees concerning hygiene, pharmaceuticals, etc. may enhance the usage experience, in the same way that the mere knowledge that one drinks a well-known brand of beer gives more satisfaction (Allison and Uhl, 1964). The fact that IKB reduces perceived quality risk will also be a factor in consumer satisfaction. Higher satisfaction with the usage experience should lead to a greater commitment to IKB pork (cf. Jacoby and Chestnut, 1978).

One hypothesis is that reduced risk and increased commitment as consumer consequences have a positive effect on the *consumption* of IKB pork. More specifically, it is hypothesized that for consumers who attach much value to the IKB label, the relative proportion of IKB pork in the total consumption of pork will be higher, and, more speculatively, that for these consumers introduction of IKB will have a positive effect on the total consumption of pork (IKB plus regular pork). Moreover, *price sensitivity* may decrease for these consumers which offers opportunities for charging higher prices.

Design
A large scale consumer survey was carried out in close cooperation with the Dutch Commodity Board for Livestock, Meat, and Eggs.

Stimuli

Based on the results of a qualitative pilot study, the IKB-concept was defined as: 'IKB pork comes from authorized farms and slaughter houses where additional inspection is conducted on the fodder (including the use of medicines), transport and hygiene. The extra inspection is carried out by an independent organization'.

Data collection

The main study was conducted in May and June 1993 among a representative sample of 505 Dutch households from which the member most responsible for purchasing fresh meat participated. Respondent selection was based on a two-stage cluster sampling technique on Dutch postal codes. Respondents were individually approached with a computerized questionnaire to reduce interviewer bias and to stimulate consumer motivation. As part of a larger data collection task, they were asked to indicate their purchase and consumption behaviour with respect to meats. They then judged a number of meat products on a set of attributes including overall quality and evaluative and descriptive attributes. In addition, consumers were asked to indicate the distribution of their meat consumption across a number of meat products (pork, beef, poultry, fish, veal, lamb, minced meat, convenience meats and non-meat). For this purpose a constant-sum scaling technique was applied in which consumers indicated the number of days out of 100 days that they consume each of the different meat products. Subsequently, consumers were confronted with the IKB-concept, and were asked a number of questions related to their primary reaction to the concept in terms of perceived need for such a concept and willingness to devote time and effort to obtaining IKB-pork. Next, subjects were asked their opinions about IKB in terms of overall quality, evaluative judgments and descriptive attributes. The reported consumption procedure with the constant-sum methodology was repeated, this time with IKB-pork included.

Methodology

Perceived quality was operationalized through a five-point bipolar scale ranging from 'poor quality' (1) to 'good quality' (5). Equity of IKB was operationalized as the difference in overall attitude between IKB and regular pork (Aaker, 1991), with attitude taken to be the mean score on three five-point bipolar scales ranging from 'bad'-'good', 'not attractive-attractive', 'not pleasurable- pleasurable'. Subjects rated both regular and IKB-pork on a number of experience and credence associations (see Table 3.1). The two components of perceived quality risk, quality uncertainty at the moment of purchase and the possible consequences of a wrong decision, were operationalized through the statements: 'Quality of pork is easy to judge' and 'Pork has constant quality', respectively. Both statements were scored on five-point Likert scales ranging from 'completely agree' (1) to 'completely disagree' (5). The overall perceived quality risk score was estimated by multiplying these two scores. Risk reduction was operationalized as the perceived quality risk of regular pork minus perceived quality risk associated with IKB pork.

Commitment to IKB was measured through five statements. These statements, all scored on three point scales with category labels 'yes'(+1), 'no' (-1) and 'don't know' (0), were:

(a) 'Do you consider IKB a good thing?';
(b) 'Do you feel a need for IKB?';
(c) 'Are you willing to pay somewhat more for pork with the IKB label?';
(d) 'Would you be willing to visit another shop to obtain pork with the IKB label?';
(e) 'Would you increase your pork consumption if pork with the IKB label were made available?'.

IKB-commitment was operationalized as the summed score of the five items, overall scores thus ranging from -5 to +5.

The constant-sum task allowed us to compute two different measures concerning consumption: the relative share of IKB-pork in total pork consumption, and the relative share of pork (IKB plus regular) in total consumption of meat after introduction of IKB.

Two elements are not included: awareness and prices/margins. The IKB label had not been introduced at the time of this study and hence the IKB concept was described in the interview. Awareness is not an issue in this study as by definition it is 100%. Prices/margins were not included on the explicit wish of the sponsor of this study.

Results

Table 3.1 shows a comparison of IKB and regular pork for the main components of our model: perceived quality, associations, attitude, perceived risk, and the relative share of pork (IKB plus regular) in total consumption of meat after introduction of IKB, using paired t-tests.

IKB pork outperformed regular pork on IKB-equity, product quality, all credence attributes and a number of experience attributes. The lack of a significant difference for the associations 'goes with many dishes' and 'easy to prepare' serves as a validity check on our results (whether the responses are due to halo effects) as there is nothing in the IKB concept that would make a difference on these aspects.

In terms of consequences, IKB reduces perceived quality risk relative to regular pork. Although consumers do not expect that the quality of IKB pork would be easier to judge, they are confident that the IKB quality guarantees will result in more constant quality levels, thereby reducing overall perceived quality risk. This finding lends support to the result that IKB most strongly differentiates on the credence attributes that cannot be directly verified upon consumption. Finally, it was found that the relative share of pork (IKB plus regular) in total consumption of meat after introduction of IKB increased by about 3% from 19% to 21.8 % (IKB pork: 13.37%, regular pork 8.43%). Van Trijp, Steenkamp and Candel (1997) show further empirical evidence for the validity of the distinction between sources and outcomes of IKB equity.

	IKB	Regular	Difference
IKB equity			
Overall attitude	4.0	3.4	0.6 *
Product Quality			
good quality	4.4	3.7	0.7 *
Experience attributes			
tender	4.1	3.8	0.3 *
good taste	4.0	3.9	0.1
lean	3.3	2.9	0.4 *
goes with many dishes	4.2	4.2	0.0
suitable for guests	3.8	3.5	0.3 *
easy to prepare	4.5	4.6	-0.1
Credence attributes			
special	3.5	3.1	0.4 *
exclusive	3.1	1.8	1.3 *
healthy	3.8	2.7	1.1 *
free of hormones	4.2	2.5	1.7 *
animal friendly	4.0	2.4	1.6 *
free of additives	4.1	3.1	1.0 *
Quality risk			
Uncertainty	3.0	3.2	-0.2
Consequences	2.1	3.3	-1.2 *
Overall risk perception	6.1	10.1	-4.0 *
Consumption			
Total pork consumption (%)[**]	21.8	19.0	2.8 *

Table 3.1 Comparison of consumer perceptions of IKB-pork relative to regular pork

*   p<0.01
** Note that these figures refer to the market share after and before IKB-introduction respectively

Conclusions

This study shows that consumers' quality perception may also be influenced by extrinsic cues such as a quality label. Also important to note is that the added value is not restricted to the characteristics actually captured by the label but extends to consumer beliefs about quality attributes that may subsequently be verified through personal consumption. As such, quality labelling may be used to achieve competitive advantage in the marketplace, even for commodity-type products such as pork. However, awareness of the label (100% in our experimental study) is a necessary condition and in the 'real world' will have to be created through marketing communication.

In the present study we investigated equity of labelling for a new product *concept*. At the time of this research the IKB label had not been introduced into the market. It is important to note, however, that the procedure outlined in this paper applies equally to quality labels already in the market. Such research would provide insight into important managerial questions, such as:

Does our labelling achieve its purposes? At what level (e.g. awareness, associations, perceived quality, risk reduction, commitment) does it fall short? Is additional effort needed, in terms of criteria and communication?

Despite the usefulness of the brand equity framework, it is important to outline some distinguishing features of IKB equity. First, IKB is a generic seal that any producer satisfying the IKB criteria can obtain. This limits the individual company's opportunity for long-term competitive differentiation on the basis of IKB equity. On the other hand, generic seals such as IKB tend to be supported by whole industries, public bodies and/or government. This may result in higher credibility to the consumer than messages on company-specific brands. Together these considerations may explain why certain national brand producers tend to consider IKB equity as a base-line level upon which they build competitive equity through strong brands.

3.6 Conclusions

In this chapter we have systematically reviewed the basic principles of consumer-oriented NPD, and applied them to food product quality improvement. We illustrated various elements of the advocated approach in case studies pertaining to improvement of perceived food product quality through adjustment of the physical product characteristics and the application of food quality labelling.

It is our firm conviction that successful NPD should take the consumer's needs and desires as point of departure for its R&D and NPD activities. This basic philosophy forms the heart of marketing theory and has now gained considerable acceptance in most companies. However, for this philosophy to be put into practice so as to expand it beyond mere lip-service, it is of paramount importance that food companies implement a formal and structured procedure for the NPD process. Formalized procedures, such as Quality Function Deployment, can be particularly helpful in improving the communication and integration between marketing and R&D. This in turn constitutes a critical step in the effective and efficient translation of consumer needs and desires all the way through to physical product offering and marketing support, designed to satisfy those needs and desires.

We expect the consumer focus in NPD to become even more important in the future. As Wind and Mahajan (1997) conclude in a recent analysis of the new product development process, one of the key challenges for future success lies in the transition from the current focus on incremental innovations addressing consumers' current problems to a more radical approach where *discontinuous* innovations will be aimed at less familiar consumer segments (new geographical areas; future consumer problems etc.). Thorough understanding of the driving forces behind consumers' current consumption behaviour patterns, as well as the dynamics and latitude for change therein will be critically important. Wind and Mahajan (1997) warn that current consumer behaviour theory and research methodology may not be adequate to address this new challenge.

Others (e.g. Woodruff, 1997) have also argued that future sources of competitive advantage will no longer come from internal orientation on quality improvement of the food product per se, but rather from outward customer orientation aimed at superior customer value delivery. This will encompass a shift from competition surrounding consumer choice criteria that are relatively well established ('doing the same thing better') to competition over product dimensions that the consumer has not yet encountered or even thought of ('radically new elements of consumer delivery'). As input to this continuous and more radical innovation process, consumer behaviour research needs to be of a more strategic and on-going nature, encompassing all phases in the 'consumption chain' (MacMillan and McGrath, 1997) ranging from early need recognition all the way through usage experience and disposal. Also, it will require high levels of creativity in consumer behaviour theory and methodology development, and a higher degree of consumer involvement in the idea generation phase (Wind and Mahajan, 1997). Advanced applications of modern information technology will become more important in the process of collecting and collating consumer response (Urban et al., 1997) and its transformation into knowledge and customer understanding on which new product development creativity can build.

Notes

1   Hans C.M. van Trijp is Consumer Behaviour Scientist at Unilever Research Laboratory, PO Box 114, 3130 AC Vlaardingen, The Netherlands. Jan-Benedict E.M. Steenkamp is Professor of Marketing at the Catholic University of Leuven, Belgium and the GfK Professor of International Marketing Research at Wageningen Agricultural University, The Netherlands. The authors are indebted to Mr. J.A. Bijkerk for his support in data analysis and preparing the Figures.
2   Note that the importance issue concerns differences in need importance within a particular consumer (e.g. consumer X may consider health delivery more important than taste) as well as differences between consumers (one consumer may be more health-oriented while another finds taste more important). The latter differences provide a basis for market segmentation, in which case the House of Quality would be constructed for each of the various segments separately. We do not consider the segmentation issue here.
3   This assumes that the list of engineering characteristics is complete and accurate.
4   Note that this formulation captures the notion that the relative importance of quality cue perceptions in quality expectation judgments may be psychologically moderated through perceived cue-attribute relationships.
5   Extrinsic cues may also be affected by physical product characteristics and intrinsic cues by marketing efforts, but the dominant influence on extrinsic cues is likely to be marketing efforts while intrinsic cues will be primarily affected by physical product characteristics. In this chapter, we concentrate on these dominant relations.

References

Aaker, D.A. (1991), Managing Brand Equity: Capitalizing on the Value of a Brand Name. New York: Free Press.

Allison, R.I. and K.P. Uhl (1964), Influence of beer brand identification on taste perception. Journal of Marketing Research 1, 36-39.

Ansoff, H.I. (1957), Strategies for diversification, Harvard Business Review, 35 (Sept/Oct), 113-124.

Audenaert, A. and J-B.E.M. Steenkamp (1997), Means-end theory and laddering in agricultural marketing research. In: B. Wierenga, A. van Tilburg, K. Grunert, J-B.E.M. Steenkamp and M. Wedel (Eds), Agricultural Marketing and Consumer Behavior in a Changing World. Boston: Kluwer Academic Publishers, 217-230.

Bech, A.C., E. Engelund, H.J. Juhl, K. Kristensen and C.S. Poulsen (1994), QFood - Optimal Design of Food Products. MAPP working paper no 19. Aarhus: The Aarhus School of Business.

Booz, Allen and Hamilton (1982), New Product Management for the 1980's. New York: Booz, Allen and Hamilton.

Buzzell, R.D. and B.T. Gale (1987), The PIMS Principles: Linking Strategy to Performance. New York: The Free Press.

Churchill, G.A. and C. Suprenant (1982), An investigation into the determinants of customer satisfaction. Journal of Marketing Research 19, 491-504.

Cooper, R.G. (1993), Winning at New Products: Accelerating the Process from Idea to Launch, 2nd ed. Reading, Ma: Addision-Wesley.

Cooper, R.G. and E.J. Kleinschmidt (1990), New products: The Key Success Factors. Chicago: American Marketing Association.

Craig, A. and S.J. Hart (1992), Where to now in product development research? European Journal of Marketing 26, 3-49.

Cunningham, S.M. (1967), The major dimensions of perceived risk. In: D.F. Cox (Ed.), Risk Taking and Information Handling in Consumer Behavior. Boston, Ma: Harvard University Press, 82-108.

Darby, M.R. and E. Karni (1973), Free competition and the optimal amount of fraud. Journal of Law and Economics 16, 67-88.

Engel, J.F. and R.D. Blackwell (1982), Consumer Behavior, 4th ed. Chicago: The Dryden Press.

Fishbein, M. and I. Ajzen (1975), Belief, Attitude, Intention and Behavior. Reading, Ma: Addison-Wesley.

Griffin, A. and J.R. Hauser (1992), Patterns of communication among marketing, engineering and manufacturing - a comparison between two new product teams. Management Science 38 (3), 360-373.

Griffin, A. and J.R. Hauser (1993), The voice of the customer. Marketing Science 12(1), 1-27.

Griffin, A. and J.R. Hauser (1996), Integrating R&D and marketing: a review and analysis of the literature. Journal of Product Innovation Management 13, 191-215.

Grunert, K., A. Baadsgaard, H. Hartvig Larsen and T. Koed Madsen (1996), Market Orientation in Food and Agriculture. Boston: Kluwer Academic Publishers.

Grunert, K., H. Harmsen, H. Hartvig Larsen, E. Sorensen and S. Bisp (1997), New areas in agricultural and food marketing. In: B. Wierenga, A. van Tilburg, K. Grunert, J-B.E.M. Steenkamp and M. Wedel (Eds), Agricultural Marketing and Consumer Behavior in a Changing World. Boston: Kluwer Academic Publishers, 3- 30.

Gupta, A.K., S.P. Raj and D. Willemon (1986), A model for studying R&D - marketing interface in the product innovation process. Journal of Marketing 50, 7-17.

Gutman, J. (1982), A means-end chain model based on consumer categorization processes. Journal of Marketing, 46 (spring), 60-72.

Haley, R.I. (1968), Benefit segmentation: a decision oriented research tool. Journal of Marketing 32 (July), 30-35.

Hart, S. (1996), New Product Development: a reader. London: The Dryden Press.

Hauser, J.R. and D. Clausing (1988), The House of Quality. Harvard Business Review 66(3), 63-73.

Hauser, J.R. and P. Simmie (1981), Profit maximizing perceptual positioning: an integrated theory for the selection of product features and price. Management Science 27 (2), 33-56.

Heeler, R.M., C. Okechuku and S. Reid (1979), Attribute importance: contrasting measurements, Journal of Marketing Research 16 (Feb), 60-63.

Hoyer, W.D. and S.P. Brown (1990), Effects of brand awareness on choice for a common repeat-purchase product. Journal of Consumer Research, 17 (Sept), 141-148.

Hughes, D. (1994), Breaking with Tradition: Building Partnerships and Alliances in the European Food Industry. Wye: Wye College Press.

Jacoby, J. and R.W. Chestnut (1978), Brand Loyalty: Measurement and Management. New York: John Wiley & Sons, Inc.

Janiszewski, C. (1988), Preconscious processing effects: the independence of attitude formation and conscious thought. Journal of Consumer Research, 15 (Sept), 199-209.

Kahn, B.E. and L. McAlister (1997), Grocery Revolution: the New Focus on the Consumer. Reading, Ma.: Addison-Wesley.

Kotler, P. (1994), Marketing Management: Analysis, Planning, Implementation and Control, 8th ed. Englewood Cliffs: Prentice Hall.

Lancaster, K. (1966), A new approach to consumer theory. Journal of Political Economy, 74, 567-585.

MacMillan, I.C. and R.G. McGrath (1997), Discovering new points of differentiation. Harvard Business Review (July/August), 133-145.

Meulenberg, M.T.G. (1997), Evolution of agricultural marketing institutions: a channel approach. In: B. Wierenga, A. van Tilburg, K. Grunert, J-B.E.M. Steenkamp and M. Wedel (Eds), Agricultural Marketing and Consumer Behavior in a Changing World. Boston: Kluwer Academic Publishers, 95-108.

Myers, J.H. and M.I. Alpert (1968), Determinant buying attitudes: meaning and measurement. Journal of Marketing 32 (Oct), 13-20.

Myers, J.H. and M.I. Alpert (1977), Semantic confusion in attitude research: salience vs. importance vs. determinance. In: W.D. Perrault (ed.), Advances in Consumer Research, Vol. 4 Atlanta: Association for Consumer Research, 106-110.

Monroe, K.B. and R. Krishnan (1985), The effect of price and subjective product evaluations. In: Jacoby, J. and J.C. Olson (eds), Perceived Quality. Lexington: Lexington Books, 209-232.

Narasimhan, C. and S.K. Sen (1992), Measuring quality perceptions, Marketing Letters 3, 147-156.

Olson, J.C. (1972), Cue utilization of the Quality Perception Process: a Cognitive Model and an Empirical Test. Unpublished doctoral dissertation, Purdue University.

Porter, M.E. (1980), Competitive Strategy. New York: The Free Press.

Ram, S. and J.N. Sheth (1989), Consumer resistance to innovations: the marketing problem and its solutions. The Journal of Consumer Marketing, 6 (2), 5-14.

Reynolds, T.J. and J. Gutman (1988), Laddering theory, method, analysis and interpretation. Journal of Advertising Research 28(1), 11-31.

Souder, W.E. (1987), Managing New Product Innovations. Lexington: Lexington Books.

Steenkamp, J-B.E.M. (1989), Product Quality: an Investigation into the Concept and How it is Perceived by Consumers. Assen: Van Gorcum

Steenkamp, J-B.E.M. (1990), A conceptual model of the quality perception process. Journal of Business Research, 21, 309-333.

Steenkamp, J-B.E.M. (1997), Dynamics in consumer behavior with respect to agricultural and food products. In: B. Wierenga, A. van Tilburg, K. Grunert, J-B.E.M. Steenkamp and M. Wedel (Eds), Agricultural Marketing and Consumer Behavior in a Changing World. Boston: Kluwer Academic Publishers, 143-188.

Steenkamp, J-B.E.M. and J.C.M. van Trijp (1986), Consumentenbeoordeling van de sensorische vleeskwaliteit [Consumer evaluation of sensory quality of meat]. Rijswijk: PVV (in Dutch).

Steenkamp, J-B.E.M. and J.C.M. van Trijp (1988), Sensorische Kwaliteitsbeoordeling en Bereidingsgewoonten Vers Vlees [Sensory Quality Evaluation and Preparation Habits of Fresh Meat]. Rijswijk: PVV (in Dutch).

Steenkamp, J-B.E.M. and J.C.M. van Trijp (1989), A methodology for estimating the maximum price consumers are willing to pay in relation to perceived quality and consumer characteristics. Journal of International Food and Agribusiness Marketing, 1: 7-24.

Steenkamp, J-B.E.M. and J.C.M. van Trijp (1996), Quality guidance: a consumer-based approach to food quality improvement using partial least squares. European Review of Agricultural Economics, 23: 195-215.

Steenkamp, J-B.E.M. and J.C.M. van Trijp (1997), Attribute Elicitation in Consumer Research: A comparison of three methods. Marketing Letters 8 (2), 153-165.

Stenson, H.H. (1982), Multidimensional psychophysics. In: N. Hirschberg and L.G. Humphreys (eds.), Multivariate Applications in the Social Sciences. Hillsdale: Lawrence Erlbaum.

Urban, G.L. and J.R. Hauser (1993), Design and Marketing of New Products, 2nd ed. Englewood Cliffs: Prentice Hall.

Urban, G.L., J.R Hauser, W.J. Qualls. B.D. Weinberg, J.D. Bohlmann and R.A. Chicos (1997), Information Acceleration: validation and lessons from the field. Journal of Marketing Research 34 (Feb), 143-153.

Van Trijp, J.C.M., J-B.E.M. Steenkamp and M.J.J.M. Candel (1997), Quality labeling as instrument to create product equity: the case of IKB in the Netherlands. In: B. Wierenga, A. van Tilburg, K. Grunert, J-B.E.M. Steenkamp and M. Wedel (Eds), Agricultural Marketing and Consumer Behavior in a Changing World. Boston: Kluwer Academic Publishers, 210-215.

Wierenga, B. (1997), Competing for the future in the agricultural and food channel. In: B. Wierenga, A. van Tilburg, K. Grunert, J-B.E.M. Steenkamp and M. Wedel (Eds), Agricultural Marketing and Consumer Behavior in a Changing World. Boston: Kluwer Academic Publishers, 31-55.

Wind, J. and V. Mahajan (1997), Issues and opportunities in new product development: an introduction to the special issue. Journal of Marketing Research, 34 (Feb), 1-12.

Woodruff, R.B. (1997), Customer value: the next source for competitive advantage. Journal of the Academy of Marketing Science 25 (2), 139-153.

Zajonc, R.B. (1980), Feeling and thinking: preferences need no inferences. American Psychologist 35, 151-175

4 Product Development in the Food Industry

Matthijs Dekker and Anita R. Linnemann

4.1 Introduction

On his journey from Troy to reclaim his threatened home on Ithaca Odysseus lands on the island of the nymph Calypso. Calypso takes Odysseus to her cavern and there, "The nymph placed at his side the various kinds of food and drink that mortal men consume, and sat down facing the noble Odysseus. Her maids set ambrosia and nectar beside her, and the two helped themselves to the meal spread before them." (Book V, 195-200). Gods apparently consume merely one type of food, namely ambrosia, and drink nothing other than nectar. This is apparently all they need, and all they want. This consumption pattern is completely different for us humans. We desire a variety of foods and demand a large choice of beverages. No single product is good enough to satisfy our demands in terms of taste or nutrition.

This chapter is about the continuous quest for new foods and beverages that are required to fulfil the demands of consumers.

4.2 Historical developments in food production and preparation

Long ago man obtained food by hunting, fishing and gathering. The invention of the use of fire in food preparation -approximately 500,000 years ago- gave rise to a range of new food products. Many, particularly starchy, plant parts could be made digestible by heating, and many animal food products became more attractive for consumption.

The start of deliberate plant production, agriculture, was the next dramatic change in food supply. Walstra (1996) describes changes in food processing that occurred concurrently. Pieces of food were initially put in hot ashes or on hot stones. This heating process was improved by the development of the spit and grid. The invention of pottery-making made it possible to cook food above a fire. Pots also turned out to be very useful for storing foods. Storage of food, and its preservation, were a matter of life and death due to the periodicity of crop production.

Heating of foods improved their preservation potential. However, heat treatment alone was insufficient since this only resulted in a temporary reduction of the number of micro-organisms and not in their permanent exclusion. Smoking foods was a better form of preservation due to two simultaneous effects: drying and the application of chemical compounds with a preserving effect. Drying in the open air was practised too, preferably in the sun. Cold storage was possible in some regions. Later on, salt and sugar became available as preservatives. Mostly preservation methods were combined.

Milling of grain was the next important development in food preparation. This practice allowed the separation of grain and chaff. Very soon many uses for flour were developed, including making porridge or bread. During storage porridge and dough could start to ferment. Fermenting porridge eventually yielded beer. Fermented dough or sourdough rose during baking and produced more attractive bread. Gradually many other fermented food products were developed such as wine, cheese, yoghurt, sauerkraut and tempeh (fermented soya). Fermentation contributed to preservation (for example due to the presence of lactic acid or alcohol), but it also improved taste and/or reduced harmfulness (tempeh).

Furthermore new processing methods were developed to concentrate valuable substances or to isolate them. Examples include the extraction of fat and protein from milk to make butter and cheese, respectively; edible oil was obtained from olives, nuts or seeds by pressing. In addition starch was produced from roots and tubers by grinding, washing and concentrating.

These historical developments in technological possibilities for food preparation and processing have eventually led to the range of food products available to the present-day consumer. The goals of food preparation have remained more or less unaltered over time, in spite of the wide variety of observed changes in food preparation methods. Three categories of methodologies are discerned, namely those aiming at i) the production of microbiologically safe food products with sufficient shelf life (i.e. no reduction in quality during a certain period, the length of which depends on the type of product), ii) the production of tasty and digestible food products, iii) the production of foods with a high nutritional value which contain the essential components to maintain and, if possible, improve human health and iv) more recently the production of foods using environmentally friendly methods (sustainable production methods).

4.3 Industrialisation of food production

Some decades ago, a certain homogenisation of food production took place. This development occurred when traditional methods were replaced by mechanized, large-scale industrial production processes. Uniformity in consumer needs formed the basis of the success of the products that the newly developed industries offered.

In the course of time, industries started to diversify their supply of products. This diversification was stimulated in particular by increasing prosperity after World War II. Advances in technology facilitated the production of an ever-increasing amount of diverse products, without violating industrial productivity levels (van Asseldonk, 1995).

Nowadays, consumer behaviour is considered to be increasingly unpredictable. Marketing specialists describe the present consumer as 'capricious, impulsive, spontaneous and irrational' (Andrea, 1995). This description reflects the frustration resulting from the inadequacy of present marketing strategies. These once successful strategies were based on the assumption that consumers can always be divided in target groups with similar needs.

The observed unpredictability of consumers' needs and wishes makes it increasingly difficult to make products according to fixed production plans (van Asseldonk, 1995). The ultimate result of this development is that initiation and control of production chains will be in the hands of the consumers. This presents a great challenge to the food production industry. Instead of exploiting similarities in consumer needs, as in the past, industries will have to exploit differences between consumers to be successful in the future.

4.4   Reversal of production chains

Traditionally, production chains (as schematically shown in figure 4.1) are characterized by two distinct features: i) the one-way communication from producers of raw materials (most often farmers) to the users of end products (consumers), and ii) the understanding of the concept of quality. Quality was, and in a number of cases still is, predominantly based on production costs and productivity (i.e. at the level of primary production: kg per hectare, and at industrial level: kg product per kg raw material). Nowadays many actors in the production chain still have these two aspects of quality in common. However, each actor may also employ a number of additional quality determinants, such as homogeneity and storability of raw materials at industrial level and ease of handling at retail level. Such quality determinants are sometimes incompatible, whereby the quality determinants formulated by one actor in the chain may conflict with those used by another actor, or even with those of consumers.

The traditional approach observed in the operation of production chains was also found in the organisation and implementation of scientific research. Research was organized by discipline and could not deal with the new challenges that arise from rapidly changing consumer preferences. In the past, agronomists focused their efforts predominantly on raising crop yield levels through improved cultivation practices and efficient use of inputs such as fertilizer and pesticides. Plant breeders were concerned with creating new high-yield varieties that were less susceptible to pests and disease. The combined efforts of breeders and agronomists resulted in products that were delivered to the industry for further processing. Industries asses-

Figure 4.1
The food production
chain

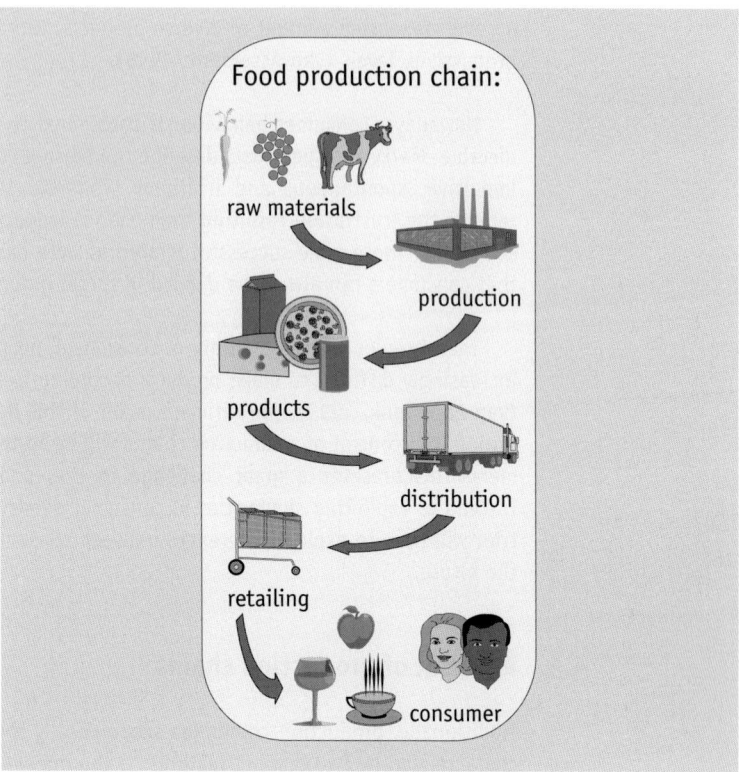

sed the quality of the raw material they received and consequently tried to make the most of it.

This traditional approach to research and production leaves many possibilities for improving product quality open, and as such is inadequate to respond to the changes that the present market developments dictate. First of all it is necessary to integrate the complete production chain, and consumers' demands must act as the driving force for the production chain (Jongen *et al.*, 1996).

4.5 Perspectives on traditional product development

The development and introduction of new food products require large investments, in terms of money as well as manpower. And yet the rate of success is very disappointing. Failures are commonly attributed to the predominantly empirical methods that are used in product development. According to Keuning (1994), it takes on average 7 to 10 years from the first idea about a possible new product to actual market introduction. Most ideas never even reach the marketing stage. For every product entering the test market, 13 others have not survived the development process at laboratory or pilot-plant scale (Fuller, 1994). Of the products that are finally launched, fifty percent does not survive the test market. More than twenty percent of newly introduced food products disappears within three years from the market, and after five years less than twenty percent of these products is still on the market. Figure 4.2 shows this funnelling effect from ideas to a successful product.

Figure 4.2
The innovation funnel from ideas to successful products

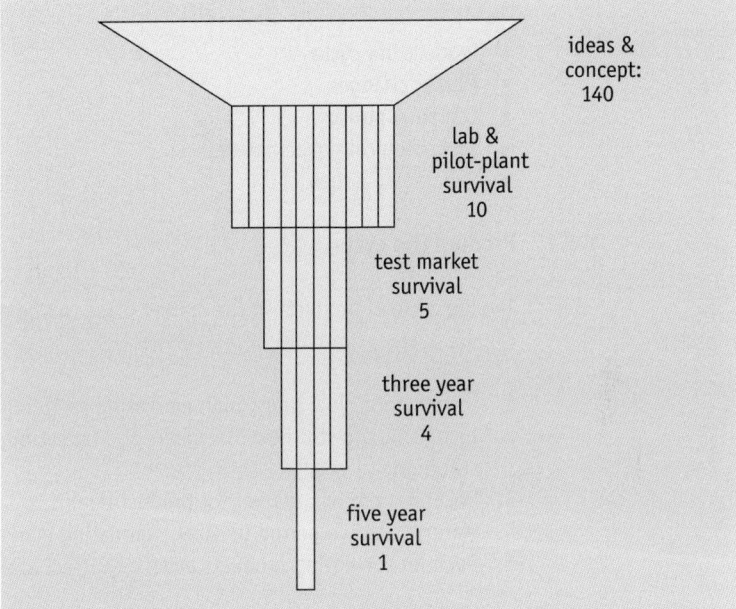

The history of product development shows a number of consecutive generations of products. These generations are characterized by an increase over time in the complexity of the quality standards they have to meet. The most important criterion for the first generation of products was improvement in preservation and the prevention of spoilage. The important feature of the second generation was that products had to comply with specific demands regarding nutritional value and taste. The third generation was characterized by convenience for use. The additional requirement for the present, fourth generation is that food products must fulfil a role in the preservation and improvement of human health (Jongen, 1995).

4.6 Reasons for developing new food products

Taking into account the very high rate of failure of developing and introducing new food products, one must have very strong reasons for putting time and money into the endeavour. Apparently industry has these reasons more and more, judging by the ever increasing number of product launches which take place. In the USA the number of product launches was 1030 in 1970,

2016 in 1980 and had risen to 9192 by 1990 (Kantor, 1991)!

The final consideration which has to be made when planning product development is always the profitability of the company in the longer term. Despite the huge costs involved in the process, future earnings should always more than compensate these. The reasons for initiating product development can be divided into five categories (Fuller, 1994) which are discussed in the following sections:

- Product life cycle
- Market changes
- Company policy
- Technological developments
- Regulatory issues

4.6.1 Product life cycle

The life cycle of products in the market place can be divided into five phases (Figure 4.3):

1. Introduction: low sales, high marketing spending.
2. Increasing growth: new consumers and repeat-buyers, promotional costs still high.
3. Declining growth: market for product begins to saturate.
4. Maturity: stable period in sales, stagnating market.
5. Decline: competing products adversely affect sales.

The length of these phases varies for each product. A food company will of course have many different products in different phases of their life cycles. To maintain its overall profitability it is therefore essential for a company to initiate new life cycles regularly by introducing newly developed products.

Figure 4.3
Product life cycle in terms of sales volume (a) and profit (b)

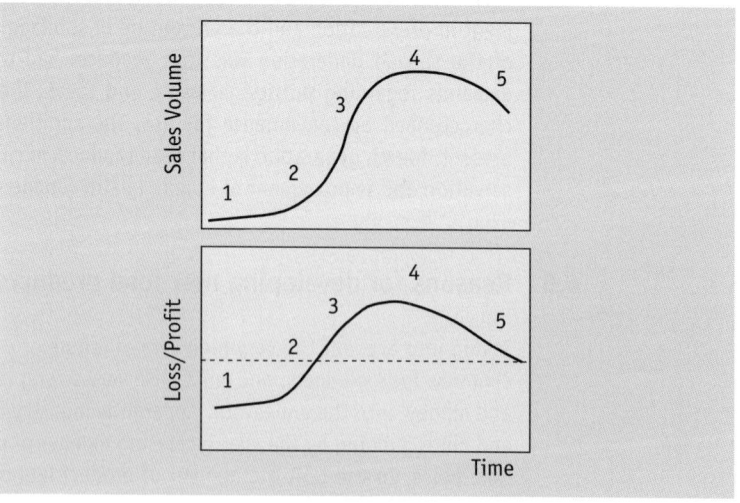

4.6.2 Market changes

The marketplace is constantly changing as a result of a number of predictable and unpredictable trends. Retail outlets for food are currently taking on many new forms; department stores, mail catalogue shopping, electronic shopping and internet shopping are changing consumers' buying habits. The traditional supermarket is also adopting new concepts in retailing, and is becoming a collection of specialized food stores (Fuller 1994). 'Shop-around-the-clock' convenience stores are increasing in numbers. Less time is spent on preparing food, and convenience foods are popular. Dining in restaurants and buying take-away food is becoming more popular. More people are becoming aware of the relation between their health and the food they consume.

All these changes are taking place because the consumers makes decisions which are based on convenience for daily life. Food manufacturers serving this market sector must respond quickly to changes.

Another important factor in the market is the competition. The launch of an improved product by a competitor can be a serious threat to the position of a company. Retaliatory actions may therefore be required. These can be very short term actions like new pricing strategies, promotional gimmicks, or medium term actions in the form of the development of comparable products (the 'me too' approach).

The fluidity of the market place must be accepted by the food manufacturer as a challenge. It should be kept in mind that no single product will answer all the demands of consumers. New products are required to satisfy emerging market niches.

The use of the marketplace (i.e. consumer demands) as the basis for structured product development is incorporated in the tool "Quality Function Deployment" which is discussed in 4.8.

4.6.3 Company policy

Each company has the desire to grow and make profit in a certain area. The area in which the company has chosen to be active is often translated into a mission statement. This mission statement can be extended with a more practical strategy (Keuning, 1994). A strategy should contain the following elements: objectives, resources required, and timing. Usually the objectives contain an element of growth (Fuller, 1994), e.g. in terms of market share (relative to a competitor), entering a new geographical area, or selling more profitable products.

Historical developments, available resources and the competition are issues that influence the content of company strategies. It is essential that the strategy is known throughout the entire company and that practical decisions reflect its implementation to all employees (Keuning, 1994).

4.6.4 Technological developments

The developments in scientific research and their implementation in new technologies or new materials create novel products and services that were simply not possible in the past.

Good examples can be found in the area of food packaging. The start of the large scale food industry was the introduction of the three-piece can, which enabled safe canning and sterilisation of foods. Nowadays a multitude of materials in all shapes and sizes are available for food packaging: steel, aluminium, glass, plastics, coated paper, laminates of paper, plastic, aluminium and even glass. These materials have permitted the manufacture of a wide range of containers with unique properties to preserve and protect the high quality of foods. Novel forms of packaging can be microwaveable, edible, degradable, and/or recyclable.

Greater knowledge of food quality deterioration processes has given rise to new products with good stability in combination with higher quality (improved flavour, colour, texture, etc.) and nutritional value (higher levels of vitamins, etc.).

Knowledge in the area of nutrition and health has led to a growing awareness of the role of food in health. The relation between certain foods and the occurrence of cancer and cardiovascular disease in particular is receiving more attention. The development of functional foods is a consequence of this knowledge (see 4.9).

Developments in computers linked with telecommunications and information databases through the internet have enabled even the smallest food processing company to use the latest information in their product development activities (Fuller, 1994).

4.6.5 Regulatory issues

The objectives of (US) government food legislation are (Wood, 1985):

1. To ensure that the food supply is safe and free from contamination within the limits of available knowledge and at a cost affordable by the consumer.
2. To develop standards for composition of foods and labelling of foods together with food manufacturers.
3. To maintain fair trading and competition among retailers and manufacturers in such a way as to benefit consumers.

The first and second objectives will influence technical development of food products. The second and third will influence the marketing and sales possibilities. Besides national legislation there are international bodies which can affect food product development through international trade laws or other legislation. Examples are the General Agreement on Trade and Tariffs (GATT), the European Union (EU), the International Standards Organisation (ISO), the Codex Alimentaris of the FAO/WHO and many bi- or tri-lateral trade agreements between countries (Fuller, 1994).

4.7 Quality determinants

End product quality in and of itself does not exist (Jongen, 1995). Consumers buy and consume products for a number of reasons. These reasons relate predominantly to the characteristics of the product, but they are also influenced by, for instance, production methods. These quality attributes can be divided into the so-called intrinsic quality determinants and the extrinsic quality determinants. This terminology has been discussed extensively in chapter 3.4.

The intrinsic factors refer to physical product characteristics such as taste, texture and shelf life. These intrinsic factors can be measured in an objective manner. Take, for example, the texture of a product. Texture can be defined in a physical-chemical way in terms of the composition of cell wall material and structure. Consumers describe these attributes with words such as crisp, floury or tough. In addition there are several other attributes like taste, nutritional value, shelf life, freshness, safety, appearance and health. The combination of all these attributes together determines the intrinsic end product quality.

Extrinsic factors relate to the way in which the food was produced, such as the use of pesticides, the type of packaging material, a specific processing technology or the use of genetically modified organisms during the production of ingredients. These extrinsic factors have no direct influence on the characteristics of the product, but they can be of overriding importance in the purchasing policy of consumers.

The sum of the intrinsic and extrinsic factors finally determines the attractiveness of products to consumers.

4.8 Structured approach for product development: Quality Function Deployment

In the previous section it has become clear that in order to make product development more successful one has to obey the voice of the customers. This seems to be an obvious way of approaching the process of designing new products. However, in practice there are a large number of reasons why this is difficult to achieve. In companies each separate department usually specializes in one particular activity: market research, research and development, engineering production, quality control, finance, purchasing, sales and marketing. Coordinating these activities is incredibly difficult. Product development involves the input of the expertise of all these departments and is therefore an extremely complex process. Quality Function Deployment (QFD), a planning tool, is used by the automotive, electronics, computer software, defence, health care and more recently also food industries to aid in the management of this process and to bring better products to the market (Hofmeister, 1991).

QFD originated in 1972 at Mitsubishis's Kobe shipyard in Japan (Kogure and Akao, 1983). Since then it has been widely used in Japan, particularly among the major exporting companies. More than half of the Union of Japanese Scientists and Engineering-member companies were using QFD by 1986 (King, 1987). QFD was introduced to the USA by Yoji Akao in 1983 and the 3M Corporation became the first company to apply QFD in the USA (Adams and Gavoor, 1990). Since then QFD has spread to nearly every industry and has been used in the food industry since 1987 (Hofmeister, 1991; Charteris, 1993).

QFD is a systematic means of ensuring that customer or market requirements are accurately translated into relevant technical requirements and actions through each stage of product development (Fortuna, 1988). As such, it is a planning process that ensures that quality is engineered into a product or process at the design stage (Charteris, 1993).

QFD will help an organisation to (Hofmeister, 1991):

- Gain an understanding of customer wants and needs.
- Recognize and incorporate company and regulated requirements.
- Develop product requirements to ensure that customer wants are being addressed.
- Evaluate the competition from a technical as well as a customer viewpoint.
- Establish long- and short-term priorities.
- Document the work as a knowledge base for the future.
- Formalize the communication process.
- Institutionalize continuous improvement.

4.8.1 The QFD method

The QFD method begins with by seting up a conceptual map (Hauser and Clausing, 1988). This map consists of various types of matrices that are linked together. The first matrix is often referred to as the "House of Quality" because of the shape of the matrix (Figure 4.4).

This chart is complex at first glance, as it contains a great deal of information. However, once one is familiar with a few simple conventions, it becomes second nature to read and understand the chart. The "house" can be divided into various rooms and segments. The next part of this section will explain the methodology of using the matrix approach for product development. The development of an improved tomato ketchup is given by way of an example (de Vries, 1996; Costa, 1996). We have simplified the account of the development process to a large extent here for the sake of readability, but the principle of the QFD concept remains the same.

4.8.2 The voice of the customer (WHAT's)

The first room of the house of quality is known as the WHAT's. This is a list of customer requirements, which often is referred to as the 'voice of the customer'. These items are usually vague, general, and difficult to implement directly. This information can be obtained from market research. Often

Figure 4.4
The simplified house
of quality for tomato
ketchup

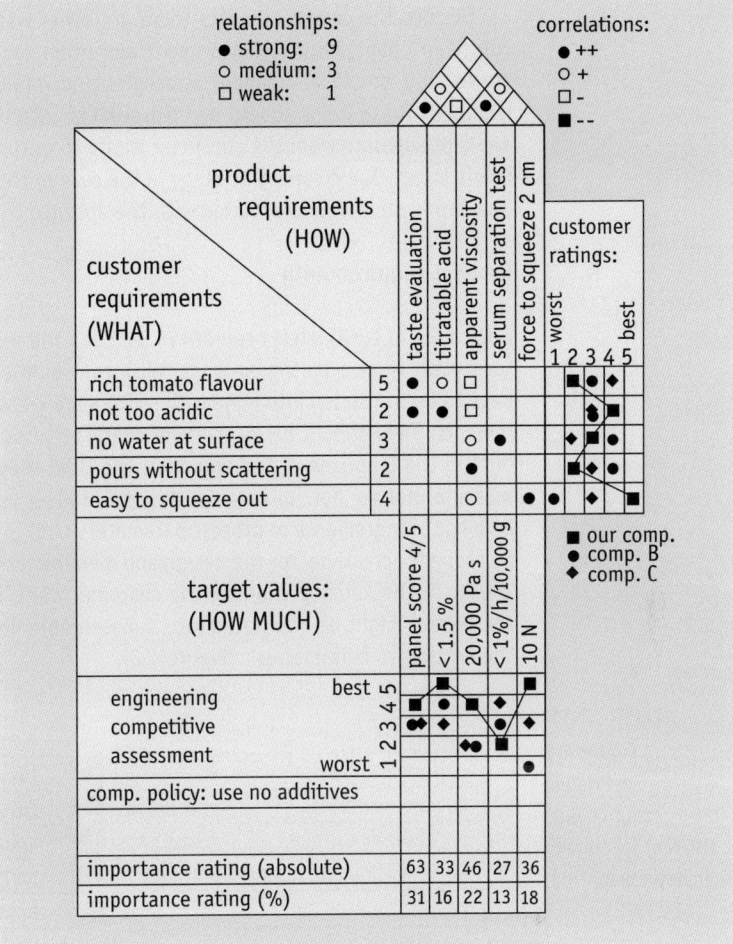

the most powerful customer wants are never verbalized, but are observed (Hofmeister, 1991). Other sources of information include customer complaints about previous similar products. Some of these customer wants for the tomato example are given in Figure 4.5.

Figure 4.5
Voice of the
customer for
improved tomato
ketchup (simplified)

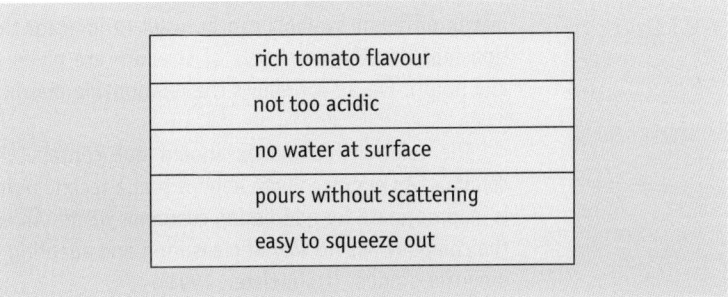

Besides the customer wants there are other wants to consider, as discussed in Chapter 4.6.3. Government and other regulations (these 'wants' are usually 'musts'!), company strategies and retailer wants should all be included. These items should be incorporated into the first QFD matrix but are kept separate from the consumer wants to ensure the consumer's voice is left intact. The company strategy in the case of tomato ketchup might be: 'Our brand should be associated with the absence of additives'.

4.8.3 Product requirements

Once a list of WHAT's has been drawn up, each will require further definition to explain what a particular want will mean for the product itself: WHAT's have to be translated into HOW's. The HOW's are known as the product requirements. They should be measurable characteristics that describe the product in the language of the engineer. The HOW should be read as: 'how to measure' not as 'how to accomplish'. The product requirements should not be a list of ingredients or process parameters, and in this way there will still be scope for creativity for the design and manufacturing people (Hofmeister, 1991). In the ketchup example the customer want 'easy to squeeze out of the bottle' might be translated into a measurable 'force needed to squeeze the bottle two centimetres'. (Figure 4.6).

Figure 4.6
Product requirements (HOW's) for tomato ketchup (simplified)

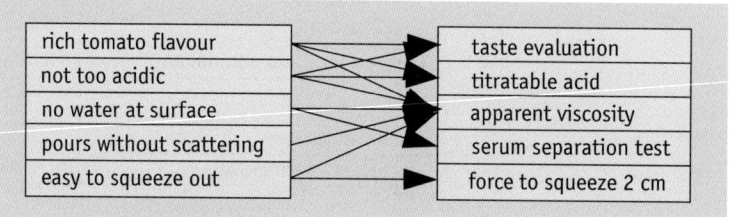

rich tomato flavour	taste evaluation
not too acidic	titratable acid
no water at surface	apparent viscosity
pours without scattering	serum separation test
easy to squeeze out	force to squeeze 2 cm

4.8.4 Relationship matrix

Looking at Figure 4.6 it can be seen that the process is more complex than just translating each WHAT into one or more HOW's: some of the HOW's will affect more than one WHAT. This complexity can be reduced by introducing the relationship matrix between the WHAT's and HOW's (Figure 4.7). In this matrix different symbols can be used to indicate the strength of the relationship. Usually four levels of strength are given (strong, medium, weak and none). Figure 4.7 shows the relationship matrix for the ketchup.

The relationship matrix should not contain empty or weak rows or columns. An empty column implies that a technological product requirement is inappropriate for addressing customer wants. An empty row indicates that the company has no way of measuring and adapting a customer want regarding the product (Hofmeister, 1991).

Figure 4.7
The relationship matrix for the tomato ketchup (simplified)

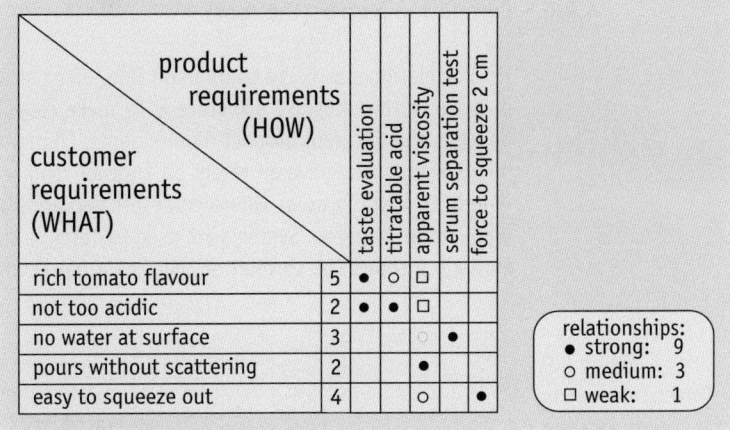

4.8.5 Objective target values (HOW MUCH)

Target values should be assigned to all the product requirements (HOW's). These levels should represent the customer wants and not necessarily the current performance levels. The customer want 'easy to squeeze out' was translated to 'force to squeeze bottle 2 cm', and through consumer research this can be given a value, e.g. 10 Newton. The HOW MUCH's provide specific objectives that drive the subsequent product design by means of objectively assessing progress, thus minimising 'opinion-eering' (Hofmeister, 1991). Figure 4.8 shows how the target values are introduced into the QFD matrix.

Figure 4.8
Target values for the HOW's of tomato ketchup (simplified)

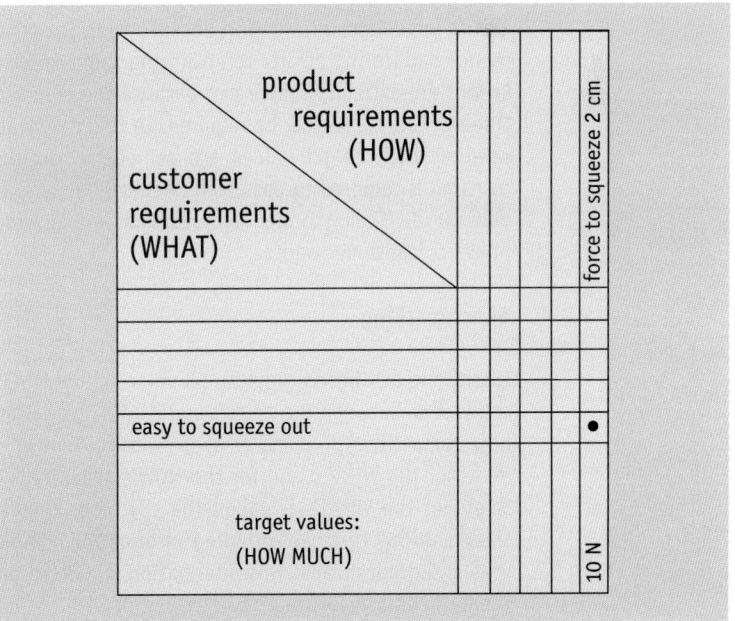

4.8.6   Correlation matrix (the roof)

The correlation matrix is a triangular table, often attached to the HOW's. The purpose of this roof-like structure is to make clear what correlations exist between the different product requirements. Changing one of these requirements will usually have an effect on another requirement. Using the roof it is easy to identify areas where trade-off decisions and research and development are required. Symbols are used to describe the types of correlations. Figure 4.9 shows the correlation matrix for our ketchup example.

**Figure 4.9
Correlation matrix
for tomato ketchup
(simplified)**

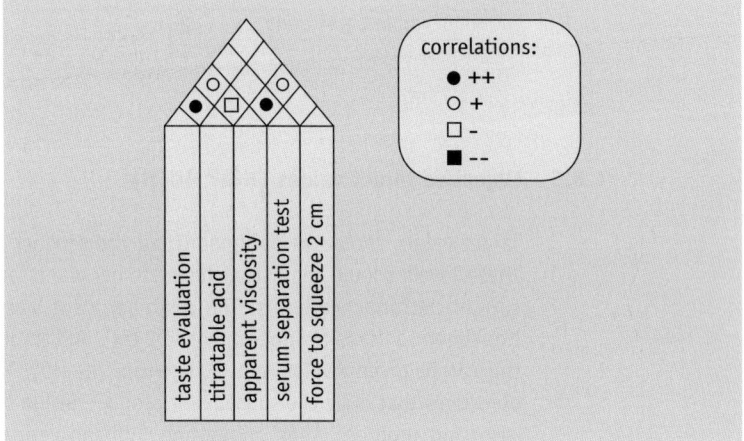

Strong positive correlations means that one requirement supports another. This is important information because resource efficiencies may be gained by not duplicating efforts to attain the same result. Strong negative correlations are extremely important because they represent conditions in which trade-off decisions may be required. In this case it is necessary to discover whether both target values are achievable or whether more innovative research is required to pass technological barriers. In this way QFD is valuable for identifying longer-term research and development projects that are linked to consumer wants.

4.8.7   Benchmarking

In order to establish proper target values (HOW MUCH's) and to ensure good correlation between the WHAT's and HOW's it is extremely important to know how competitive products compare with current company products. This is done for the WHAT's and for the HOW's separately. The competitive assessment of the WHAT's is called the customer competitive assessment, and should utilize customer-oriented information, gained through market surveys and other means. This information is plotted on the right-hand site of the QFD chart in Figure 4.10.

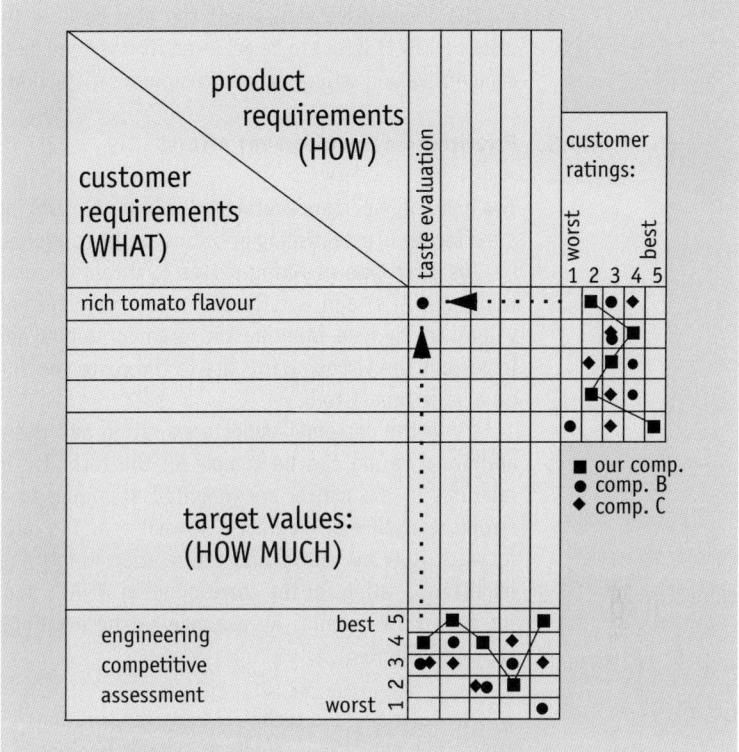

The competitive assessment of the HOW's is called the engineering competitive assessment. In order to obtain this information the competitive products are analysed by the company's own techniques (the same as establishing the values for the HOW's) It is strongly recommended that the product
engineers be directly involved in this process in order to gain the most complete understanding of competitive products (Hofmeister, 1992). This information is plotted graphically, in an area below the HOW MUCH's (Figure
4.10).

These two graphs yield very powerful information. If WHAT and HOW
items are strongly related to each other, then the customer and engineering
competitive assessments should also be consistent with each other. In our
tomato example the 'taste evaluation' product requirement (judged by the
company taste panel) is strongly related to the 'rich tomato flavour' customer want. This means that the competitive assessments for these items
should be consistent. In the example shown in Figure 4.10 the 'taste evaluation' rates the company's existing product as good (the best) while the
customer scores show exactly the opposite result: the company's product is
performing poorly on 'rich tomato flavour' (the worst). If such conflicts are
not solved properly there is a serious risk that the company will develope the
best possible product according to its in-house tests, but fail in the eyes of
the customers.

The competitive assessment can also be used to determine the target values (HOW MUCH's) to be achieved. This is done by selecting values that are competitive and reflect the real customer satisfaction (Hofmeister, 1991).

4.8.8 Priorities for development efforts

Two types of importance ratings usually are brought into QFD charts, and they are effective in establishing priorities for the continuous improvement efforts.

The first type of rating serves to establish customer priorities for the wants (WHAT's) and is reflected in the customer importance rating. These values are derived from market research studies and should indicate how important the various wants are to the customer. They are usually reported on a scale from 1 to 5.

Using the customer importance rating and the relationship matrix, an additional rating can be computed: the technical importance rating. The relations in the matrix are weighted according to a certain scheme: e.g. strong relation = 9; medium = 3; weak = 1. The ratings are now calculated for each HOW by multiplying the relation weight factor with the customer importance rating for the corresponding WHAT's and summing up the total for each HOW-column. An example of these ratings in the QFD matrix is shown in Figure 4.11.

The customer and technical importance ratings should not be taken literally , but serve as a guide to establish product development priorities (Hofmeister, 1991).

Figure 4.11
Importance ratings for the tomato ketchup (simplified)

customer requirements (WHAT)		taste evaluation	titratable acid	apparent viscosity	serum separation test	force to squeeze 2 cm
rich tomato flavour	5	●	○	□		
not too acidic	2	●	●	□		
no water at surface	3			○	●	
pours without scattering	2			●		
easy to squeeze out	4			○		●
importance rating (absolute)		63	33	46	27	36
importance rating (%)		31	16	22	13	18

4.8.9 The complete first 'house of quality'

The product planning matrix we have built is often called the 'House of Quality'. It may be difficult to understand at first glance, even using this simplified example. For food products the house may contain a matrix of up to a hundred different WHAT's and HOW's. However, the house is built up of graphically depicted elements, all of which are crucial for effective product development decision making.

It is very likely that the information discussed thus far will already be available somewhere within a company. The key advantages to using the QFD approach are: one is forced to take the time to pull all information together and actually use it to satisfy the customer; cross functional teams are working on avoiding problems instead of solving them later on; the 'voice of the customer' is systematically used to drive all aspects of the product development process.

It is important to realize that QFD is not a fixed process; it can be adapted in many ways to make it suit the particular needs for the development of the company's products (Hofmeister, 1991).

4.8.10 Cascading to the next 'houses'

The product planning matrix that has been built should now be translated into matrices for design, process, production and packaging of the product.

Figure 4.12
Cascade of the QFD matrices for product and package

This cascading from matrix to matrix is done by making the HOW (MUCH)'s of the previous chart the WHAT's of the next chart. To keep all charts manageable, the items which are going to appear on the next chart

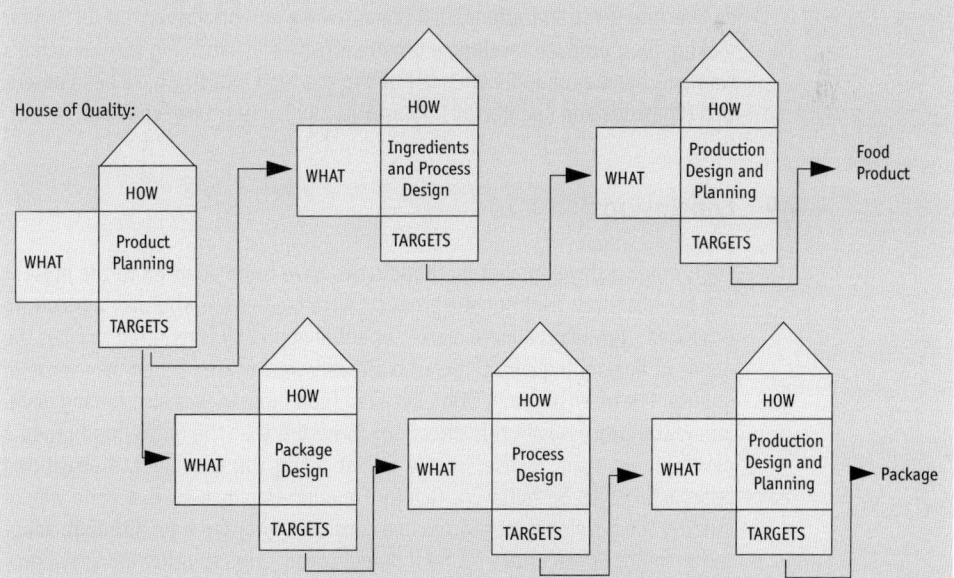

should be selected carefully. Usually only the 'new', 'important' (for the customer!) and the 'difficult' HOW's are taken to the next chart.

After the product planning matrix two separate development routes are usually made: one for the product and one for the package (Hofmeister, 1991). These are shown in Figure 4.12.

The package development route usually consists of the following matrices: product planning, package design, manufacturing process design and production design and planning.

In the food product development route the matrices for the design of composition of the product and the design of the processes usually have to be combined because of the many interactions between ingredients and process conditions.

4.8.11 Application of QFD for food products

QFD was not developed specifically for food product development. In fact it was a long time before the technique was even taken up by the food industry. There are a number of reasons for this:
- Foods can be very complex products; many ingredients show interactions and affect the way processes should be designed and optimized. This gives rise to a very large and complicated relationship matrix.
- Ingredients for foods show a natural variation which may require continuos adaptation based on their specifications.
- Customer wants can be very diverse and variable. This can result in very large lists of WHAT's and HOW's which are difficult to capture in a very precise target value (HOW MUCH).

Despite these limitations, QFD seems to be a potentially very useful tool for making food product development more effective in satisfying the consumer's wants. A number of applications of QFD in the food industry have been described (Charteris and Keogh, 1991; Charteris, 1992, 1993; Charteris et al., 1992).

4.9 Conclusions

Food product development methodologies have to be adapted to the present market situation. Traditionally products were made from whatever agriculture produced. Nowadays a more market oriented approach is required to meet the needs of demanding consumers who are very well aware of their own sense of quality. The intense competition between food industries is also forcing developmental processes in this direction. To ensure that the entire food product development team focuses purely on satisfying the consumer, a structured approach has to be followed. Quality Function Deployment is a good way of guiding the development process in a consumer oriented way. Although adaptation might be necessary for food products compared to other industrial products, QFD can be an extremely useful tool for food product development.

References

Adams, R. & M. Gavoor, 1990. Quality Function Deployment: its promise and reality. ASQC Quality Congress Transactions 44, 33-38.

Andrea, J.G., 1995. 15 miljoen markten. Conferentie Massaindividualisering. WTC Rotterdam. October, 24.

Asseldonk, A.G.M. van, 1995. Een goed bedrijf is op zijn toekomst voorbereid. Conferentie Massa-Individualisering. WTC Rotterdam. 24 oktober 1995.

Charteris, W.P. & M.K. Keogh, 1991. Table spreads - trends in the European market. Journal of the Society of Dairy Technology 44, 3-8.

Charteris, W.P., 1992. Food quality by design in product development and processing. Food Ireland 2, 44-45.

Charteris, W.P., P.M. Kennedy, M. Heapes & W. Reville, 1992. A new very low fat table spread. Farm and Food Research 1 [3] 18-19.

Charteris, W.P., 1993. Quality Function Deployment: a quality engineering technology for the food industry. Journal of the Society of Dairy Technology 46, 12-21.

Costa, A.I.A., 1996. Development of methodologies for quality modelling: an application on tomato ketchup. MSc. thesis, Department of Food Technology and Nutrition Sciences Agricultural University Wageningen. 98pp.

Fortuna, R.M., 1988. Beyond quality: taking SPC upstream. Quality Progress 21 [6], 23-28.

Fuller, G.W., 1994. New food product development: from concept to marketplace. CRC Series in Contemporary Food Science. CRC Press, Boca Raton, USA. 275 pp.

Hauser, J.R. & D. Clausing, 1988. The house of quality. Harvard Business Review 66 [5/6], 63-73.

Hofmeister, K.R., 1991. Quality Function Deployment: market success through customer-driven products. In: Food Product Development. Graf, E. & I.S. Saguy, eds. Van Nostrand Reinhold, New York, 189-210.

Jongen, W.M.F., 1995. Op functionele wijze naar een gezonde toekomst. Inaugural lecture, April 27, 1995. Wageningen Agricultural University. 33pp.

Jongen, W.M.F., A.R. Linnemann & M. Dekker, 1996. Productkwaliteit uitgangspunt bij aansturen product(ie)technologie vanuit keten. Voedingsmiddelentechnologie 29(26): 11-15.

Kantor, D., 1991. New product proliferation: are the benefits worth the cost? Prepared Foods, 160, 28, no 7.

Keuning, R., 1994. Produktontwikkeling in de levensmiddelenindustrie. Lecture notes; Department of Food Technology and Nutrition Sciences, Wageningen Agricultural University.

King, B. 1987. Better designs in half the time: Implementing Quality Function Deployment in America, Methuen MA: QOAL/QPC.

Kogure, M. & Y. Akao, 1983. Quality Function Deployment and CWQC in Japan. Quality Progress 16 [10], 25-29.

Vries, E. de, 1996. Quality Function Deployment: modelling the quality of ketchup. MSc. thesis, Department of Food Technology and Nutrition Sciences, Wageningen Agricultural University. 82pp.

Walstra, P., 1996. Historische ontwikkeling. In: Lecture notes, Voedsel en Voeding. Department of Food Technology and Nutrition Sciences, Wageningen Agricultural University.

Wood, S., 1985. Food law enforcement - where next? An industry viewpoint. Proceedings of the Institute of Food Science and Technology 18, 89-97.

5 Developments in technologies for food production

M.A.J.S. van Boekel

5.1 Introduction

Foods in Western society are to a large extent produced on an industrial scale. A rough estimate would be that 80-90% of the foods has undergone some treatment, from very simple to very complex. Over the past 100 years food processing methods have gradually changed into more scientifically oriented approaches, although the traditional roots of many food processes can still be recognised. There is still even a market for foods produced (or claimed to be produced) in the traditional way. For the sake of clarity, we would like to define technology as the use of scientifically based techniques to reach a goal in society; in this particular case the goal is production of foods. Defined in this way, the word technology is different from the word technique, which is not necessarily scientifically based (techniques exist as long as mankind) whereas technology only emerged in the late 19th century.

Today, technologies for food production are subject to many changes for several reasons. First, the market for food products has drastically changed in the last decades, from 'bulk' production in large quantities to a more consumer-oriented approach. For the food manufacturer this comes down to paying much more attention to food quality, as this has become a decisive factor in keeping or obtaining a market position. Such an approach has, of course, a large impact on the technologies to be applied. The basic point is: what technologies are available to help the manufacturer meet consumer demands. Another reason for changing technologies may be an economic push, in order to achieve a higher productivity and/or cost reduction (for instance, by making a process less labour intensive) and to increase process reliability. Environmental demands or a more general desire for sustainable food production may be reasons for change. Other reasons may include changes in the availability and composition or properties of raw materials, outside normal biological variability, for instance due to genetic modification. Remarkably, changes caused by technology push are rare in the food industry, although they do exist, high pressure treatment of foods and extrusion cooking being examples. Irradiation technology is another example but which has had limited success because of consumer rejection.

In this chapter we will try to put changes in technologies for food production into perspective. In order to do so, we will first give an overview of food technology and its role in food production. Within that framework, we will discuss new and existing technologies for food products. We will not go into detail but rather refer to relevant literature. An extensive impression of new and existing food technologies can be found in recent conference proceedings (Yano et al., 1994) and in a multi-authored book (Gaonkar, 1995). In addition, the Journals 'Trends in Food Science and Technology' and 'Food

Technology' offer frequent reviews of new developments in Food Science and Technology.

5.2 Food technology and its goals

It is perhaps useful to define the field of food technology more precisely for the remainder of this chapter. In our view, food technology comprises the combination of food process engineering and food science. Food process engineering uses chemical engineering principles (e.g. Niranjan, 1994), i.e. the application of mass, energy and momentum balances (the combination of which is called transport phenomena) in so-called unit operations. A unit operation is a basic process such as crystallization, filtration, extraction, centrifugation, fluid flow, pasteurization, etc., and a whole process is built up of a limited number of unit operations. Mass transfer occurs, for instance, in the extraction of oil from oil seeds or during distillation or crystallization; energy transfer occurs during pasteurization and sterilization in heat exchangers, momentum transfer is of importance in pumping of fluids, flow in pipes, etc. Frequently, mass, energy and momentum transfer occur at the same time in food processing. Knowledge of transport phenomena is necessary for process design, while it is also necessary to take into account phase changes and biochemical reactions that may happen during the process, and for this knowledge of thermodynamics and kinetics is necessary. What makes food process engineering different from chemical engineering is that foods are complex heterogeneous materials, and the relevant physico-chemical properties are often not well-known, such as thermal, colligative, mass transfer, rheological properties. In addition, such properties vary with the inherent variation in biological materials, and most importantly, they may drastically change during processing. More information on such properties can be found in Rao & Rizvi (1986). To complicate matters even further, reactants in a biochemical reaction may be separated at first, e.g. by cell walls, but may come together as a result of the process, for instance because cell walls are disrupted. It is here where food process engineering is inextricably entwined with understanding of the systems involved, i.e. with food science. Food science studies physical, chemical, biochemical and microbiological properties of foods, and, as indicated above, knowledge of these properties and of their changes due to processing is necessary for the food engineer to be able to design processes. The synthesis of process engineering and food science is food technology (including economic aspects of a process as well). Another aspect that distinguishes food engineering from most chemical engineering is the required safety of the food and consequently the special hygienic design of food processes, which may sometimes seriously limit possibilities; fouling of equipment (especially membranes and heat exchangers) can be quite severe in some cases and the subsequent cleaning which is necessary requires special design of the equipment and the process.

The goal of food technology is to convert raw materials into high-quality food products at the lowest possible cost; the objectives of food technologies can be classified into four categories (Figure 5.1). There are, of course, several other ways of classifying (see Niranjan (1994) for another one), but we found this classification useful for discussing new and existing technologies.

Figure 5.1
Overview of types of
food processes

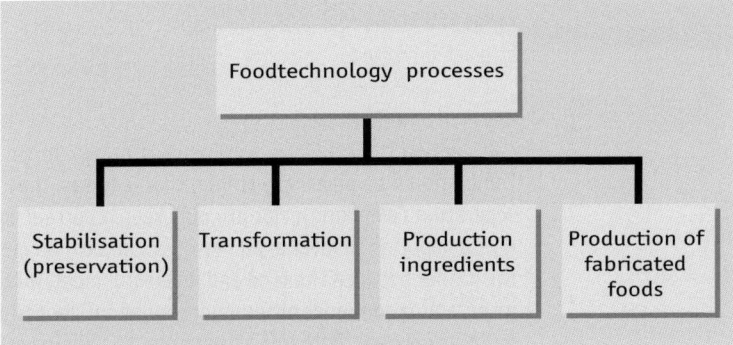

5.2.1 Processes to preserve foods (stabilization processes)

Food products are usually non-equilibrium systems, i.e. they are in a state of thermodynamic instability. A very important goal of food technology is to bring the food in a (pseudo) stable state, meaning that the stability of the food is greater than its lifetime. In order to achieve that, several aspects can be recognised.

Microbial stabilization:

First and foremost foods ought to be safe from a microbiological point of view. Pathogenic micro-organisms (or sometimes their metabolites) should be removed or eliminated. Furthermore, spoilage due to micro-organisms should be prevented: e.g. to prevent souring of milk, mould growth in bread, yeast fermentation in fruit juices. The most frequently used process in this respect is heating: pasteurization (often the minimal heat treatment to ensure absence of pathogens) or sterilization (no micro-organisms left, complete microbial stability).

Chemical stabilization:

Some chemical reactions cause a decrease in quality of foods. Examples are the Maillard reaction (non-enzymatic browning reaction, causing discoloration, off-flavours, loss of nutritional quality, perhaps formation of toxicologically suspect compounds), and fat oxidation (causing off-flavours and loss of nutritional quality). In such cases, it is necessary to minimize unwanted reactions as much as possible.

Biochemical stabilization:

Raw materials from both plant and animal origin contain enzymes that can cause deterioration of the materials, e.g. protein breakdown by proteases, fat breakdown by lipases, enzymatic browning by polyphenol oxidase. In as far as these changes are undesirable, such enzymes should be destroyed, or at least inhibited.

Physical stabilization:

Foods should be physically stable, that is to say, they should not show phase separation (demixing), not dry out, keep a certain consistency, etc.
A very important aspect of all preservation technologies is packaging. It forms the barrier between the food and its environment, it can protect the food from recontamination and other undesirable influences from the environment (such as oxygen). Packaging, therefore, has a large effect on food quality.

5.2.2 Transformation processes

Raw materials are transformed into foods by means of a variety of processes, such as fermentation (using micro-organisms or enzymes, e.g. cheese, olives, tea leaves, cocoa, beer, wine), extrusion (e.g. snacks from starch containing raw materials), hydrogenation of fats, emulsification, extraction (e.g. fruit juices). Frequently, the resulting food product does not resemble the raw material in appearance or properties. For instance, cheese is completely different from milk, bread is different from wheat, orange juice different from oranges.

5.2.3 Separation processes

Separation processes are used to obtain components or ingredients from raw materials, e.g. processes to obtain starch from potatoes or maize, milk proteins from milk, sugar from sugar cane or beets, oil from soy beans or olives. Typical processes used are phase separations (filters, membranes, centrifugation) and molecular separations (crystallization, distillation).

5.2.4 Manufacture of fabricated foods

Fabricated foods are foods that are made from various ingredients and they are coming up strongly in the food market these days. Traditional foods such as bread or cheese can be seen as fabricated foods. Examples of 'new' foods are cheese in which milk fat is replaced by a fat from plant origin, replacement of milk proteins in milk products by soy protein, cocoa-butter substitutes, bakery products and ready-made meals. A very successful fabricated food has been margarine, basically an imitation of butter. An example that has not been very successful is TVP ('texturized vegetable protein'), an attempt to produce a meat substitute. Functional foods, which are claimed to have specific health effects, also belong to the category of fabricated foods.

Figure 5.2
Position of food
technology (shaded
area) in the food
production chain

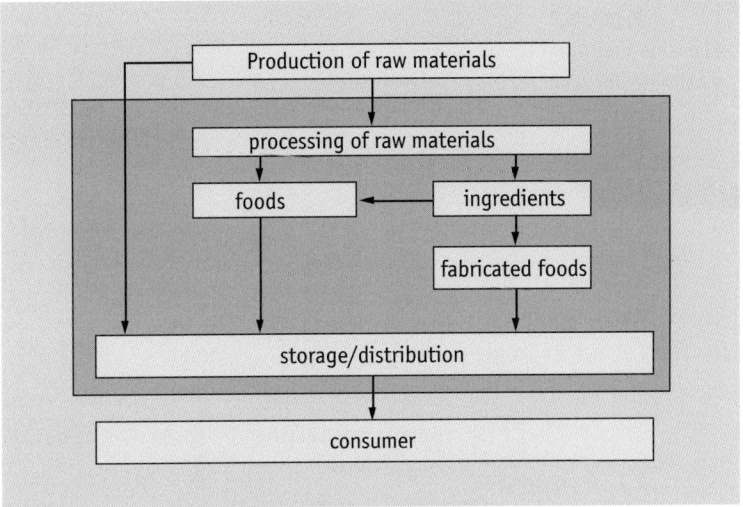

5.3 Position of food technology in the food production chain

The position of food technology in the food production chain is shown in
Figure 5.2.
Raw materials for food products are produced in the chain element of primary production, i.e. crop growing, cattle husbandry, fishing, milking and
the like. As soon as the raw materials are harvested, they become the
domain of food technology. Admittedly, some products such as fresh vegetables and fruits do not undergo treatment before they reach the consumer,
but here also a trend can be seen, as technologies including modified and
controlled atmosphere packaging emerge, which is discussed below. After
processing, storage and distribution are still within the domain of food technology because of possible changes which can take place in the food. These
changes must be controlled during the preceding production process. In the
consumption phase, the effects of the food on the consumer become the
domain of nutritional sciences. In summary, food technology is centrally
situated between primary production of the raw materials and consumption
of the food. It is obviously a multidisciplinary field of study. Food technologists have to be aware of what is going on in the field of primary production
because this may affect quality and properties of raw materials and may have
a large impact on the process chosen. At the same time they produce foods
with a certain nutritional value, or even a health promoting effect, and, last
but not least, desired organoleptic properties. First and foremost, food technologists should produce foods that are safe from the toxicological as well
as the microbial point of view.

The boundary conditions for food technology are quite strict, as summa-
rised in Figure 5.3. In other words, new as well as existing technologies have
to take these constraints into account. Nevertheless, there are apparently
continuous changes, as described in the following sections.

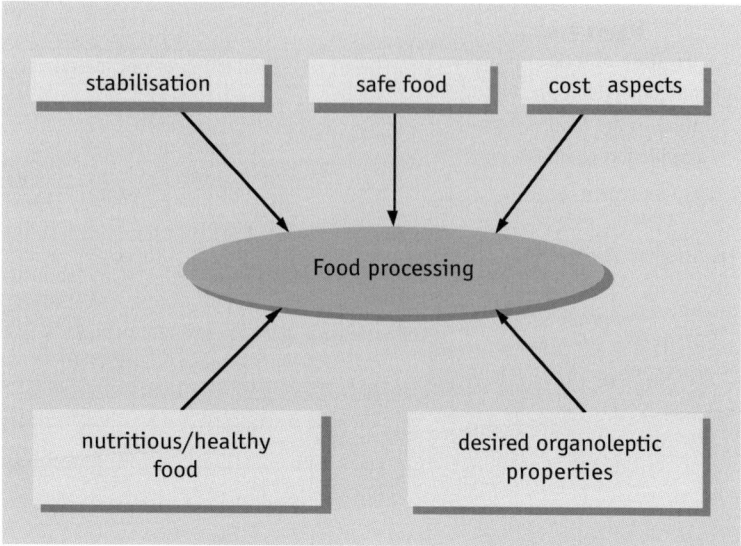

Figure 5.3
Elements that form
constraints for food
technologies

5.4 Developments in stabilization technologies

Heating processes

The most widely used existing stabilization technology is, of course, heat treatment. Heating inactivates micro-organisms and enzymes, hence enabling the production of safe, keepable foods. The drawback is, however, that heating may impair the quality of the food. Chemical reactions are accelerated at high temperature and cannot be prevented. These cause loss of nutritional value (e.g. destruction of vitamins), organoleptic changes (for instance, brown discoloration and off-flavours due to the Maillard reaction). Heating technology may be optimized, however, to produce safe and stable foods but with the least heat damage possible. Use is then made of the different temperature sensitivities of microbial inactivation (usually having a high activation energy) and 'normal' chemical reactions (mostly with lower activation energy). Figure 5.4 illustrates this phenomenon.

This approach results in the HTST (high temperature short time) and UHT (ultra-high temperature) processes (Figure 5.4), which have gained popularity, especially in the dairy industry. Many new technologies are in fact based on this optimization of time-temperature combinations (balance between microbial and enzyme inactivation on the one hand, and as little heat damage as possible on the other hand). This optimization includes attempts to reduce residence time distribution and heating-up and cooling-down periods in the equipment, to avoid overprocessing. Furthermore, aseptic packaging technology is a prerequisite for this optimization because packaging has to be done after heating.

Heating of foods containing particulates presents special problems because liquid and solid phases are heated at different rates. In addition,

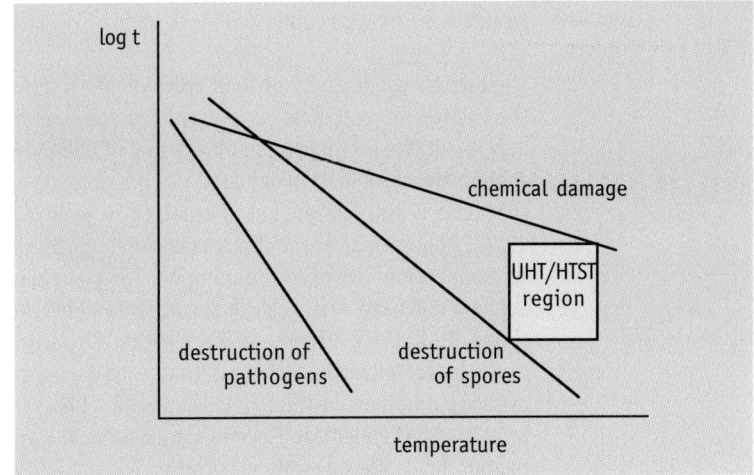

Figure 5.4
Heat treatment.
Schematic presenta-
tion of time (t) -
temperature combi-
nations giving the
same effect of
microbial inactiva-
tion and chemical
damage

particulates are easily damaged by pumps, in heat exchangers and during
the filling process. One solution is to heat solid and liquid phases separately and remix them again before filling (Bengtsson, 1994). Some new developments are discussed below, such as nonthermal processes (Mertens &
Knorr, 1992) and combinations of preservation methods (Leistner, 1992).

There are also some new developments in the traditional process of canning foods, where it has been shown that variable retort temperatures can
be more beneficial for the quality of the resulting product than holding at a
fixed maximum temperature (Durance, 1997). In addition, this results in
energy efficient processes with reduced processing time and production
costs. This can be achieved with the aid of computer simulations and automated process control.

Microwave heating

Microwave heating is widely known because of its application in the household. It can also be used on an industrial scale, though frequently in combination with conventional heating methods. The process allows a rapid
heating-up and in-depth heating of the material as the heat is generated within the food and continuous processes are possible. Rapid cooling-down is
however not possible, and neither is regeneration of heat. In addition, microwave heating can also be used for packaged food. According to Bengtsson
(1994), the largest application of microwave technology is for tempering to
just below the ice-melting temperature of frozen meats and fruits. A problem
remaining with microwave heating is that the electromagnetic field is not
homogeneous so that heating rates within the food can be different.

High-frequency heating (near 27 Mhz) is simpler than microwave heating
and can be done with larger amounts. However, high-frequency heating is
less flexible, more bulky and less frequency stable and is used, if at all, in
combination with conventional technologies (Bengtsson, 1994).

Electrical resistance heating (ohmic heating)

If electrical conductivity of food components is about equal and if neither the voltage nor electrical current applied are excessively high, this technology is suitable for rapid and mild heating of liquids and solids, though rapid cooling and regeneration of heat is not possible. Its application on an industrial scale is still limited, but is expected to grow in the future (Bengtsson, 1994). Applications are continuous cooking, pasteurization and sterilization in combination with aseptic packaging. The main advantages of the method are very rapid and even heating and absence of overheating at the tube walls (Fryer & Li, 1993, Parrot, 1992). Heating of particulate-containing foods works better with this technique than with conventional heating. A recent overview on ohmic heating (IFT Symposium, 1996) includes information on product development and economic aspects. It was concluded that ohmic heating holds considerable perspective for some food processes, especially for processing low-acid foods. Ohmic operational costs were found to be comparable to those for freezing and retort processing of low-acid products.

Infrared heating

Infrared (IR) heating transfers heat by radiation. Short-wave IR (wavelength near 1 (m) and intermediate IR (wavelength near 10 (m) make it possible to heat quickly to a penetration depth of 5 mm. Energy is converted into heat by interaction with molecules in the surface of the food, as opposed to conventional oven heating where heat is transferred through convection of circulating hot air. The features of infrared heating are (Sakai & Hanzawa, 1994):
- efficient heat transfer to the food
- the surrounding air is not heated
- more uniform heating and rapid heating rates
- compact and automatic constructions are possible.

Possible industrial applications are in continuous baking, drying and grilling, thawing and pasteurization, but the technique is not yet widely used in the food industry (Bengtsson, 1994). Regeneration of heat is not easy.

High electric field pulses

High-voltage micro or milliseconds pulses (field strengths in the order of 15-30 kV/cm) cause damage to microbial cells ('electroporation'), thus inactivating them. Damage to food components does not seem to occur, so the sensorial quality is not impaired (retention of flavour, nutrients and resemblance of freshness). Inactivation of proteases is also reported (Vega-Mercado et al., 1997), but a limitation of the technique is that it does not inactivate spores (Knorr et al., 1994), though Marquez et al. (1997) claim that spores can be inactivated at increased temperature or increased time gap between pulses. Inactivation depends on factors such as electrical field intensity and/or number of pulses, temperature, pH, ionic strength and conductivity of the medium. The advantage is that an instant distribution throughout a conductive food system is reached using short treatment times and very little heating. However, this nonthermal stabilization technique does not yet seem to be commercially attractive (Bengtsson, 1994), though prototype equipment is available and products such as fruit juices and liquid eggs could be industrially processed using this technology in the future (Vega-Mercado et al., 1997, Qin et al., 1995).

Pulsed light

Pulsed light with the power of an intense flash of sunlight-like light, with a spectrum between 200 nm and 1 mm and maximum emission between 400-500 nm, has bactericidal power, and the technique can thus be used to extend shelf life of foods and to kill micro-organisms on packaging materials (Dunn et al., 1995). Pulsed light is reported to have a higher bactericidal effect than conventional UV light and may have potential for treating baked goods, meat and seafood (Dunn et al., 1995). However, the killing effect on micro-organisms is limited to surfaces and to transparent media.

Ultrasound

This technology can be divided in two applications: low- and high-intensity ultrasound. Low-intensity ultrasound (power < 1 $W(cm^{-2})$ is useful as an analytical tool for studying physico-chemical properties of foods (McClements, 1995); it could also be used in-line during production as it is a non-invasive and non-destructive method. High-intensity ultrasound (typically in the power range of 10-1000 $W(cm^{-2})$ causes physical disruption and promotes chemical reactions involving radicals (such as oxidation) by generating intense pressure, shear and temperature gradients (McClements, 1995). Although enzyme and micro-organism inactivation is possible, its largest potential is probably in emulsification, deaggregation, degassing, induction of crystallization and phase separation. It may also facilitate heat and mass transfer in drying processes. The potential of high-intensity ultrasound still needs to be translated into low-cost equipment before it can be used in food processing (IFT Symposium, 1994a).

Irradiation by γ-waves

This was a competely new technology for stabilising foods which was developed in the 1940-1950s. The principle is based on inactivation of micro-organisms and enzymes due to formation of radicals induced by the radioactive waves. If the radiation intensity becomes too high, chemical damage to the food itself also occurs. For instance, fat oxidation may become a problem, as fat oxidation is initiated by radicals. However, processing conditions are well established and good quality foods can be produced (IFT Symposium, 1994b). This technology has not been a success, however, because of rejection by the consumer, who associates the technique with radioactive foods. Although this is of course a misconception, because the foods do not come into contact with radioactive material, the technology is at present not able to demonstrate its potential. It is now being used for limited purposes only, such as sterilization of spices and condiments, or to prevent some unwanted physiological changes in stored fruits and vegetables, such as potatoes, strawberries, mushrooms. Irradiation is not suitable for inactivation of specific parasites but is more useful in ensuring safety from a variety of foodborne pathogens and in prolonging shelf life (Loaharana & Murrell, 1994). Perhaps irradiation will be used more in the future in combination with other methods of food preservation (Thakur & Singh, 1995). An example is the combination of refrigeration and irradiation to improve the safety and shelf life of fresh meat and poultry (Murrano, 1995).

High-pressure treatment

This is probably the most promising new technology for stabilising and preserving foods, and is already used, especially for fruit and vegetables. The potential of high-pressure treatment was already known for a long time, but its application was limited by technical difficulties, which now seem to have been overcome. The pressure range of interest is between 400-600 MPa and the working principle is based on inactivation of enzymes and micro-organisms, probably because of irreversible protein denaturation. Because high-pressure treatment can be given at low temperatures, heat damage does not occur; pressure is distributed evenly throughout the food and the resulting product almost resembles fresh food. High-pressure technology also opens up possibilities for inducing some structure, as gelation of proteins or starch can be the result of the treatment (e.g. Messens et al., 1997). However, less desirable changes may also occur; it was found that lipid oxidation in fish muscle was enhanced by high pressure (Oshima et al., 1993). One drawback of high-pressure treatment is that it cannot yet be carried out in continuous mode, though a semi-continuous process can be used by overlapping batch units. There is much research being carried out on high pressure treatment at the moment, see for instance, Ledward et al. (1995), IFT Symposium (1993).

Cooling and freezing

Stabilization by cooling and freezing is also a frequently used process. The working principle is the slowing down of reaction rates (both chemically and physiologically). Sensorial and nutritional quality are not usually impaired by the process itself, apart from possible damage in the case of freezing when ice crystals are formed (which damages cell structures) and changes induced by the resulting high ionic strength and pH changes. Cooling and freezing cannot result in completely stable products: even at low temperatures chemical and biochemical reactions continue, albeit at a slow rate. As soon as the temperature increases, degradation (including growth of micro-organisms) becomes prominent. There are not really any new developments in this field (apart from technical improvements, such as savings in energy requirements, rate of freezing, and improved process control, George, 1993). Perhaps new possibilities will arise with increased knowledge on control of ice crystallization, and growth and manipulation of the phase states of frozen water. Another possibility would be the addition of a sugar like trehalose to prevent ice crystal growth due to its ability to form a glass (Scher, 1993, Roser, 1991) Using extremely high freezing rates, it may be possible to go directly into the glassy state region even from high levels of unfrozen water (Bengtsson, 1994). Osmotic concentration of cut fruits and vegetables changes the solid matter content so that the glassy state is reached at higher temperature than normal when freezing; such a process should result in higher quality retention (Bengtsson, 1994). The effect of deep-freezing and the glassy state has been discussed by Goff (1992). Another development is the use of antifreeze proteins to block undesirable nucleation and ice-crystal growth (Swienteck, 1992), but whether this is a realistic option in food technology remains a question. High-pressure technology in combination with low temperatures also provides the means to control freezing and thawing of foods (Bengtsson, 1994).

Minimal processing

Minimal processing is becoming a popular way to satisfy consumer demand for fresh foods which nevertheless have a substantial shelf life. Minimal processing is a somewhat vague concept, as it may actually involve substantial processing, but what is meant is that foods are produced which retain a fresh-like quality and contain only natural ingredients. Minimal processing can be described as processing which is invisible to the consumer, and can be applied at various stages of the food distribution chain (processing, storage, packaging, Ohlsson, 1994). It is especially of interest for fruits and vegetables. Ahvenainen (1996) has provided a recent overview and distinguishes two purposes of minimal processing: i) to keep the produce fresh, yet supply it in a convenient form without losing nutritional quality, ii) to ensure a sufficiently long shelf life so that distribution to the consumer is feasible.

Hurdle technology

The concept of hurdle technology is not new, but is currently receiving renewed attention in relation to minimal processing of foods. It means that existing and novel preservation techniques are combined to give a series of preservative factors, called hurdles, that cannot be overcome by micro-organisms (Leistner & Gorris, 1995). Examples of hurdles are temperature (heating, cooling), water activity, pH, redox potential and preservatives (chemical agents, bacteriocins). Novel preservative factors are gas packaging, ultra-high pressure treatment, edible coatings, use of bacteriocins (Leistner & Gorris, 1995). Hurdles should not be taken too literally: in most cases it is not so much that micro-organisms overcome one hurdle and then face another; rather, it is the synergistic effect of factors (e.g. the combination of pH and water activity).

The concept of hurdle technology has been more or less reinvented in the meat industry for the production of sausages, and can now also be used in the production of fruits and vegetables, bakery, dairy and fish products (Leistner & Gorris, 1995).

Sous-vide

Sous-vide cooking is vacuum cooking of raw materials and/or foods in heat-stable vacuum pouches under controlled conditions of temperature and time (Schellekens, 1996). The process is especially suitable for ready-made meals and is claimed to provide better quality (sensorial as well as nutritional) than normally cooked meals. Long heating times and relatively low heating temperatures are used to avoid thermal damage. However, the use of a low heating temperature results in only a small pasteurizing effect and hence a limited shelf life at 0°C. The microbiological safety of sous-vide cooked products can be improved by introducing the concept of hurdle technology.

The packaging material in which the foods are heated is subject to strict requirements: it should be heat-stable, have low permeability for gases, sufficient mechanical strength, and it should, of course, be food-grade (no migration of components from the package to the food). Sous-vide cooking is a semi-continuous process and is used mostly in catering (Schellekens, 1996).

Drying and concentration

Water is a very important compound in food and has a great impact on the chemical, microbiological and physical stability of foods. Food preservation and food quality depend to a large extent on appropriate management of food moisture (van den Berg, 1991). The reactivity of water is the key factor, more so than water content. Food scientists are accustomed to use water activity as the important factor in this respect. However, there is some debate in the literature as to whether this is the correct parameter (van den Berg, 1991, Franks, 1991, Slade & Levine, 1991, Roos et al., 1996, Fennema, 1996). It is beyond the scope of this chapter to go into detail; suffice it to say that the concept of water activity in relation to food stability is still useful but it should not be taken as the definitive parameter as is sometimes suggested in textbooks.

Removal of water from foods is done for stabilization purposes, and/or to reduce transport costs. Removal of water can be done in three ways:
- as gas/vapour, by evaporation (usually under reduced pressure to avoid too high a temperature)
- as liquid (water) by reverse osmosis
- as solid (ice) by freeze concentration.

An overview of dehydration techniques can be found in Cohen & Tang (1995). Evaporation can be seen as the traditional method for concentration and is frequently used for liquid foods such as fruit juices and milk products. The oldest drying technique is undoubtedly solar drying (in the open air), used for fruit, vegetables, meat, fish. Another technique from antiquity is smoking of meat and fish. (In addition to drying, antimicrobial agents are transferred from the smoke to the product, thus improving stability.) A somewhat more sophisticated technique than solar drying is convection drying in drying chambers, mostly done by passing hot air over the product.

Modern drying technology uses spray drying, in which a liquid product is atomized through a nozzle or a fast rotating wheel into small drops surrounded by hot air. Fast evaporation takes place and powder particles result. Products such as instant coffee, tea and milk powder are examples. Spray drying is often used in combination with fluidized-bed drying, in which particulate solids are levitated in an upward-flowing gas (mostly hot air). It is often useful to agglomerate powder particles to some extent, thus improving properties such as free flowing, bulk density and instant properties. Jet agglomeration is a newer technology used to agglomerate particles in turbulent free jets of steam (Schuchmann et al., 1993). It has the advantage that materials containing volatile compounds can be processed, due to the short residence time and a narrow residence time distribution.

Drum-drying is a technique in which water is evaporated from a liquid product on the surface of a heated drum; the technique is used for the production of gelatin, but is not used very much otherwise because of possible heat damage.

Freeze-drying (lyophilization) is a technique in which frozen water is removed from frozen food under high-vacuum without the water going through the liquid phase. Freeze-drying results in very little damage to the product and the resulting powder is usually very easily redispersable. However, the process is slow and expensive, and therefore not much used in the food industry.

Osmotic drying is a dehydration technique in which products are soaked in a concentrated sugar or salt solution. In such processes, three types of mass transfer take place: i) water flow out of the product, ii) solute transfer from solution to product, iii) a leaching out of the product's own solutes. As opposed to traditional soaking techniques (salting, candied fruit), osmotic dehydration involves significant water removal with limited and controlled solute incorporation (Raoult-Wack, 1994). Optimization of the process is now possible and new applications could be developed, for instance with fruits and vegetables, meat and seafood. Industrial application has been limited until now to semi-candied fruit production (Raoult-Wack, 1994). Osmotic dehydration will be used mainly as a pre-processing step (to save energy and improve product quality) since the process will not generally yield a stable product when used on its own.

Novel dehydration techniques employ lower temperatures and/or decreased drying times. Examples are microwave drying, dielectric drying, and microwave augmented freeze-drying (Cohen & Tang, 1995). Drying by microwave in combination with hot air allows controllable water transport in relation to surface evaporation for accelerated dehydration and less volume change. Drying with microwave under strong volume expansion provides possibilities for new fat-free snacks (Bengtsson, 1994). Centrifugal fluidi-

zed-bed drying is the same as conventional fluid-bed drying but uses a rotating chamber to speed up the drying process. Ball drying uses a screw con-
veyer in hot air, and the material within the drying chamber comes into
direct contact with heated balls made from ceramic or heat-conductive
material; drying occurs primarily by conduction. Ball drying is only useful for
small particles; the advantage is that lower temperatures can be used (e.g.
70 °C). Ultrasonic drying produces small droplets through a nozzle and then
by further cavitation using ultrasonic energy within a drying chamber. Cohen
& Tang (1995) concluded that there is no one best drying technique, it
depends on the type of product and the susceptibility of the products to
heat, and of course on the cost of processing.

Reverse osmosis is a relatively new technology, and is used in the dairy
industry to remove water from whey. Freeze concentration is also relatively
new and is used for fruit juices, coffee extracts, beer, wine and tea
(Deshpande et al., 1984). The possibilities for using the technology for milk
products have also been explored (van Mil & Bouman, 1990). The advantages of freeze concentration are that the process takes place at low temperature, hence no flavour loss and no significant microbial or enzymatic activity, and little or no undesirable physical or chemical changes. In principle,
there are two stages in the method, i) crystallization (e.g. in a scraped-sur-
face heat exchanger) and ii) separation of the ice crystals by centrifugation
or wash column. A major drawback of freeze-concentration is that the costs
are three to four times higher than for evaporation or reverse osmosis, so a
cost-benefit analysis should be made (van Mil & Bouman, 1990).

Packaging

Packaging is important to keep processed foods stable. Packaging of foods
can be done using traditional canning and bottling, or using aseptic packaging technology in the form of cartons and pouches. Aseptic packaging
means that a product is packed free from undesirable micro-organisms
(removed or eliminated in a preceding operation) in packaging material that
is also free from undesirable micro-organisms (EHEDG report, 1993). There
have been no new packaging technologies developed recently, but there is a
constant search for better packaging materials such as plastic materials and
flexible aluminium pouches. As was pointed out by Cleland (1996), it is not
just packaging but rather the combination of stabilization/preservation and
packaging that counts.

Another development in packaging technology is controlled atmosphere
(CA) and modified atmosphere packaging (MA) in which metabolic processes
in the food are controlled through gas composition. CA is done in a storage
room with monitoring and active adjustment of gas composition, and is used
mainly for bulk storage and transport of fruits and vegetables (Kader et al.,
1989, Church, 1994, Peppelenbos, 1996). The proportion of the gas mixture
in CA is maintained at the original level throughout. MA refers to a different
gas composition from that of ambient air without active control of gas composition; the gas composition within the package is the result of the balan-

ce between metabolic rates of the product and diffusion characteristics of the package and, as a result, the gas composition will change over time. Gases used in MA are oxygen, nitrogen or carbon dioxide. MA is used for fruits and vegetables, fresh pasta, cooked and chilled meat and seafood and prepared salads (Church, 1994). Gas packaging also has an effect on micro-organisms and can thus influence shelf life with regard to microbial stability (Labuza et al., 1992).

Vacuum packaging is another method whereby air is removed from the product in a package, resulting in low oxygen permeability.

Active packaging means packaging methods and agents that actively influence shelf life of food, such as oxygen scavengers (Ohlsson, 1994).

For environmental reasons, research is being conducted into edible coatings made of proteins, starches and waxes, for use as biodegradable films to package foods. Limitations to these include the fact that such films are sensitive to moisture and are thus not well-suited for packaging dry, frozen and semi-moist foods (Ohlsson, 1994).

5.5 Developments in transformation processes

The most important, centuries-old but still widely used transformation process is fermentation. Fermentation can be regarded as a precursor of modern biotechnology. It is the process by which micro-organisms or enzymes are used to transform raw materials into foods. The success of this transformation is undoubtedly that it involves (usually) a lactic acid fermentation as a result of which the food becomes safe (no pathogens can grow at low pH) as well as keepable. Although fermentation processes and fermentation products have been known for centuries, a major change has occurred in this century because the general principles are now well understood so that the process can be controlled. In addition, genetic modification of micro-organisms has made it possible to tailor the properties of micro-organisms or enzymes to the needs of the specific process. It has also opened up the possibility of obtaining non-traditional sources of enzymes. An example is the use of rennet (chymosin) in the cheese industry to clot milk. Traditionally, this enzyme was obtained from the stomachs of young calves, but nowadays the enzyme is also produced by genetically modified microbes.

As far as new fermentation technologies are concerned, traditional batch methods are replaced by continuous methods, for instance in the brewing of beer, or the manufacture of yoghurt. Use of immobilised enzymes can greatly reduce production costs, but care must be taken that the resulting products are of the same quality as the traditional products. These methods involve more an optimization of existing technologies than the application of really new technologies. Some new developments can perhaps be found in solid state fermentation, as it becomes possible to control this process better.

A subject related to fermentation is the use of 'probiotics', bacteria that are claimed to support the bacterial flora in the gut so as to help in preventing infectious diseases, or even colon cancer. It remains to be firmly established whether probiotics indeed have beneficial effects on the intestinal tract (O'Sullivan, 1992). In any case, foods containing probiotics are on the market, and much research is being carried out in this field. For food technologists it is of importance to develop technologies for probiotics containing foods, so that these foods are acceptable to the consumer as well as able to carry the probiotic bacteria to the place of destination without loss of their activity.

Solid-state, or solid-substrate fermentation are processes in which raw materials are used without addition of water for fermentation by micro-organisms. An example of a product produced in this way is tempeh, which is the result of fermentation of soya beans by the mould *Rhizopus oligosporus*. The design of solid-substrate ferments is still largely empirical, and the potential for optimizing these kinds of (mostly traditional) processes needs to be explored (de Reu, 1995).

Physical transformation processes, such as extrusion and emulsification, are discussed in the section on technologies for fabricated foods.

5.6 Developments in separation technologies

A recent review of methods for bioseparations is provided by Singh & Singh (1996). They consider four sequential steps: removal of insolubles (e.g. by filtration, centrifugation), isolation of fractions (e.g. by extraction, adsorption), purification of components or fractions (e.g. by chromatography) and refining of the product (e.g. by water removal, crystallization). According to Singh & Singh (1996) the cost of the final product is invariably dominated by the concentration in the initial raw material; isolation is the key step to controlling cost.

Membrane technology

Membranes can be used to concentrate, fractionate and purify materials. Membrane technology is a pressure-driven process. The technology can be subdivided into microfiltration (membranes retain particles in the size range of microns), ultrafiltration (membranes retain molecules of the size of proteins, several thousands of daltons, depending on the cut-off value of the membrane) and reverse osmosis (only water is removed). There is also nanofiltration which lies between ultrafiltration and reverse osmosis. Applications are found in the dairy and fruit juice industries and are used to concentrate milk, whey, fermentation broth, fruit juices. Production of alcohol-reduced beers and wines is also possible using membrane technology, as is the extraction of colours and aromas. Membrane technology is energy efficient, easy to scale up and thermal damage can be limited to a minimum. Limitations are encountered in fouling of the membranes and lack of durability. However, new membrane materials are continuously being introduced, such as ceramic membranes that can withstand high temperatures and organic solvents and are resistant over a wide pH range (Cuperus & Nijhuis, 1993).

Pervaporation is a membrane technique whereby the permeate is directly evaporated on the other side of the membrane, followed by condensation in a low temperature condenser. It results in a vapour permeate (later on condensed) and a liquid retentate. The driving force for the mass transfer of permeants from the feed to the permeate is a gradient in chemical potential achieved by applying a difference in partial pressures of the permeants across the membrane. Difference in partial pressures can be achieved by reducing the total pressure on the permeate side or by sweeping an inert gas on the side of the membrane (Karlson & Trägårdh, 1996). The technique can be used for recovery of aromas or aroma concentration and de-alcoholization of beer, wine and liquor is also possible (Singh & Singh, 1996, Karlson & Trägårdh, 1996).

Electrodialysis is a membrane technology whereby molecules or ions are separated in an electric field using charged membranes (Bengtsson, 1994). Desalination of whey is an application.

Membrane reactors also form a new technology: they integrate catalytic conversion, product separation and/or concentration, and catalyst recovery into a single operation (Prazeres & Cabral, 1994). For instance, a biochemical reaction can take place and the products of the reaction are removed through the membrane, thus preventing product inhibition, and enzyme loss. Continuous processes are possible in this way, allowing better process control, higher productivity, more uniform products and the integration of a purification step in the process (Prazeres & Cabral, 1994). These authors also provide an overview of possible applications: hydrolysis of proteins and polysaccharides, synthesis of amino acids and peptides, lactate, aldehydes, alcohols, hydrolysis of fats and oils and production of mono- and diglycerides, to name but a few.

Industrial chromatography

Chromatography is a technique that is widely used for analytical purposes because of its superior separating possibilities. However, application on industrial scale it is not so easy because of scaling-up problems and the associated costs. Affinity chromatography, in which the target molecules adsorb onto a solid phase (the ligand), is used commercially for the production of native biologically active substances (Singh & Singh, 1996). Applications are in the isolation of proteins and peptides, for instance from milk and whey. Proteins isolated in this way are expensive and are only used in foods for special applications, for instance, the use of lactoferrin, or bioactive peptides. Another chromatography application is in the separation of fructose from a glucose-fructose mixture using calcium-loaded ion-exchange resins (Singh & Singh, 1996).

The use of immobilized enzymes can also be considered a kind of chromatography: enzymes are immobilized onto a solid carrier in a column and the substrate is fed through the column. Applications are in the continuous production of beer using immobilized yeast, hydrolysis of galactose using β-galactosidase to produce sweet syrups of glucose and galactose, and hydrolysis of proteins (Singh & Singh, 1996).

Conventional and supercritical fluid extraction

Components can be removed from raw materials by extraction using an immiscible solvent. The most widely-used form of extraction is probably oil extraction from oilseeds, but many other applications exist. Solvents used should be nontoxic, highly efficient and selective, stable, non-flammable, nonexplosive, environmentally safe and inexpensive (Singh & Singh, 1996).

A supercritical fluid is a fluid that is above its critical temperature and pressure, and exhibits characteristics which are intermediate between liquid and gas. The liquid-like high density makes it a good solvent while the low gas-like viscosity and lack of surface tension (between the gas and liquid phase) achieves good penetrating and mixing abilities (Rizvi et al., 1995). Supercritical fluids leave residual-solvent-free products (Singh & Singh, 1996). The supercritical fluid for foods *par excellence* is carbon dioxide because it is inert, nontoxic, non-flammable, recyclable, readily available in high purity and leaves no residues (Palmer & Ting, 1995). Its main application until now has been in the production of decaffeinated coffee beans and extraction of hop flavours. A general overview of potential applications for supercritical fluid technology in food processing can be found in Palmer &Ting (1995).

Much research is also being carried out on the production of fractionated fats in which the solid-liquid balance is changed. This process is of interest because the technological possibilities of the fractions are greatly enhanced. The greatest applications are for palm oil and milk fat (Hamm, 1995, Rizvi & Bhaskar, 1995). Fractionation possibilities include dry fractionation (crystallization), solvent fractionation, and detergent fractionation (Hamm, 1995). With regard to solvent extraction, supercritical fluid extraction has received much attention because there is less retention of liquid phase in the separated solid material, and the fractions obtained melt more homogeneously and provide superior selectivity. However, supercritical fluid extraction is not as popular as crystallization due to high capital investment and operating costs, though Rizvi & Bhaskar (1995) state that 'the estimated economic profile of the large-scale commercial plants indicates that supercritical-CO_2 is economically viable for fractionation of milk fat contrary to what may be the generally-held belief'.

Enzymatic and microbial synthesis

Enzymes are mostly used in the food industry to degrade components, and less to synthesize components. It may well be that enzymatic synthesis will gain interest in the near future because it can yield components of high purity with very little contamination. Biotransformations of proteins and fats are possible to produce components, as well as synthesis of emulsifiers, flavours, peptides and oligosaccharides (Vulfson, 1993). The use of enzymes in low-water media has several advantages, as discussed by Vulfson (1993). In principle, biotechnological methods may offer attractive alternatives compared to conventional chemical approaches, but the cost of some enzymes may be too high for manufacturing products with low added value. On the other hand, genetic engineering may offer possibilities for increasing specificity of enzymes at reduced costs (Vulfson, 1993).

Micro-organisms may also be used to synthesize flavour compounds (Belin et al., 1992) or food colorants (Arad & Yaron, 1992).

Extraction of proteins with reversed micelles

In the search for novel protein foods, protein sources may come from micro-organisms. Production of protein by fermentation, using modern biotechnology, is possible, but separation and purification of proteins from the fermentation media is still a bottleneck in downstream processing. Use of liquid-liquid extraction to isolate protein is a possible method, using selective solubilization of proteins in reversed micelles as a bioseparation technique (Pires et al., 1996). These authors also discuss strategies of operation and scale-up and conclude that the use of reversed micelles shows potential for application in large-scale continuous mode operations.

5.7 Developments in technologies for fabricated foods

Extrusion

In the extrusion process, mixing, shearing, cooking and shaping can occur, as mechanical and thermal energy is used to transport the material by means of rotating helical screws through a die; chemical and physical changes take place and the visco-elastic mass (consisting of biopolymers) can be formed into certain shapes (Rizvi et al., 1995). The process can be used for a multitude of products. Cold-extrusion, in which only shaping takes places (without cooking), can be used for the manufacture of pasta, cookies, candies, dough and pastry. Cooking-extrusion is the process in which raw ingredients are cooked by the combined action of shear, heat and pressure, resulting in homogeneous or heterogeneous phases which are fixed by rapid conversion into a rubber-like or glassy state. Swelling on exiting the die may induce a porous structure. New technological possibilities are co-extrusion (e.g. cereals with a soft stuffing) and co-expansion (two extruders with a common die). Twin-screw extruders can be used to emulsify fat, sterilize spices, produce microparticulates from proteins and to restructure and shape minced fish and meat with a high water content (Bengtsson, 1994). The use of supercritical fluids in extrusion technology is described by Rizvi et al. (1995); this allows for simultaneous occurrence of expansion, solute incorporation and reduction of melt viscosity, and in the case of carbon dioxide it can also be used to adjust the melt pH. Upon exiting the die, most of the carbon dioxide evaporates. All in all, extrusion technology is very suitable for production of fabricated foods from all kinds of materials. It is *the* technique for texturizing protein-containing foods, and shows promise for the development of novel protein foods (Cheftel, 1992, Ledward & Tester, 1994).

Encapsulation technology

Encapsulation is a technology whereby solid, liquid or even gaseous materials are packaged in small particles that are suspended in the food. This technology enables substances to be protected to some extent (for instance, minerals, micro-organisms, enzymes), or be subject to slow, controlled release (e.g. of flavours) (Reineccius, 1989, Jackson & Lee, 1991, Pothakamury & Barbosa-Cánovas, 1995). The microparticulate particles can be made from proteins such as gelatin, or by coacervation of biopolymers (e.g. proteins and polysaccharides). Alternatively, liposomes can be used (Kim & Baianu, 1991). For production of microparticulates, spray-drying, coating, extrusion and freeze-drying methods can be used (Pothakamury & Barbosa-Cánovas, 1995). Water-soluble polymers can be used to encapsulate hydrophobic materials, and water-insoluble polymers for encapsulation of aqueous materials. The problem for foods is that the materials should be food-grade, and use must be made of food biopolymers, if necessary modified.

Products can also be encapsulated via solid-melt technology (extrusion-type processes), resulting in commercially stable glasses. The primary feature is stability which is particularly significant in minimally packaged products (Popplewell et al., 1995). The authors claim that the new process is versatile, scaleable and economically feasible.

Fat replacers

In the search for fat-free or low-fat food products to satisfy consumer demands, attempts have been made to find fat substitutes. The problem with low-fat or fat-free foods is that they lack the taste and structure of the corresponding fat-containing foods. Fat contributes to structure and texture because it is one of the structural elements of the food. Fat is also a good solvent for flavour substances which tend to often be somewhat hydrophobic in character, hence removal of fat also removes a source of flavour components, or causes a shift in the balance of flavour compounds (Plug & Haring, 1993, IFT Symposium, 1997a). Fat replacers should therefore also be substitutes for structure and flavour. There are three types of fat replacers (Lucca & Tepper, 1994): i) based on proteins (total milk protein, whey protein), ii) based on carbohydrates (modified starch, maltodextrins, cellulose, guar gum), iii) fat-based (emulsifiers, medium-chain triacylglycerols, acaloric lipids, i.e. lipids resistant to digestive enzymes). A serious problem with fat replacers based on proteins or carbohydrates is that they are not well-suited for use in cooking oils or for frying.

Glassy foods

Low moisture foods (confectionery, cereals, snacks, powdered foods) are often solid, amorphous materials with a glassy structure that may become plasticized as a result of an increase in water content or temperature. The amorphous state of these foods may result from a rapid removal of water from food solids that occur during such processes as extrusion, spray drying and freezing. Amorphous states (rubber or glass) are non-equilibrium states with time-dependent properties; in contrast, crystals, solutions and melts are physically stable equilibrium states. Physical properties of low-moisture and frozen foods have been related to the glass transition temperature (which is actually a temperature range rather than one specific temperature). Below the glass transition temperature an amorphous solid is a glass, and above the glass transition temperature it is a rubber (usually a more viscous state, though not necessarily). There is a drastic change in molecular mobility above the glass transition temperature resulting in a dramatic decrease in stability of a food. It is actually a glass-rubber transition. Water plasticizes food polymers and (even when present in trace amounts) drastically decreases their glass transition temperature and may thus have a detrimental effect on food quality.

The glass transition temperature is therefore very important for food quality and shelf life of amorphous foods, such as powders. It is also important for frozen foods, as ice formation causes freeze-concentration of dissolved components and, as a result, the temperature at which freezing takes place decreases for the remaining water. At a sufficiently low temperature the freeze-concentrated phase may solidify into the glassy state and ice formation stops. The freeze-concentrated phase contains unfrozen water within the ice-phase. In the glassy state, foods are very stable because the molecular mobility of components is very limited which means that degradative reactions cannot occur. However, above the glass transition temperature all kinds of changes take place in dehydrated foods: caking, stickiness, oxidation, non-enzymatic browning reactions (Maillard reaction).

The glass transition temperature obviously depends on the composition of foods (especially the water content), and on the temperature at which the procees takes place. State diagrams are useful tools to predict and control the stability of dehydrated foods (Roos et al., 1996, Slade & Levine, 1995, Fennema, 1996). Knowledge about glass transitions in general represents a powerful tool for food technologists, and this development has been a major breakthrough in the past decade. With knowledge from state diagrams, it is easier to select ingredients that raise the glass transition temperature and thus extend shelf life. In addition to food composition, choice of processing conditions is equally important in choosing rate of drying, final moisture content and temperature.

Emulsification

Many fabricated foods are emulsions, e.g. infant formulae, clinical foods, creams, desserts, sauces, dressings and ice cream. There are oil-in-water emulsions, in which the oil is dispersed in the aqueous phase (e.g., mayonnaise), water-in-oil emulsions, in which water is dispersed in a lipid phase (e.g. margarine) and multiple emulsions (W/O/W) are also possible.

In order to make emulsions, emulsifiers are necessary, i.e. surface active agents. It is important to distinguish between the manufacture of emulsions and the stability of emulsions (Walstra, 1996). Emulsifiers are necessary both for the formation and the stabilization of emulsions, but they may act differently in both processes. A thorough discussion about formation of emulsions is provided by Walstra (1983), including the effect of various types of emulsifiers and ways to produce emulsions. Attention is also given to emulsifying machines. Industrial production of emulsions is mostly done using high-pressure homogenizers, rotor-stator stirring, ultrasonic vibration, or a colloid mill, and combinations are of course also possible.

Emulsions need to be stable during processing and during storage. However, emulsions are inherently unstable from a thermodynamic point of view: they tend to separate. There are various types of instability possible: flocculation, creaming, (partial) coalescence and Ostwald ripening (Walstra, 1996). In general, the size of emulsion droplets needs to be in the order of one micrometre (there is in fact a globule size distribution). Emulsion stability depends on the surface active agents present (often named stabilisers), partial crystallization of the oil phase (and hence on temperature), flow conditions, viscosity of the continuous phase, etc. (Walstra, 1996). Emulsion droplets greatly contribute to the structure (consistency) of a food product, and are carriers of essential fatty acids, vitamins and flavour substances, and therefore important from a nutritional and sensory point of view.

A large number of emulsifiers and stabilisers are available. Proteins can fulfil both tasks, as can numerous low molecular surfactants, such as lecithins and monoglycerides. An overview can be found in Dickinson (1993).

Structuring by phase separation

Hydrocolloid mixtures can be used as functional food additives. Interactions between macromolecules may result in thermodynamic incompatibility or in complexing, thereby affecting physico-chemical properties and structure (Ledward, 1993, Tolstoguzov, 1995). Synergistic as well as antagonistic effects are possible. The macromolecules of interest are proteins and polysaccharides. An example of exploiting such macromolecular interactions is the production of a caviar analogue (Tolstoguzov, 1995). Other applications are conceivable, for instance, water-in-water emulsions, consisting of spherical drops of a protein solution in a polysaccharide solution and vice-versa. Knowledge of phase-behaviour of macromolecule components in foods in both liquid and solid systems is of great importance for controlling the structural functions of food hydrocolloids. For instance, development of low-fat products leads to more usage of macromolecules and their interactions. Also, use of natural food ingredients puts more emphasis on physical interactions and physical processes (heating, drying, high pressure or extrusion) rather than on chemical modification. Applications are conceivable for infant formulae, sports drinks, functional foods, convenience foods and snacks.

5.8 Conclusion and future prospects

This chapter provides an overview of current technological possibilities in food processing. Consumer trends towards healthy, fresh and natural foods have their impact on the technology applied, and stimulate the search for processes that can supply the consumer with the type of food products demanded. Some real new developments can be seen, but most effort seems to go into optimization and combination of existing technologies. Table 5.1 gives an overview. Increasing emphasis is on scientifically based food processing and on attempts to convert batch processes into mechanized continuous automated processes. A trial-and-error attitude is no longer sufficient, it is necessary to understand what is happening in the food at a molecular level (microscopic) as well as at the structural (mesoscopic) level in order to understand the macroscopic properties of food, and how processing affects these aspects. An ever complicating fact with foods is that they are heterogeneous and complex, and that their properties change during processing. Because of that, new technological developments in other industries are not directly applicable to the food industry. We have not paid much attention to process control techniques because it was considered beyond the scope of this chapter. However, it goes without saying that developments in this field are also of importance: these enable maintenance of high product quality while operating at the highest possible processing rates, so that food manufacturing operations can be improved (Haley & Mulvaney, 1995). Novel developments such as fuzzy-logic control and artificial neural networks can be used in this respect (Eerikäinen et al., 1993). Developments in on-line sensors are also very useful, but again, food quality and safety are not easily measured on-line because of the complexity involved.

In the near future, mathematical modelling will be needed to predict and control processes as well as product quality. Statistical process control systems as well as Total Quality Management (TQM) and Hazard Analysis of Critical Control Points (HACCP) systems need to be implemented (Rizvi et al., 1993) and quantitative data on the kinetics of chemical, physical and enzymatic changes and on physical properties of foods are a prerequisite for the mathematical modelling. Scott and Richardson (1997) argue that computational fluid dynamics can be used to understand the dynamics and the underlying physics of a processing operation and thus aid in the design of existing and new processing equipment. It will be possible to predict flow behaviour of fluid foods and particulates in fluids, mixing efficiency, residence time distribution and convection patterns in chillers or ovens. Development of process simulation software packages and knowledge-based expert systems will be useful. The achievements in predictive microbiology provide a good example of what can be done (Wijtzes, 1996, IFT Symposium, 1997b). Much current research seems to be going in this direction, so that processes can indeed be optimized in order to satisfy the needs of the consumer. Thus, both new and existing technologies need to maximize product quality while minimizing production costs within the physical constraints of

Table 5.1 Overview of new developments in food technology

Type of technology	Developments	Characteristics	Suitable for	Drawbacks
Preservation by thermal treatment	HTST, UHT	Less heat damage, heat regeneration	fluids, fluids containing particulates	not suitable for 'solid' foods
	Ohmic heating	rapid and even heating	fluids and fluids containing particulates; low-acid foods	no heat regeneration
	Infrared heating	efficient and rapid heat transfer	baking, drying, grilling, thawing	no heat regeneration, low penetration depth
	Microwave	rapid heating	all kinds of foods	uneven heating, no heat regeneration
	Sous-vide	mild heating in vacuum pouches, sensory quality improved	all kinds of foods, catering	shelf life limited
Preservation by non-thermal treatment	High-pressure	no thermal damage, fresh-like quality	fruits, vegetables	not continuous, expensive
	high-electric field pulses	little thermal damage, high sensoric quality	conductive foods	no inactivation of spores, high cost
	pulsed light	no thermal damage	packages	only active at surfaces, or in transparent liquids
	γ-irradiation	no thermal damage	fruits, vegetables, spices, condiments, meat	not accepted by consumer
	ultrasound	facilitates heat and mass transfer, physical disruption	to be used in combination with other techniques	high cost, little microbial stabilization
	drying, concentration	removal of water, glassy foods	all kinds of foods	
	glassy foods	solid amorphous materials, very stable below glass transition temperature	low moisture foods (confectionery, cereals, powders, frozen products)	stability critically dependent on glass transition temperature
Preservation in the cold	rapid freezing	formation of glass	all kinds of foods	

Hurdle technology & minimal processing	combination of preservation technologies	less quality loss	dry meat products, fruits, vegetables	microbial safety is critical
Packaging	aseptic packaging	combination with continuous processes	fluids, fluids containing particulates	special hygienic design of equipment
	modified atmosphere (MA) and controlled atmosphere packaging (CA)	interference with metabolic processes of the food	fruits, vegetables, meat, seafood	
Fermentation	continuous processes	higher production rates, standardized quality	milk products, alcoholic beverages	
	solid-substrate	better control of fermentation	solids, such as soy beans	
Separation	membranes	separation of ingredients at large scale	liquid foods	fouling of membranes
	chromatography	separation of ingredients in high purity	liquids	expensive
	enzymatic synthesis	high purity	peptides, colorants, emulsifiers, flavours	expensive
	supercritical fluid extraction	efficient extraction of ingredients	coffee beans, hops, oils and fats	high cost
	reversed micelles	protein extraction	novel protein foods	
Fabricated foods	extrusion	shaping and/or cooking	snacks, pasta, pastry, novel protein foods	
	emulsification	emulsion droplets contribute to structure, flavour, nutritional value	fat-containing products	
	phase separation	structure formation by food hydrocolloids	gel-like foods, novel protein foods, meat and fish-like products	

the processing equipment (Haley & Mulvaney, 1995).It is probably the very complex nature of foods and food processing that causes progress to be slow. This becomes particularly instructive if one looks back at research priorities of 10 years ago (Mälkki, 1988): many of these priorities are still high on the agenda. Nevertheless, progress, slow as it is, has indeed been made and the developments in the field of food technology continue to be both interesting and necessary. To be able to keep up, it is stressed again that knowledge of food properties (i.e. food science) is invariably linked to process development (i.e. food process engineering).

Acknowledgements

The author would like to thank Dr G. Meerdink, Dr A. Linnemann and Prof. Dr P. Walstra for critical reading of the manuscript.

References

Ahvenainen, R., 1996. New approaches in improving the shelf life of minimally processed fruit and vegetables. Trends in Food Science and Technology 7, 179-187.

Arad, S. & A. Yaron, 1992. Natural pigments from red microalgae for use in foods and cosmetics. Trends in Food Science and Technology 3, 92-97.

Belin, J.M., M. Bensoussan, & L. Serrano-Carrean, 1992. Microbial biosynthesis for the production of food flavours. Trends in Food Science and Technology 3, 11-14.

Bengtsson N., 1994. New processes and products. An updated guide for people active in food processing, product development and marketing. SIK, Swedish Institute for Food Research, SIK-report no. 606, 55p.

Cheftel, J.C. 1992. New protein texturization processes by extrusion cooking at high moisture levels. Food Review International 8, 235-275.

Church, N. 1994. Developments in modified-atmosphere packaging and related technologies. Trends in Food Science and Technology 5, 345-352.

Cleland, A.C., 1996. Package design for refrigerated food: the need for multidisciplinary project teams. Trends in Food Science and Technology 7, 269-271.

Cohen, J.S. & T.C.S. Yang, 1995. Progress in food dehydration. Trends in Food Science and Technology 6, 20-25.

Cuperus, F.P. & H. Nijhuis, 1993. Applications of membrane technology to food processing. Trends in Food Science and Technology 4, 277-281.

De Reu, J.C. 1995. Solid-substrate fermentation of soya beans to tempe. PhD thesis, Wageningen Agricultural University, 154 p.

Deshpande, S.S., M. Cheryan, S.K. Sathe & D.K. Salunkhe, (1984). Freeze concentration of fruit juices. CRC Critical Reviews in Food Science and Nutrition 20, 173-248.

Dickinson, E., 1993. Towards more natural emulsifiers. Trends in Food Science and Technology 4, 330-333.

Dunn, J., Th. Ott, & W. Clark, 1995. Pulsed-light treatment of food and packaging. Food Technology 49 (9), 95-98.

Durance, T.D., 1997. Improving canned food quality with variable retort temperature processes. Trends in Food Science and Technology 8, 113-118.

Eerikäinen, T., P. Linko, S. Linko, T. Siimes & Y.H. Zhu, 1993. Fuzzy logic and neural network applications in food science and technology. Trends in Food Science and Technology 4, 237-242.

EHEDG report, 1993. Microbiologically safe aseptic packaging of food products. Trends in Food Science and Technology 4, 21-25.

Fennema, O. 1996. Water and Ice. In: Food Chemistry, 3rd edition. Ed. O. Fennema, Marcel Dekker, New York, pp. 17-94.

Franks, F. 1991. Water activity: a credible measure of food safety and quality? Trends in Food Science and Technology 2, 68-72.

Fryer, P. & Z. Li, 1993. Electrical resistance heating of foods. Trends in Food Science and Technology 4, 364-369.

Gaonkar, A.G. (Ed.). Food processing. Recent developments. Elsevier, Amsterdam, 1995, 315 p.

George, R.M. 1993. Freezing processes used in the food industry. Trends in Food Science and Technology 4, 134-138.

Goff, H. D., 1992. Low temperature stability and the glassy state in frozen foods. Food Research International 25, 317-325.

Haley, T.A. & S.J. Mulvaney, 1995. Advanced process control techniques for the food industry. Trends in Food Science and Technology 6, 103-110.

Hamm, W. 1995. Trends in edible oil fractionation. Trends in Food Science and Technology 6, 121-126.

IFT Symposium, 1993. Use of hydrostatic pressure in food processing. Food Technology 47 (6), 149-172.

IFT Symposium, 1994a. Ultrasonic applications in the food industry. Food Technology 48 (12), 67-84.

IFT Symposium, 1994b. Food irradiation: recent developments and future prospects. Food Technology 48 (5), 123-144.

IFT Symposium, 1996. Ohmic heating for thermal processing of foods: government, industry and academic perspectives. Food Technology 50 (5), 242-273.

IFT Symposium, 1997a. The chemistry of flavor interactions. Food Technology 51(1), 59-80.

IFT Symposium, 1997b. Predictive Food Microbiology: where do we go from here? Food Technology 51(4), 81-103.

Jackson, L.T. & K. Lee, 1991. Microencapsulation and the food industry. Lebensmittel Wissenschaft und Technologie 24, 289-297.

Kader, A.A., D. Zagory, & E.L. Kerbel, 1989. Modified atmosphere packaging of fruits and vegetables. CRC Critical Reviews in Food Science and Nutrition 28, 1-30.

Karlsson, H.O.E. & G. Trägårdh, 1996. Applications of pervaporation in food processing. Trends in Food Science and Technology 7, 78-83.

Knorr, D., M. Geulen, Th. Grahl, & W. Sitzmann, 1994. Food application of high-electric field pulses. Trends in Food Science and Technology 5, 71-75.

Kim, H.-H.Y. & C. Baianu, 1991. Novel liposome micro-encapsulation techniques for food application. Trends in Food Science and Technology 2, 55-61.

Labuza, T.P., B. Fu, & P.S. Taoukis, 1992. Prediction for shelf life and safety of minimally processed CAP/MAP chilled foods: a review. Journal of Food Protection 55, 741-750.

Ledward, D.A., 1993. Creating textures from mixed biopolymer systems. Trends in Food Science and Technology 4, 402-405.

Ledward, D.A. & R.F. Tester, 1994. Molecular transformations of proteinaceous foods during extrusion processing. Trends in Food Science and Technology 5, 117-120.

Ledward, D.A, D.E. Johnston, R.G. Earnshaw & A.P.M. Hastings, (Eds.), 1995. High pressure treatment of foods. Nottingham Press, Loughborough, UK.

Leistner, L.L., 1992. Food preservation by combined methods. Food Research International 25, 151-158.

Leistner, L.L. & L.M. Gorris, 1995. Food preservation by hurdle technology. Trends in Food Science and Technology 6, 41-45.

Loaharana, P. & D. Murrell, 1994. A role for irradiation in the control of foodborne pathogens. Trends in Food Science and Technology 5, 190-195.

Lucca, P.A. & B.J. Tepper, 1994. Fat replacers and the functionality of fat in foods. Trends in Food Science and Technology 5, 12-19.

Mälkki, Y., 1988. Research needs and priorities in food technology. Lebensmittel Wissenschaft und Technologie 21, 71-75.

Marquez, V.O., G.S. Mittal & M.W. Griffiths, 1997. Destruction and inhibition of bacterial spores by high-voltage pulsed electric field. Journal of Food Science 62, 399-401,409.

McClements, D.J. 1995. Advances in the application of ultrasound in food analysis and processing. Trends in Food Science and Technology 6, 293-299.

Mertens, B. & D. Knorr, 1992. Developments of nonthermal processes for food preservation. Food Technology 46(5), 124-133.

Messens, W., J. van Camp & A. Huyghebaert, 1997. The use of high pressure to modify the functionality of food proteins. Trends in Food Science and Technology 8, 107-112.

Murrano, E.A., 1995. Irradiation of fresh meats. Food Technology 49 (12), 52-54

Niranjan, K. 1994. Chemical engineering principles and food processing. Trends in Food Science and Technology 5, 20-23.

O'Sullivan, M.G. 1992. Probiotic bacteria: myth or reality. Trends in Food Science and Technology 3, 309-313.

Ohlsson, Th., 1994. Minimal processing-preservation methods of the future: an overview. Trends in Food Science and Technology 5, 341-344.

Ohshima, T., H. Ushio & C. Koizumi, 1993. High pressure processing of fish and fish products. Trends in Food Science and Technology 4, 371-375.

Palmer, M.V. & S.S.T. Ting, 1995. Applications for supercritical fluid technology in food processing. Food Chemistry 52, 345-352.

Parrot, D.L., 1992. Use of Ohmic heating for aseptic processing of food particulates. Food Technology 46 (12), 68-72.

Peppelenbos, H.W. The use of gas exchange characteristics to optimize CA storage and MA packaging of fruits and vegetables. PhD thesis, Wageningen Agricultural University, 1996.

Pires, M.J., M.R. Aires-Barros & J.M.S. Cabral, 1996. Liquid-liquid extraction of proteins with reversed micelles. Biotechnology Progress 12, 290-301.

Plug, H. & P. Haring, 1993. The role of ingredient-flavour interactions in the development of fat-free foods. Trends in Food Science and Technology 4, 150-152.

Popplewell, L.M., J.M. Black, L.M. Norris & M. Porzio, 1995. Encapsulation system for flavors and colors. Food Technology 49 (5), 76-82.

Pothakamury, U.R. & G.V. Barbosa-Cánovas, 1995. Fundamental aspects of controlled release in foods. Trends in Food Science and Technology 6, 397-406.

Prazeres, D.M.F. & J.M.S. Cabral, 1994. Enzymatic membrane bioreactors and their applications. Enzyme and Microbial Technology 16, 738-750.

Qin, B.L., U.R. Pothakamury, H. Vega, O. Martín, G.V. Barbosa-Cánovas & B.G. Swanson, 1995. Food pasteurization using high-intensity pulsed electric fields. Food Technology 49 (12), 55-60.

Rao, M.A. & S.S.H. Rizvi, 1986. Engineering properties of foods. Marcel Dekker, New York, 1986, 398 p.

Raoult-Wack, A.L. 1994. Recent advances in the osmotic dehydration of foods. Trends in Food Science and Technology 5, 255-260.

Reineccius, G., 1989. Flavor encapsulation. Food Reviews International 5, 147-176.

Rizvi, S.S.H., R.K. Singh, J.H. Hotchkiss & D.R. Heldman, 1993. Research needs in food engineering, processing and packaging. Food Technology 47 (3), 26S-35S.

Rizvi, S.S.H. & A.R. Bhaskar, 1995. Supercritical fluid processing of milk fat: fractionation, scale-up, and economics. Food Technology 49 (2), 90-97,100.

Rizvi, S.S.H., S.J. Mulvaney & A.S. Sokhey, 1995. The combined application of supercritical fluid and extrusion technology. Trends in Food Science and Technology 6, 232-240.

Roser, B. 1991. Threhalose, a new approach to premium dried foods. Trends in Food Science and Technology 3, 166-169.

Roos, Y.H., M. Karel & J.L. Kokini, 1996. Glass transitions in low moisture and frozen foods: effects on shelf life and quality. Food Technology 50 (12), 95-108.

Sakai, N. & T. Hanzawa, 1994. Applications and advances in far-infrared heating in Japan. Trends in Food Science and Technology 5, 357-362.

Schellekens, W. 1996. New research issues in sous-vide cooking. Trends in Food Science and Technology 7, 256-262.

Scher, M. 1993. Biotech food - and no controversy. Trehalose to find more food functions as cost falls. Food Processing, April issue, 95-96.

Schuchmann, H., S. Hogekamp, & H. Schubert, 1993. Jet agglomeration processes for instant foods. Trends in Food Science and Technology 4, 179-183.

Singh, P.C. & R.K. Singh, 1996. Choosing an appropriate bioseparation technique. Trends in Food Science and Technology 7, 49-58.

Scott, G. & P. Richardson, 1997. The application of computational fluid dynamics in the food industry. Trends in Food Science and Technology 8, 119-124.

Slade, L. & H. Levine, 1991. Beyond water activity: recent advances based on an alternative approach to the assessment of food quality and safety. CRC Critical Reviews in Food Science and Nutrition 30, 115-360.

Slade, L. & H. Levine, 1995. Glass transitions and water-food structure interactions. Advances in Food and Nutrition Research 38, 103-269.

Swienteck, 1992. Frozen foods with "fresh" qualities. Food Processing, October Issue, 55.

Thakur, B.R. & R.K. Singh, 1995. Combination processes in food irradiation. Trends in Food Science and Technology 6, 7-11.

Tolstoguzov, V.B. 1995. Some physico-chemical aspects of protein processing in foods: multicomponent gels. Food Hydrocolloids 9, 317-332.

Van den Berg, C. 1991. Food-water relations: progress and integration, comments and thoughts. In: Water relations in foods. Eds. H. Levine and L. Slade, Plenum Press, New York, pp. 21-28.

Van Mil, P.J.J.M. & S. Bouman, (1990). Freeze concentration of dairy products. Netherlands Milk and Dairy Journal 44, 21-32.

Vega-Mercado, H., O. Martín-Belloso, B.L. Qin, F.J. Chang, M.M. Góngora-Nieto, G.V. Barbosa-Cánovas, & B.G. Swanson, (1997). Non-thermal food preservation: pulsed electric fields. Trends in Food Science and Technology 8, 151-157.

Vulfson, E.N., 1993. Enzymatic synthesis of food ingredients in low-water media. Trends in Food Science and Technology 4, 209-215.

Walstra, P. 1983. Formation of Emulsions. In: Encyclopedia of Emulsion Technology, Vol. 1. Ed. P. Becher, Marcel Dekker Inc. New York, 57-128.

Walstra, P. 1996. Emulsion Stability. In: Encyclopedia of Emulsion Technology, Vol. 4. Ed. P. Becher, Marcel Dekker Inc. New York, 1-62.

Wijtzes, T. 1996. Modelling the microbial quality and safety of foods. PhD thesis Wageningen Agricultural University. 138 p.

Yano, T., R. Matsumo & K. Nakamura, 1994. Developments in Food Engineering, Parts 1 & 2. Blackie Academic & Professional, London.

6 Logistics and ICT in Food Supply Systems

P. van Beek, A.J.M. Beulens, H.F.Th. Meffert

6.1 Introduction

During the 1970s and 1980s industry, trade and also academia became heavily involved in the development of instruments primarily directed towards more effective planning and control of logistical operations. Developments include: manufacturing resource planning and the just in time approach. Interest originated mainly from within businesses concerned with production and/or assembly of semifinished and final products. Planning and control of distribution operations also received considerable attention. Developments in this area include: distribution resource planning, routing and location/allocation.

In the 1980s and 1990s these approaches began to be directed towards food supply chains and agri-chains in general. The latter are chains which are based on raw materials of agricultural origin but not necessarily leading to food products. Successful and competitive food supply chains require that the crucial elements costs, quality and technology (including information and communication technology) be taken into account in a multidisciplinary way. Furthermore, the environmental impact of production, processing and distribution is an increasing priority both in industry and in research.

This chapter discusses some general aspects of food supply systems. Previous chapters are devoted to specific aspects including market, quality and technology. Here we direct our attention to the following subjects: logistics, information and communication technology (ICT) and environmental issues. We begin with a general introduction to food supply systems paying attention to special properties of products, the role of ICT, planning and control issues, and environmental aspects. ICT is discussed in depth in Section 6.3, and environmental issues (specifically the concept of 'green supply chain') are dealt with in Section 6.4.

6.2 Logistics in Food Supply Systems

This section provides an overview of the most important logistical characteristics of Food Supply Systems. We do not pretend to offer an exhaustive discussion here.

6.2.1 Some aspects of agri-chains

Special characteristics
Agri-chains and the problems arising in them can no longer be treated solely from the perspective of independent production units. In many cases primary products are processed into articles or into components (grain into

flour, carcasses into parts). Agri-chains differ fundamentally from industrial production or assembly chains in a number of ways (Van Beek, 1990; Bloemhof-Ruwaard et al., 1995):

- restricted quality life of primary, intermediate and final products. This implies that storage technology and conditioning play a prominent role.
- large variation of quality, quantity and availability of primary products, due to regional and seasonal conditions, which require storage and/or transportation (fruits and vegetables, plants and flowers).
- unintended and/or unwanted by-products, remainders and refuse (especially from decomposition processes such as slaughtering, cheese making or potato processing).
- high turnover of volume products.
- many suppliers of primary products, centralized marketing for only a few product groups.
- substantial environmental impacts of production, processing, distribution and consumption (packaging material, surplus product, used product).
- large public interest of organisations in all links of the chain (health and safety aspects of food, animal friendly production and environmentally friendly processing and distribution).

Changing conditions
The operating functions and level of agri-chains under changing conditions requires continuous attention from all actors. The current chains may not offer adequate solutions in an environment of innovative technologies and demand-driven marketing. Moreover, increasing social commitment and awareness of environmental effects of production and distribution processes require close attention (see also Chapter 2, Food Marketing Systems).

Special attention has to be paid to Efficient Consumer Response (ECR), the development of which is stimulated by new scanning technologies for stock management. The result is a more efficient chain operation through reduction of buffer volumes together with improved services and quality for the consumers. ECR, chain logistics and marketing are most closely related. As a consequence, design and operation, control and management of processes in chains must be adapted to the requirements of traditional and new markets. The main characteristics of logistical planning are reviewed in Section 6.2.2.

Growing interest in logistical processes
The increasing interest in logistics of agri-chains stems from the relatively high logistical costs involved and the high quality levels required. Logistical costs can account for 25 to 40 % of the total added value, for example where ornamentals and meat are concerned (Van Beek, 1990; De Boer, 1993).

The growing interest also stems from the fact that logistical systems should not only operate cost effectively but also should be responsive and flexible. The design and control of such systems, taking into account cost effectiveness and flexibility issues, is a very complex task.

6.2.2 The nature of logistical planning

A brief general introduction to logistical planning is provided here. It is based on Chapter 1 of Hax and Candea (1984).

Logistical systems are concerned with the effective management of the total flow of goods from the acquisition of raw materials to the delivery of final products to the customers.

A logistical system is composed of a large number of elements which have to be managed properly in order to deliver final products in the right quantities at the desired time and quality, and at a reasonable cost. Furthermore the quality of the different logistical processes (production, storage and distribution) should be kept as high as possible. This means that processes should be designed in such a way that environmental aspects like emissions are dealt with adequately.

The most important elements are the following: plants, distribution centres, products (including raw materials, supplies, semifinished and final products), transportation infrastructure, information and communication systems, people. The acquisition and utilization of these elements are subject to a wide variety of constraints. Examples include: productivity constraints, capacity constraints, labour availability, technological options, lead times, demand uncertainties, service requirements.

In order to determine effective ways to acquire and use logistics elements subject to these constraints, several cost components have to be taken into account. Important factors contributing to cost include: purchasing costs, production costs, setup/changeover costs, inventory costs, investment costs, hiring and firing costs.

It is clear that the underlying decision processes related to design and control of logistical systems can be extremely complex. They usually encompass several echelons of an organization, and thus require a great deal of coordination within the chain (see also Section 6.2.3).

To cope with the complexities mentioned earlier we present a framework which was originally proposed by Anthony (1997), in which decisions related to design and control of logistical systems can be considered, taking into account all interdependencies. Anthony classified decisions into three categories: strategic planning, tactical planning and operations control. We will briefly comment on the characteristics of each of these categories.

Strategic Planning
Strategic planning is concerned mainly with establishing managerial policies and with developing facilities needed to satisfy all requirements and goals. In the area of logistical management the most important decisions that can be supported by model-based systems are those concerned with the design of production and distribution facilities. They include the determination of location and capacity of new plants and distribution centres, the design of transportation facilities, and so on. These decisions are extremely important because they are responsible for maintaining the competitive capability of individual enterprises and the chain as a whole. An essential characte-

ristic of these strategic decisions is that they have long-lasting effects, thus forcing long planning horizons in their analysis.

Tactical Planning
Tactical planning emphasizes the process of utilization of resources in the chain. Once the facilities (like plants, distribution centres and transportation means) have been decided upon the basic problem to be resolved is the effective allocation of resources to satisfy demand and technological requirements, taking into account the costs and revenues associated with the operation of the resources in the chain.

Whereas strategic planning is concerned with the process of *creating* capacities, tactical planning tries to *utilize* these capacities in the most effective way. Typical decisions to be made are allocation of retailer branches to distribution centres and utilization of work force.

Operational control
After making an aggregate allocation of resources in a logistical chain it is necessary to focus on day-to-day operational decisions. This stage of the decision-making process is called *operational control*. The operational control decisions require the information generated at the level of strategic planning and tactical planning be separated out into the details of daily activities. Typical decisions at this level are sequencing of (customer) orders, vehicle scheduling and inventory control.

The three types of decision cannot be studied in isolation. An integrated approach is necessary in order to avoid weaknesses in the chain. For example: there is a strong interdependency between the production capacity of a machine and the way of scheduling the production of that machine. Sometimes it could be better to allocate more capacity in order to make the scheduling process simpler. In the next section we examine the integral aspects of chain management.

6.2.3 Integral chain management

In the past research efforts have been directed to the quality of primary, intermediate and final products and to the control of logistic processes in parts of the chain. Only recently has research focused on the integral approach to logistic problems in agri-chains. Some progress has been made, but problems have not been solved completely (Van Dalen; 1995, Hagelaar, 1994). The range of problems is so diverse, that it appears impossible to study them under one heading.

We mention a number of these problems:
- Pressure of time on chain processes. Long distance transport of perishable products. Long preparation times and traffic congestion, short periods for deliveries in cities.
- Veterinary and phytosanitary restrictions for certain products under way to certain markets.

- Lack of willingness to cooperate effectively in chains by adhering to autonomy of the enterprise, and unwillingness to accept chain responsibility. Insufficient knowledge about methods for cooperation in win-win relations. Value adding partnerships are especially important where no prevailing power factor exists, and can reinforce design and operation of the chain.
- Increasing need for effective and efficient chains with regard to international competition, implying a great variation of (new) products to satisfy market-demand, which must be high quality on delivery, cost-effective, and produced under increasingly restrictive conditions.

Opportunities and bottlenecks

The opportunities for adopting an integral approach are increasingly, especially as a result of the increasingly refined requirements of customers. A growing wish for information on the history of a product is manifest. This issue is recognised as an aspect of quality. Furthermore, mutual coordination of activities between links of a chain provides opportunities for cost reduction. Information and communication technology plays an important role in this process.

Bottlenecks are mostly caused by incomplete and suboptimal control and information models, a lack of means with which to implement chain management, and by the fact that an integral approach to problems of sustainable production and logistics has still to be developed.

Research efforts

Solving the problems mentioned by adopting an integral approach to agrichains requires paying special attention to all the separate links of the chain, to all interfaces (with regard to mutual adjustment), and to the chain as a whole. Research efforts can be divided into two parts:

- Design, adjustment and control of chains (see also section 6.2.2). This requires the integration of knowledge from a great number of disciplines (management, marketing, information technology, food science and technology, operations research, agrotechnology).
- The supporting disciplines can be stimulated by carrying out interdisciplinary supply chain research projects.

The interaction stimulates the process of asking the right questions, related to design and control of chains from an integral management view. Answers have to be found by using accumulated knowledge from a range of disciplines.

6.2.4 Information

Adequate control and management of the flow of products in all links of the supply chain requires various resources and the management of the related processes. Besides manpower, equipment, buildings and energy, the supply and processing of information is also of great importance. Information constitutes an important part of products and/or services. Moreover information is also essential for the control and management of organisational processes (Beulens, 1991; Beers et al., 1994). Up-to-date information is necessary in order to be able to make the right decisions concerning supply chains.

Example: quality change of perishable products is a time-temperature related process. The management of the process factors is split up between different disciplines in the organisation. To identify performance indicators for the involved parameters, information also has to be split up into the contributing components. This can only be done by using time-temperature recording or logging instruments, which range from purely mechanical to smart card devices.

It is also necessary to have or to generate information on the expected demands in the future. At the same time information on competitors and related parties is required, together with information on decisions to be taken and their expected consequences. In this field, management information systems and decision support systems reveal their operational value. Besides the information supply from within the chain, external information (on markets and on suppliers of primary products and auxiliaries) is essential. With inadequate information systems no satisfactory logistic management can be established.

6.3 ICT in food supply systems and - chains

6.3.1 Introduction

We are continuously faced with the overwhelming and ever growing impact of information and communication technology (ICT) on our daily lives. ICT affects domestic appliances that we use, information sources that we have access to and use, as well as transport and leisure. For professional and clerical workers in and outside offices, including managers, ICT provides 'tools' and applications, giving them access to both internal and external databases, and provides them with model-based support for transaction processing, decision making, communication and coordination. Production workers in turn are also confronted with ICT applications, in the administrative, communication and coordination tasks within and between organisational or production units and in their operational tasks using automated production machines that contain computers with software applications that need instructions and control from 'operators'. In research and development we see similar developments. R&D workers are supported by the above mentioned applications. In addition, they may use sophisticated design tools and databases in the execution of their primary tasks, which may include activities such as designing systems, machines, products, buildings, (production or organisational) processes, etc. Researchers in laboratories may be supported by automated equipment, imaging, measuring tools, sensors, simulation tools, etc.

This by no means exhaustive list of ICT applications gives a clear picture of the overwhelming impact of ICT on our daily lives. The enormous amount of information sources and the immense volumes of information contained in them, which are accessible through public (Internet) and private (Intranet) networks, confront us with an important paradigm shift in the work of information technology specialists. Briefly described, professional and clerical workers have moved from a situation of technically difficult access to limited information sources, to one of easy access to gigantic sources of information. Limited information processing power means that these people have to be able to find their way around these vast data sources both efficiently and effectively in order to do their job. The problem of technical access has thus been replaced by a problem of routing and selection!

In the remainder of this chapter we confine ourselves to the importance of ICT for food production systems and chains. In particular we will discuss the role of ICT in supporting or automating operational (transaction) processes and in supporting cooperation, negotiation and decision-making processes within chains.

6.3.2   Business Process Redesign (BPR) using ICT in food production chains

In the previous section we have introduced a variety of current business applications of ICT. In this section we briefly discuss important changes and trends that businesses are encountering. Some of these have been covered extensively in other sections of this book and are reiterated here in order to provide a comprehensive set of factors leading to or contributing to the need for BPR with ICT at the company or chain level. The trends include:

- An enormous leap in the availability of ICT, in particular cheap, powerful computers and automated equipment. Moore's law of doubling capacity and halving the price each year has been true for computers for many years and is expected to hold for at least the next five to six years. A 300 mips (million instructions per second) desktop computer (PC) currently costs about US$2000. Compare this with a 1 mips mainframe computer from 1980 that cost more than US$ 1 million.
- Other technologies which are partly dependent on ICT are also developing very rapidly, and at affordable prices. These range from biotechnology to production, storage, conditioning and transport technology.
- A variety of these technological developments associated with political, social and market developments have led to expanding geographical markets for businesses or chains. Changing market demands and consumer requirements have led to a change in focus from production-oriented chains towards consumer demand controlled chains and global competition. As a result (chains of) companies have to be more responsive to market requirements, provide a greater variety of products and associated information (composition, use, storage, etc.), services and guarantees, all at the lowest possible cost. Social and political developments have resulted in social policies with respect to labour conditions and to regulations regarding product and process quality, product responsibili-

ty, tracking and tracing, the environment, quality information, social, ecological and financial reporting, etc.

- The trends described above have clearly provided both great challenges to and opportunities for the business community. Companies are faced with the challenge of having to acquire and maintain a competitive position in a rapidly changing market, with technological, social and political constraints. They are also presented with opportunities for incorporating technologies into their strategies which will result in better products at lower prices while satisfying regulations and requirements. Organisations have to be innovative and thus are seeking answers in different directions. The configuration and establishment of (virtual) supply chains is one development, the objective of which is to better fulfil consumer wishes, both more rapidly and at less cost, while satisfying all requirements previously mentioned. It is now widely accepted that a supply chain can drastically improve the performance of the whole of a value chain by working together closely. Value chains may consider different scopes ranging from suppliers of ingredients (e.g. primary producers) and packaging for products, manufacturers, wholesalers, distributors/ transportation companies, to retailers and consumers. (See P. van Beek, A.J.M. Beulens & J.Chr. Van Dalen 1996, A.J.M. Beulens 1996, Coopers & Lybrand 1996, M.T.G. Meulenberg & D.F. Broens 1996, A.M. Pearce 1996.) It is now widely accepted in both in the business community and politics that there is a need for continuous business and chain innovation using ICT in order to become and stay responsive and competitive. (See e.g. Bangemann reports of commission of the European Union, and publications of A.J.M. Beulens 1992, A.J.M. Beulens 1996, C. Ciborra & T. Jelassi 1994, J. Donovan 1994, A. Penzias 1991, M.E. Porter & V.E. Millar 1985, M.S. Scott Morton 1991 and P.A. Strassmann 1991).

- The developments mentioned above have also affected management and organisation in chains. There is a rapidly growing awareness in companies and chains that effectiveness, efficiency and quality (as perceived by the customer and from a technological viewpoint) are served by a process oriented approach in the supply chain). Examples of this approach are incorporated in concepts such as total quality management (TQM), just-in-time (JIT), business process redesign (BPR), chain process redesign, autonomous groups, socio-technics, human resource management (HRM), work flow management (WFM), hazard analysis critical control points (HACCP), etc. These approaches all have in common that a purely functional approach to the organisation, execution, management and coordination of business processes has to be abandoned. They also entail decreasing the number of hierarchical levels in companies by delegation of responsibilities and by increasing coordination capabilities, facilitated by ICT applications (WFM, EDI, E-mail, etc.).

- Finally, the widespread recognition of ICT as an important production factor has resulted in businesses implementing information management at the board level and acknowledging the need for the development of a company strategy which incorporates ICT strategy as an integral part.

The trends and developments outlined above are expected to continue to be of great importance in the coming years. As a result we can expect the configuration and implementation of new chains. There will also be continuous innovation of business processes within and over these chains, using ICT as an enabling tool, in order to make them more competitive and efficient.

6.3.3 ICT in chains

Actors within chains are dependent upon information and ICT applications (and infrastructures which allow access to these) for organising, staffing, executing, managing, coordinating and controlling business activities. They are confronted with the exchange of product and process information, with suppliers and customers, with consumers requiring information, with reporting obligations within the company and to external contacts (government, business partners, etc.). For the execution and management of the business processes themselves they need enterprise resource systems which allow them to plan, execute and monitor business processes within chain constraints. At the level of the chain, systems are required which facilitate communication between business partners (EDI, PDI, E-mail, etc.) and the planning and coordination of chain activities which set constraints for participating businesses. Figure 6.1 provides an example of information interchange. Important physical and administrative logistical processes that take place in a supply chain are depicted together with dependencies (e.g. time). The supply chain consists of retail outlets (a store), a retail organisation responsible for centralised purchasing and distribution through a distribution centre (DC), and a manufacturer with a factory and its own DC for the sale of finished products from stock.

The diagram shows information exchange in both directions along the chain using three constructs: event, process and wait.

Event: an event which takes place, a short moment, represented by a circle.

Process: an activity with a relatively long duration, often triggered by an event. Represented by a square.

Wait: a significant delay before an event or process can be triggered. Represented by a 'W' placed in the circle or square.

A short explanation of the model of the chain is provided below.

Store
The first event is an individual 'purchase'. These individual purchases are aggregated (e.g. for one day) into 'purchases aggregated'. These aggregated purchases are used for calculating the 'new' stock level. If necessary (following the process 'shelf inventory check') an 'order' will be generated by the process 'generate order'. If 'generate order' takes place at a fixed point in time, there will be a 'wait' of orders before they are sent to the distribution

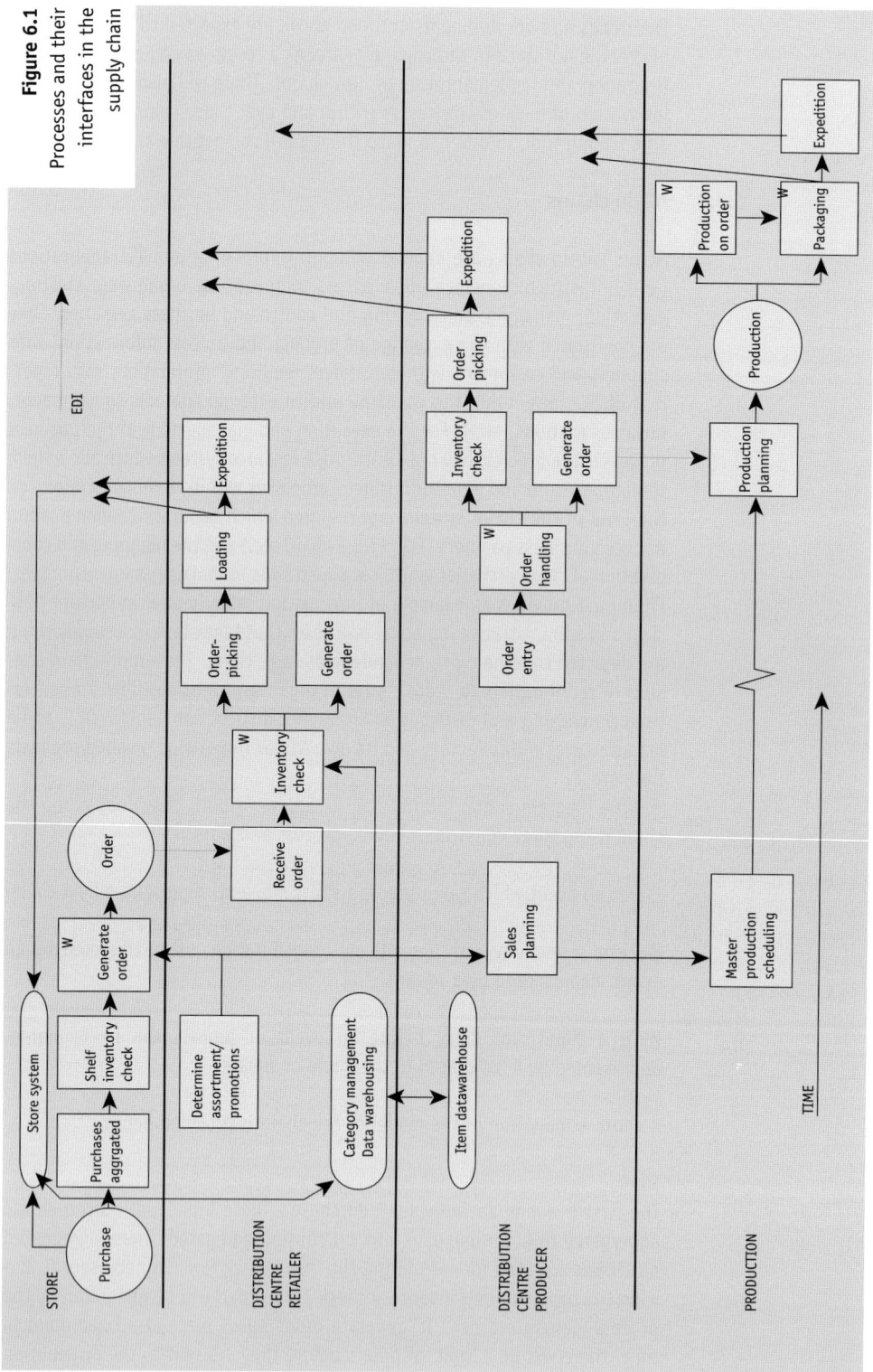

Figure 6.1
Processes and their interfaces in the supply chain

centre retailer.

Possible improvements: automated store ordering by the 'store system', sending orders using EDI, category management using point of sale information, etc.

Distribution centre retailer
The received orders are processed, usually in batches (= wait), and 'matched' with available stock. If stock is sufficient, the ordered items will be selected, loaded and transported to the store. At the same time orders are generated and sent to the producer. A process that does not really influences the throughput times of an order is 'determine assortment/promotions'. Information about this process is sent to the stores, distribution centre and to the producers.
Possible improvements: 'category management data warehousing' to support the process 'determine assortment/promotions', sending orders and advanced shipping notices using EDI, etc.

Distribution centre producer
The DC producer works in a similar way to the DC retailer, except when production on order takes place: see 'generate order' and 'production planning'.
Possible improvements: 'item datawarehousing', using EDI for sending orders and advanced shipping notices, etc.

Production
Production is based on the 'master production scheduling' and on the (less aggregated) production planning. The products are sent to the distribution centre (delivering from stock) or to the distribution centre of the retailer (production on order).
Possible improvements: using point of sale information for production planning, using EDI for sending orders and advanced shipping notices, etc.

The example above describes the information processes needed to ensure quality continuous replenishment within a chain for fresh and refrigerated products as developed in an ECR project. EDI messages have been designed to shorten lead times in the chain. Information is no longer only directly attached to goods delivered but provided at a different time from (usually ahead of or in anticipation of future events) the actual distribution or ordering processes.

Based on the above description of ICT applications in chains, we present below in some more detail the scope of ICT applications:

- *Structured or unstructured data, information or knowledge as part of the product*
  Many products are represented by information or information may form an integral part of the product. In terms of the latter we need to consider product identification, for example in the form of bar codes which may allow for automatic sales recording (POS) and for automatic physical handling in logistic processes. Further examples include product spe-

cifications and compositions provided separately or printed on the packaging of the product, as well as more 'intelligent' additions to the packaging of the product such as smart cards or heat-sensitive strips. Finally we may think about user manuals etc.

- *Structured or unstructured data, information or knowledge as part of a production machine*
  Many production machines now contain computers which when programmed and given product specifications can determine the product output level for the machine. Examples include printing machines, robots, blending machines, weighing machines, counters, automatic guided vehicles and sorters.

- *ICT- the technical component*
  Computers and software may form part of the product, or may themselves be the product. Simple examples of the latter are PCs, workstations, and other types of computers. A smart card is another example: the card is able to perform a number of functions depending on the amount of memory and the software and data it contains. Student cards, insurance cards, personal identification cards containing personal data (including fingerprint information) are examples of these chip cards. As mentioned above computers and software often form an integral part of production or logistic equipment.

- *Processes*
  Many primary support, co-ordinating and communication processes contain information processing activities. Information and messages about events and objects in the business or its environment are recorded in databases and subsequently used to generate products , decisions and messages about the process.
  The same can be said for management and control processes (production and work flow management). Management and control are supported by information obtained from administrative databases, and from knowledge and model-based systems. These help managers to design good plans and schedules and also to monitor and control the execution of these plans. See Figure 6.2.

The above discussion clearly indicates the importance of ICT for efficient and effectively operating chains and businesses. This leads us on to the issue of information management as an integral part of chain management.

6.3.4   ICT management

An important production factor, ICT needs to be managed. The management process itself must be an integral part of the management process of the business as a whole. For ICT management we can distinguish the following aspects:

Figure 6.2

Role of information system and decision support system

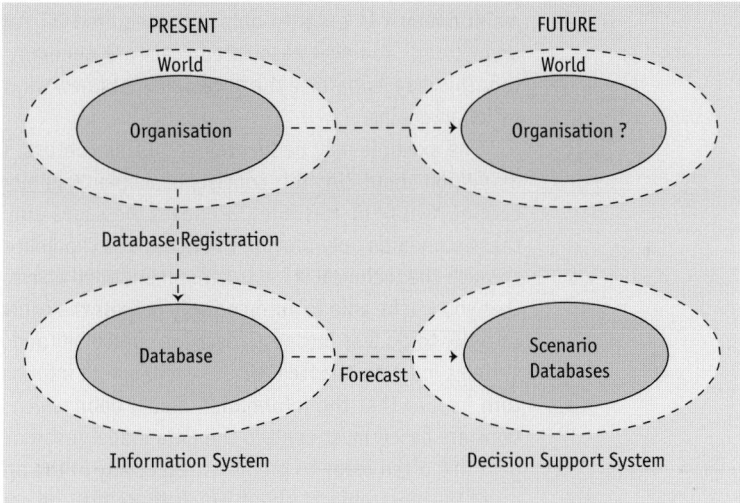

- The specification, design, development and implementation of an evolving ITC infrastructure for the organisation as part of a chain infrastructure in response to technological, business and chain developments. Important components include databases, formal procedural and modelling knowledge (model and knowledge banks, standards, (reference) information models that describe the contents of databases, etc.), applications or software systems and the technical components of the infrastructure (computers, networks, telecommunication facilities and peripheral equipment). The user has access to this infrastructure through a PC connected to a network, and through this can use software applications, communication facilities and databases.
- Facilities management: the primary task is to make sure that the infrastructure with all its components is available to the users during the periods when they are required to do their work. Currently that may mean continuous availability! For data sources in databases this means that data with the required integrity (correctness) must be available. For software applications it means that these can be accessed by users on any of the workstations to which they have access. In terms of facilities management this entails that regular backups must be made which can be used when problems occur. Further, it means that software problems must be solved when they become apparent.
- the development of an ICT strategy as an integral part of the business strategy in order to be able to satisfy future needs for ICT infrastructure elements.

We have described the role of ICT management and the components of an ICT infrastructure. It sounds easy to talk about these infrastructures at the level of businesses and chains. In practice, however, we find repeatedly that both the importance of good infrastructure and the complexity of developing and maintaining it in order to obtain the required ICT functionality are not well understood, and that associated costs are generally severely underestimated. This may jeopardise the development of new ways of working and cooperation in chains.

One example may be mentioned in this context. There is currently much discussion about EDI. This consists of simple technology, with standards concerning syntax of messages, standard messages and dictionaries. However, these standards only provide the automatic capability to exchange messages through the technical infrastructure mentioned above. They do not guarantee that you will be able to automatically process the contents of these messages. In order to do this business (decision) processes and associated information systems must be adapted for the exchange of information using EDI. This in turn implies that the information model upon which these information systems are based must contain the data model incorporated in the EDI messages. This often leads to problems, especially in the area of the identification of all business objects about which there may be communication. A simple example: using the same EAN bar code for more than one product may lead to many problems in logistics and marketing. However, the magnitude of problems that can arise as a result of incomplete or faulty infrastructure components is beyond the scope of this book. However, we hope that our remarks make you aware of the problem and cautious in strategy development, to the extent that this subject is at least taken into account.

6.4 Environmental Aspects [1]

6.4.1 Introduction

In the last few decades environmental problems have received increasing attention. Protection of the environment has become an issue at all levels of society: worldwide (UNCED 92), regional (European Union), national, sectoral and the individual consumer.

Within the field of production and logistics, attention for environmental issues is now growing rapidly. In 1991 a special issue of Transportation Science was devoted to the transportation of hazardous materials.

In order to ensure sustainable development and environmental quality production and distribution processes often have to be redesigned in such a way that economic development and environmental protection can be reconciled with each other. This section describes how environmental aspects can influence the design and control of supply chains.

6.4.2 Green supply chain management

During each step in the supply chain, from the extraction of raw materials to processing steps, consumption and then waste treatment, emissions take place that can be a threat to people, plants, animals and ecosystems. New measures are necessary to decrease emissions and waste flows. Legal requirements and changing consumer preferences increasingly make suppliers and manufacturers responsible for their products, even beyond their sale and delivery. To comply with these new regulations, producers have to apply cradle-to-grave product management covering the entire supply chain. Figure 6.3 presents a detailed view of potential environmental actions in a supply chain.

The first actions, which are quite easy to apply, are effect-directed (end-of-pipe), such as *waste treatment*. More integrated approaches include waste-directed and emission-directed adaptations in technology, such as *reuse of materials and packaging* and *recovery of products*. The most integrated approach is source-directed and deals with *adaptation of raw materials, product redesign* and *process changes*.

Barry et al. (1993) introduced a five-stage outline for analyzing environmental issues throughout the product life-cycle. This outline is used here to discuss the potential environmental actions illustrated in Figure 6.3 in more detail. First, the use of fewer raw materials is discussed. This is followed by a discussion of the manufacturing stage, covering process and product changes, distribution issues (less transport, redesign of locations and reverse logistics), the use of products, and finally, the treatment of waste.

Raw materials
In terms of raw materials, green objectives may be to minimize the use of materials whose acquisition is environmentally damaging and to maximize the use of recycled materials and renewable resources. In addition, preference can be given to suppliers which operate in an environmentally responsible manner. General Motors, for example, has embarked on an ambitious programme for material acquisition. Its WE CARE (Waste Elimination and Cost Awareness Reward Everyone) programme involves cooperation with suppliers and includes specific measures to reduce inbound packaging materials, encourage their reuse and increase their recycling ability (Barry et al., 1993).

Figure 6.3
Green supply chain

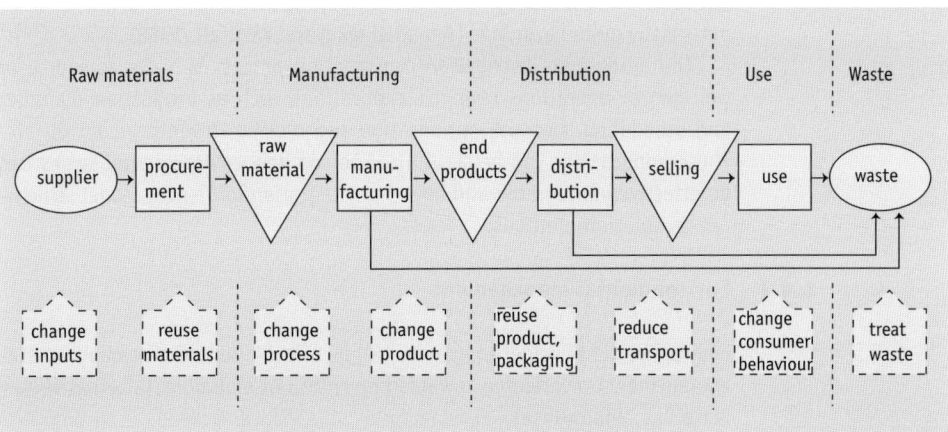

131

Manufacturing

In manufacturing, both process and product design can be improved. In process design, the goals are to reduce waste, minimize pollution, use resources efficiently and find substitutes for hazardous materials. In product design, the purpose is to design not only for cost-effective assembly but also for disassembly and recyclability. Europe's automobile manufacturers and their suppliers are considering ways to increase the use of recycled parts. BMW and Volkswagen, for example, have set up pilot plants to examine reusability of current models and to develop design requirements for new models (Kleiner, 1991).

Distribution

Reverse distribution planning is necessary for collecting packaging and used products. In Germany, consumers have the legal right to return product packaging to retailers for recycling and reuse (Töpfer Law, 1991). In response to this retailers developed the 'Duales System Deutschland' (DSD). This dual system collects used packaging and sorts it by type of material. These materials are then transported to industries that have a license to make the materials usable again (Cairncross, 1992).

Use

Efficient use means minimizing energy or other resources consumed by the product, increasing the product's durability and life span, and minimizing the pollution the product emits during use. Consumers should also be provided with instructions for using the product efficiently, so that environmental impact is minimized. The Dutch electricity company's 'efficient light bulb' campaign includes humorous advertisements and television shows aimed at changing consumer behaviour (NEPP2, 1993).

Disposal

The collection and sorting of waste requires infrastructural measures. In addition, hazardous materials should be collected according to stringent safety standards. According to the Office of Technology Assessment (USA), American industry generates approximately 250-275 million metric tonnes of industrial chemical waste annually. Most of the waste is dumped in landfills, which is potentially quite hazardous (Anandalingam and Westfall, 1988).

The production-distribution-consumption process is a classic source of well-known operations research applications such as production planning and scheduling, network optimization and routing, inventory control, etc. These applications can be scrutinized to see how environmental issues can be effectively integrated and how this integration influences model structure and solution-methods.

6.4.3 Environmental management

Environmental policy of companies can be effect-oriented (recycling, waste-management) or oriented towards prevention of emissions (alternative raw materials, energy-use).

Thinking about environmental issues in the supply chain has evolved from end-of-pipe control towards waste prevention at the source. We distinguish three stages in the increasing integration of operations research and environmental managment that correspond with the shift from an end-of-pipe approach towards a cradle-to-grave approach in supply chain modelling.

1. *Waste management*

In the first (hypothetical) stage of integration, environmental issues (waste and emissions) influence only the final processes in the supply chain, i.e. distribution, product use and waste disposal. Economic activities that have to be developed or adapted include the distribution of hazardous waste and the selection of appropriate locations for disposal sites and incinerators. Emissions to air and water are in most cases reduced through end-of-pipe techniques.

2. *Recovery management*

At the intermediate level of integration, production is also subject to change in response to environmental issues. At this level, end-of-pipe treatment and disposal of waste to reduce environmental damage are no longer sufficient. Recovery management aims at postponing the generation of waste and lengthening the lifetime of products through recycling and reuse. This requires manufacturers to feel responsible for their products after consumer use and to consider ways to increase the uses of recycled materials. It requires changes in both process and product design.

3. *Preventive management*

Prevention is the key issue in the final stage of integration. The objective of pollution prevention is to avoid the use of materials whose acquisition and transformation are environmentally damaging. Environmental burdens associated with a product or process have to be quantified. Studies to assess these are in general complex and expensive.

Below we present strategies for dealing with each of the three stages mentioned above.

i. *Waste management*

The disposal of hazardous waste at sites which are far from the production locations requires shipment of waste across a transportation network. The location and routing problem becomes one of choosing where to open disposal sites, how to assign sources to disposal sites and how to route the waste flows from each source to its assigned destination.

If the only objective is to minimize cost, the problem can be modelled in the form of a simple plant location model. ReVelle et al. (1991) combine a shortest path algorithm with a zero-one location programme and the multi-objective weighing method to solve the two-criteria problem of minimizing transportation costs and perceived risk.

Bloemhof-Ruwaard et al. (1994) consider the problem of how to design an efficient (minimum cost) distribution structure which simultaneously takes into account the location of plants and disposal sites, the coordination of the flow of goods between plants and customers and the flow of waste between plants and disposal sites. Risk related to the transport of waste is not covered in this paper.

ii. *Product recovery management*

Traditionally, manufacturers did not feel responsible for their products after consumer use. The bulk of used products were dumped or incinerated, incurring considerable damage to the environment. Today, consumers and authorities expect manufacturers to reduce the waste generated by their products.

Product recovery management is defined as the management of all used and discarded products, components, and materials for which a manufacturing company is legally, contractually, or otherwise responsible (Thierry et al., 1995). Product recovery management offers several options for handling products after consumer use: repair/reuse, refurbishing, remanufacturing, cannibalization and recycling. Each of the options involves collection, reprocessing and redistribution of the used products. The main difference is in the degree of reprocessing. Figure 6.4 illustrates the degree of required disassembly. The choice of the 'best' product recovery option in practice depends on environmental regulations, technological capabilities, costs, etc.

Uncertainties in product recovery problems occur with respect to time, quality and quantity of returned products (Flapper, 1993). The supply of used products may be highly irregular as it is influenced by various factors including alternative uses, loss of products (e.g. car accidents) and the general economic situation. Forecasting the quantity and quality of used products is therefore difficult. The varying quality of the returned product means that screening and sorting have to be done, which complicates the modelling and analysis of product recovery problems. However, these issues may have a tremendous effect on production planning and inventory control and represent a challenging research agenda.

iii. *Source-directed product management*

Examples in this part deal with environmental impacts associated with a product over its entire life cycle. They differ from the above examples, which focus solely on waste disposal and product recovery.

For some years now, people have been developing techniques for assessing environmental impacts of products and processes from cradle to grave. Such techniques require a large amount of environmental data. One of the most promising techniques is life cycle assessment (LCA), defined as a process to evaluate the environmental burdens associated with a product, process or activity by identifying and quantifying energy and materials used and wastes released to the environment (SETAC, 1993, p. 3). The knowledge obtained from LCA studies forms a valuable input to green manufacturing models.

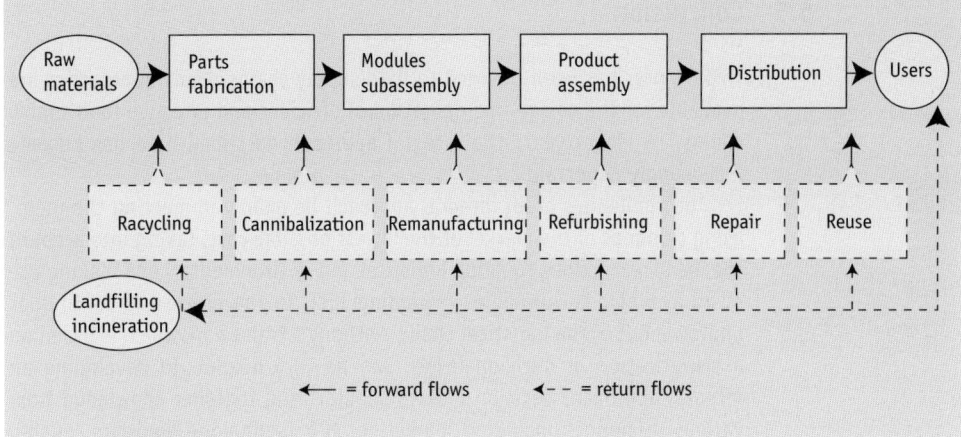

Figure 6.4
Product recovery
management
(Thierry et al., 1995)

Pirila et al. (1994) studied emission-oriented production planning in the Finnish pulp and paper industry. Their production planning model is a large multiple-period linear programme. Integration of environmental impacts within this model leads to alternative strategies, including process choices, recovery of waste products, etc.

Haasis (1994) studied production planning and control of low emission production systems. The methodologies used are based on dynamic programming, priority-based heuristics and neural networks (machine learning).

Bloemhof-Ruwaard et al. (1995) studied product blending problems in a large multinational food company. The products in this case study are spreads, usually consisting of a blend of several fats. LCA was used to assess the environmental impacts of these fats. These impacts were then converted into a single environmental index for each fat using the Analytic Hierarchy Process (AHP) (Saaty, 1980). This environmental index was used in the product mix models. Two types of linear programming product mix models were considered: one with a classical cost minimization objective and a constraint on environmental impact, and one with an environmental impact minimization objective and a constraint on costs. Results indicate that the environmental impact could be improved considerably at the expense of only a slight cost increase of the product mix.

At this point, two issues remain which need to be resolved. First, LCA studies are still pretty complex and expensive. Second, the LCA data involve all sorts of environmental effects which should somehow be combined into a single environmental index in order to be useful in an OR decision model. The practical link between LCA and OR models provides a challenging research issue: how to design LCA studies that quickly yield relevant environmental impacts and how to combine these impacts meaningfully into inputs for OR models.

6.5 Conclusions

This chapter has been devoted to food supply chains. Many approaches are available for the design and operation of efficient and effective food supply chains. In recent years the integral approach described here has become increasingly important.

The challenges of an integral approach lie mainly in meeting the increasing demands of the market at the lowest possible cost, taking into account the many restrictions (quality, logistical and environmental) and making use of all available technologies (including ICT). In the process of continuous improvement of the logistical chain, Anthony's Framework which is based on a classification of decision levels, can be very helpful. In developing an integral approach, decision makers should bring together knowledge from various disciplines including marketing, ICT, technology, logistics, quality control, environmental studies and operational research.

The bottlenecks encountered are the integral process and information models, and the fact that an integral approach to sustainability still needs to be formed. However we are not starting from scratch! The growing amount of attention paid to environmental issues within the field of supply chain management is changing from end-of-pipe control towards waste prevention.

Two main aspects of food supply systems have been discussed in depth here: ICT and environmental aspects. These complement the subjects dealt with in other chapters of this book. It is our conclusion that there is a wealth of opportunities for working out an integral approach to food supply systems, in terms of both design and control of such systems.

Notes

1) This part of Chapter 6 is largely based on an article in the European Journal of Operational Research, vol. 85, pp. 229-243, 1995 (J.M. Bloemhof et al.). Reprinted with kind permission from Elsevier Science-NL, Sara Burgerhartstraat 25, 1055 KV Amsterdam, The Netherlands.

References

Anandalingam, G. & M. Westfall, 1988. Selection of hazardous waste disposal alternatives using multi-attribute utility theory and fuzzy set analysis, Journal of Environmental Systems, 18-1, 69-85.

Anthony, R. N. & V. Govindarajan, 1997. Management Control Systems (The Irwin Series in Graduate Accounting), 9th Ed. Richard Irwin.

Barry, J., G. Girard & C. Perras, 1993. Logistic planning shifts into reverse, the Journal of European Business, September/October, 34-38.

Beek, P. van, 1990. Het bestaansrecht van agrologistiek, interview, Tijdschrift voor Inkoop en Logistiek, 6, June, 23-26.

Beek, P. van, A.J.M. Beulens & J.Chr. Van Dalen, 1996. Markgericht en efficiënt werken vereisen integrale ketenlogistiek, VMT no. 8, 11 April 1996.

Beers, G., A.J.M. Beulens & J.H. Trienekens, 1994. Global reference information models for product chains in agriculture: a case of apples and pears, in G. Hagelaar (ed.): Management Studies and Agribusiness, Agri-Chain Management, Wageningen.

Beulens, A.J.M., 1991. Informatievoorziening in de keten: veel meer dan een technologische uitdaging. In: E. van Heck & P.J.P. Zuurbier (eds.), Bedrijfskunde en Agribusiness, Agro-industriële ontwikkelingen in de jaren negentig, Wageningen.

Beulens, A.J.M., 1992. Informatie-technologie en maatschappij: intrigerende integratie, Inaugural lecture, Wageningen Agricultural University, 19 March, 1992.

Beulens, A.J.M., 1996. De rol van IT-toepassingen voor samenwerking, onderhandeling en besluitvorming in Voortbrengingsketens (Supply Chains), in: NRLO-rapport Ketenlogistiek nr. 96/3.

Beulens, A.J.M.., 1996. Continuous Replenishment in Food Chains and Associated Planning Problems, in: Workshop on Advances in Methodology and Software for Decision Support Systems, IIASA, Laxenburg, Austria, 8-10 September 1996.

Bloemhof-Ruwaard, J.M., P.van Beek, L. Hordijk & L.N. Van Wassenhove, 1995. Interaction between Operational Research and Environmental Management. European Journal of Operational Research 85, 229-243.

Bloemhof-Ruwaard, J.M., H.G. Koudijs & J.C. Vis, 1995. Environmental impacts of fat blends: a methodological study combining Life Cycle Assessment, Multi Criteria Decision Analysis and Linear Programming. Environmental and Resource Economics, 6, 371-387.

Bloemhof-Ruwaard, J.M., M. Salomon & L.N. Van Wassenhove, 1994. On coordination of product and waste flows in distribution networks, model formulations and solution procedures. European Journal of Operational Research, 79, 325-340.

Boer, A.J. de (ed.), 1993. EDI in de agrarische sector, Samsom Bedrijfsinformatie, Alphen aan de Rijn.

Cairncross, F., 1992. How Europe's companies reposition to recycle, Harvard Business Review, March/April, 34-45.

Ciborra, C. & T. Jelassi, 1994. Strategic Information Systems, John Wiley & Sons Ltd, 1994

Coopers & Lybrand, 1996. Efficient Consumer Response-Europe: Value Chain Analysis Project Overview, January 1996.

Dalen, J.Chr. van, 1995. Sustainable chain systems. In, Management studies and the Agribusiness (G. Hagelaar ed.) Wageningen 1995.

Donovan, J., 1994. Business Reengineering with IT, Prentice Hall 1994.

Flapper, S.D.P., 1993. On the logistics of recycling: an introduction, Eindhoven University of Technology, Technical Report TUE/BDK/LBS, 93-16.

Haasis, H.-D., 1994. Planung und Steuerung emissionsarm zu betreibender industrieller Produktionssysteme (Planning and control of industrial production systems with low emissions), Physica-Verlag, c/o Springer-Verlag, Berlin (in German).

Hagelaar, G (ed.), 1994. Management studies and the Agri-Business, Agri-chain Management, Wageningen.

Hax, A.C., D. Candea, 1984,. Production and Inventory Management, Prentice Hall, Inc., Englewood Cliffs, New Jersey.

Kleiner, A., 1991. What does it mean to be green?, Harvard Business Review, July/August, 38-47.

Meulenberg, M.T.G. & D.F. Broens, 1996. Inzicht in ketens helpt bij ketenvorming, VMT No. 12, 6 June, 1996.

NEPP2, 1993. National Environmental Policy Plan, Environment as Measure, Ministry of Housing, Physical Planning and Environment, 23560, Nos. 1-2, SDU, The Hague.

Pearce, A.M., 1996. Efficient Consumer Response: managing the supply chain for 'ultimate' consumer satisfaction. Supply Chain Management, Vol.1, No.2, 1996, 7-10.

Penzias, A., 1991. ICIS Lecture, New York, 1991.

Pirila, P., 1994. Emission oriented production planning in the Finnish pulp and paper industry, Joint National Meeting TIMS/ORSA, April 24-27, Boston, Mass.

Porter, M.E. & V.E. Millar, 1985/1991. How information gives you competitive advantage. Harvard Business Review, July/August 1985, 49-160.

ReVelle, C., J. Cohon & D. Shobrys, 1991. Simultaneous siting and routing in the disposal of hazardous wastes. Transportation Science, 25/2, 138-145.

Saaty, T.L., 1980. The Analytic Hierarchy Process, Planning, Priority Setting, Resource Allocation, McGraw-Hill, New York.

Scott Morton, M.S., 1991. 'The corporation of the 1990's. Information technology and Organizational Transformation, Oxford University Press, New York.

SETAC, 1993. Guidelines for Life-Cycle Assessment: a code for practice. Edition 1, Workshop at Sesimbra, Portugal, March 31 - April 3.

Strassmann, P.A., 1991. The business value of information technology. Strassmann Inc., New Canaan (Conn).

Thierry, M.C., M. Salomon , J. van Nunen & L.N. Van Wassenhove, 1995. Strategic production and operations management issues in product recovery management. California Management Review, 37/2, 114-135.

7 Quality Assurance Systems

J.P. Hoogland, A. Jellema and W.M.F. Jongen

7.1 Introduction

Throughout the world, food manufacturing, distribution and retailing is becoming a highly complex business. Raw materials are obtained from sources worldwide, an ever-increasing number of processing technologies is utilised, and a vast array of products is available to the consumer. Such complexity necessitates the development of comprehensive control procedures to ensure the production of safe and high quality food. In addition, consumer expectations are changing, with a desire for convenience, 'less-processed' and fresher foods with more natural characteristics (see Chapter 2). Against this background the total food chain has to ensure that the highest standards of quality and safety are maintained. At all stages of the food chain, from acquisition of raw materials through manufacture, distribution and sale, whether it be through retail or catering outlets, consideration must be given to quality issues associated with specific products, processes and methods of handling. There are a number of reasons why, especially in the agri-food business, implementation of quality assurance systems is an issue of the greatest importance.

- Agricultural products are often perishable and subject to rapid decay due to physiological processes and microbiological contamination.
- Most agricultural products are harvested seasonally.
- Products are often heterogeneous with respect to desired quality parameters such as content of important components (e.g. sugars), size and colour. This kind of variation is dependent on cultivar differences and seasonal variables which cannot be controlled.
- Primary production of agricultural products is performed by a large number of farms operating on a small scale.

This chapter sets out to describe the currently available systems, how they can be used as tools for quality assurance management and outlines a framework for their interaction and use. Irrespective of size and complexity all food businesses must have an appropriate food quality assurance programme (see Chapter 8). Whilst at present quality assurance programmes focus primarily on food safety issues (e.g. Hazard Analysis Critical Control Points, HACCP), the general principles are equally applicable to the management of product quality in a wider sense.

7.1.1 Food safety issues

Despite the progress in medicine, food science and the technology of food production, illness caused by foodborne pathogens continues to present a major problem in terms of both health and economic significance. In 1990, an average of 120 cases of foodborne illness per 100,000 population were reported from 11 European countries, and estimates based on a more recent study indicate that in some European countries there are at least 30,000 cases of acute gastro-enteritis per 100,000 population (Notermans and Van der Giessen, 1993).

It is clear that only a small proportion of cases of foodborne illness are brought to the attention of food inspection, control and health agencies.

In addition we have seen the emergence of bacterial pathogens in recent years which may cause serious illness in susceptible individuals e.g. *Listeria monocytogenes* and verotoxigenic *Escherichia coli* such as 0157:H7. Estimates have been made of the economic consequences of foodborne illness, where costs are incurred by individuals who become ill, their employers, families, health care agencies and the food company or business involved. For example, in England and Wales in 1991, some 23,000 cases of salmonellosis were estimated to have resulted in overall costs of £40 - 50 million (Sockett, 1991).

7.1.2 Changes in food production systems

Significant changes are taking place in animal husbandry, large scale food production and distribution methods. The increased use of a range of raw materials and products originating from a wider range of countries has increased the potential for a geographical spread of diseases associated with particular contaminants. Many new processing techniques have been introduced which alone or in combination with each other, offer distinct product quality advantages, e.g. milder thermal processing, microwave, heating, ohmic heating and high-pressure processing techniques. All present new food safety challenges which must be fully evaluated.

7.1.3 Changes in consumer requirements

There is increasing demand for convenience foods, requiring minimal handling or preparation in user-friendly packaging. In addition, consumers are seeking foods which are more 'fresh' and with enhanced natural flavours which inevitably challenge the industry to use less harsh processing and production regimes.

Whilst there is little evidence that such trends have led to increased foodborne illness, it must be appreciated that these foods will require greater care in their production, distribution, storage and preparation prior to final consumption.

7.1.4 Socio-economic changes

There is a significant worldwide trend towards increased consumption of food outside the home. A major increase in the frequency of international travel for business and vacation purposes also means that more people are in touch with new types of products.

Population changes are taking place. The young and the aged are groups at risk with regard to foodborne illness and in a number of countries the population is ageing, resulting in a stronger focus on health-related aspects.

7.2 Quality assurance strategy

7.2.1 Introduction

Quality assurance is of paramount importance to all companies and organisations involved in the production, sale and handling of food. Modern trading conditions and legislation require food businesses to demonstrate their commitment to food quality and establish an appropriate product quality programme. Such a programme should take into account the role of the business in the food chain, i.e. whether they are primary producers, manufacturers, retailers or caterers. A product quality programme contains four primary elements:
1. it meets the expectations of the consumer
2. it fits within the strategy of the company
3. it ensures that a company is clearly committed to the quality of its products
4. it aims for the highest quality level achievable.

Such programme should highlight where improvements are necessary and can usefully be applied to both organisational and technological issues. All company employees, from senior management to food handlers, should be aware of the significance a quality assurance programme. The programme should identify the key tools and their application to all stages of production, distribution and sale. An outline for such a programme is described below and illustrated in Figure 7.1.

Figure 7.1
Development of
Quality Assurance
System

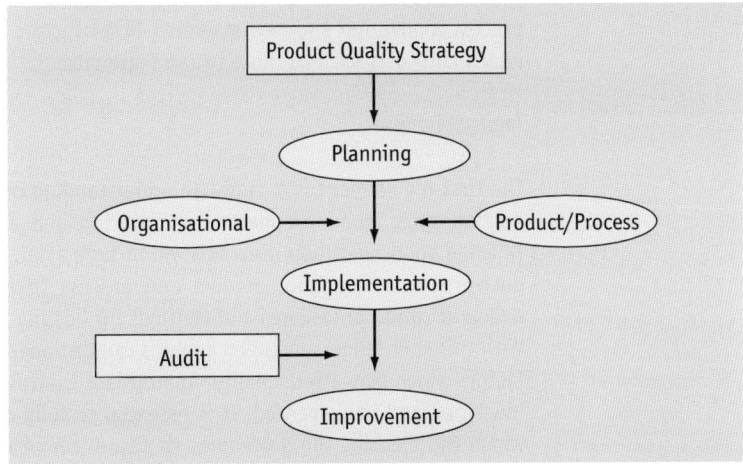

7.2.2 Development of a Quality Assurance Programme

Product Quality Strategy

Senior management in a company has ultimate responsibility for ensuring that the highest standards of food production and handling are achieved with respect to product quality. Total commitment to this aim is crucial for the successful implementation of such a programme.

The senior management should ensure a logical and structured approach to both organisational and product or process related activities.

A policy statement by senior management should outline the general approach to ensure production and handling of food products with the desired quality. The company should make sure that the food policy concerning product quality:

- is appropriate to the nature and activity of the business
- provides a commitment to continuous improvement
- complies with legislation
- is fully communicated, understood and supported by all employees

Planning

Organisational planning should include the preparation of a detailed quality assurance programme. This should clearly define aims, assignment of responsibility, resources, requirements and lines of communication to gain full commitment from all personnel to the quality assurance programme. This process, through assessment and auditing, should seek continuous improvement.

Product and process planning should result in the definition of clear and unambiguous requirements, for example with respect to food safety. All such requirements should be based on a full consideration of constraints, opportunities and other relevant factors. Constraints may include regulatory and commercial requirements. Opportunities may include product development, process innovation and new markets. Other factors may include economic issues and costs such as those of raw materials.

Implementation

The first requirement is a thorough understanding of all stages of the production cycle from raw material production and acquisition through to finished goods and their use. This will include a detailed knowledge of product-process interaction, product and process specifications, monitoring and verification procedures and methods for dealing with non-compliance. With this knowledge, a detailed analysis can be undertaken to identify those factors which may affect quality. Appropriate control measures can then be identified and implemented. It is essential to fully document this analysis which will describe the procedures to ensure compliance with quality assurance requirements and the operational criteria necessary for product and process control. A number of specific tools have been developed to carry out this analysis, some of which have already been widely used in the food industry e.g. HACCP.

Audit (Assessment of performance)

Senior management should ensure that there is a process of regular assessment of performance of the food safety programme. This can be done internally or externally and will include audit of individual stages and identification of any weaknesses. In this way an assessment can be made of whether the quality assurance requirements are being met and whether the programme is truly effective.

Improvement

The analysis and assessment process is likely to identify issues for adjustment, modification and improvement. These should be undertaken and appropriate follow-up carried out. This is an on-going review process designed to ensure compliance with changing regulations and further enhance the assurance of food safety.

7.3 Tools for quality assurance

The practical success of any quality assurance programme will depend on the proper use of appropriate methods and tools. These will include Good Hygienic Practice (GHP), Good Manufacturing Practice (GMP) and HACCP specifically targeted to food safety (Institute of Food Science and Technology of the U.K., 1986 and 1993). Other tools of more general application are quality assurance methods and systems such as the ISO 9000 series of standards and the Total Quality Management (TQM) approach.

7.3.1 Good Manufacturing Practice (GMP) and Good Hygienic Practice (GHP)

GMP covers the fundamental principles, procedures and means needed to design a suitable environment for the production of food of acceptable quality. GHP describes the basic hygienic measures which establishments should meet and which form the prerequisites to other approaches, in particular, HACCP. GMP/GHP requirements have been developed by governments, the Codex Alimentarius Committee on Food Hygiene (FAO/WHO, 1995), and by the food industry, often in collaboration with other groups and food inspection and control authorities. Development of GMP codes is taking place in various areas of industrial production. These codes establish quality assurance procedures which can be implemented in a specific field of production, both at company and sector level (horizontal integration, as shown in Figure 7.2). For several types of production, specific codes have been developed at the international level. Veterinarians have their code of Good Veterinarian Practice (GVP) and bakeries, greengrocers and farmers have also developed a number of internationally accepted codes. Sometimes the abbreviation GXP is used for this type of code.

General GHP requirements usually cover the following:
- the hygienic design and construction of food manufacturing premises
- the hygienic design, construction and proper use of machinery
- cleaning and disinfection procedures (including pest control)
- general hygienic and safety practices in food processing including:
  - the microbial quality of raw foods
  - the hygienic operation of each process step
  - the hygiene of personnel and their training in food hygiene and safety

Good Manufacturing Practice codes and the hygienic requirements they contain are the relevant boundary conditions for the hygienic manufacture of foods. They should always be applied and documented.

Figure 7.2
GXP codes: A: code for Good Agricultural Practice (GAP), applicable to all producers of carrots; B: conserved carrot production chain (vertical integration); C: fresh carrot production chain (vertical integration); D: code for Good Hygienic Practice (GHP), applicable to all greengrocers but not for the production of conserved (e.g. deep frozen or canned) carrots

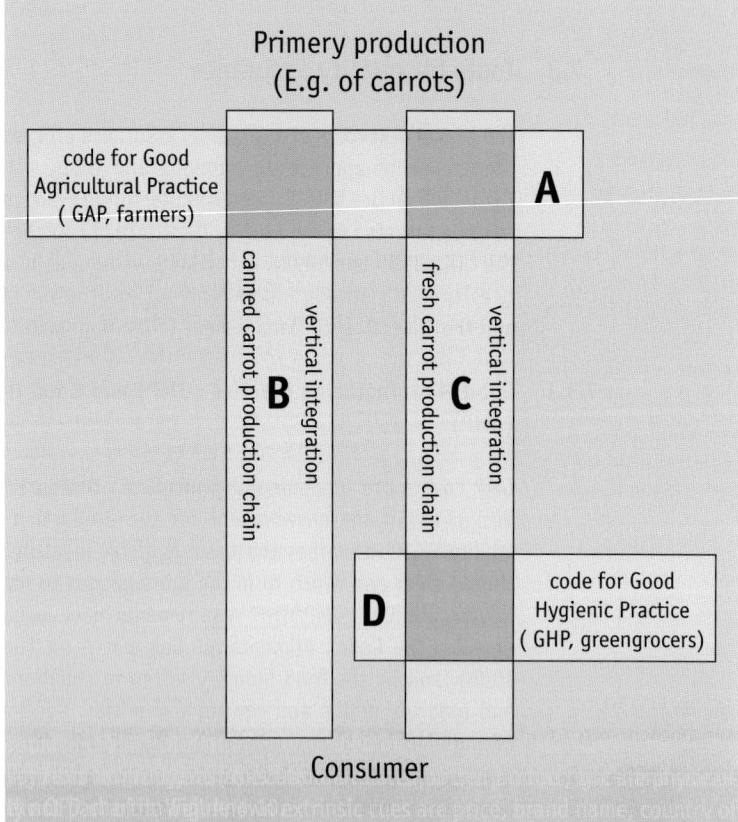

Until recently GXP codes have been implemented on a national basis for a specific branch of industry. Although implementation is most often voluntary, companies which have not adopted the code - or an equivalent quality system - may have problems staying in business, especially when vertical integration of food production chains occurs. Various quality programmes and production codes for the production of meat, milk and eggs in the Netherlands stipulate that compound animal feeds must be supplied by feed manufacturers which work according to the Dutch code for Good Manufacturing Practice. At present virtually all feed producers in the Netherlands comply with this code: they have either adopted the code or have gone out of business.

General codes have been developed by international bodies, for instance by the International Dairy Federation (International Dairy Federation, 1980) and Codex Alimentarius (Codex Alimentarius, 1985). These codes may serve as a starting point for the development of GXP codes for a specific purpose. It must be stressed that, in general, adjustments must be made with respect to specific branches of production, or to cover situations which are specific to a certain country. The same is true for companies adopting a GXP code: in most cases some fine tuning with respect to specific conditions within the company will be necessary. Care must be taken to avoid unnecessary procedures: some codes have been nicknamed 'codes for Getting More Paperwork'! GXP codes must be lightweight systems, applicable especially in small companies which either do not require a full-sized quality system, or which are not able to develop and maintain such a system.

7.3.2   The HACCP system

The development of the system which is now known as 'HACCP' (Hazard Analysis Critical Control Point) can be traced back to at least 1972. In that year cooperation between the International Commission on Microbiological Specifications for Foods (ICMSF) and the World Health Organization (WHO) was established. In 1988 the results of this cooperation were laid down in a book (Thatcher et al., 1988). Since then, the system and its application has also been described in documents of Codex Alimentarius (Codex Alimentarius, n.d., 1995a and 1995b). The European Union adopted the HACCP approach in Directive 93/43, which means that HACCP is now a part of national legislation in all member states of the European Union (Anon, 1993).

HACCP is a food safety management system which is based on systematic identification and assessment of hazards and risks associated with the production of food (Dillon and Griffith, 1996). Although originally developed to control microbiological hazards, the approach can also be used to identify and assess hazards of chemical and or physical nature. Examples of chemical hazards are residues of pesticides in plant raw materials and the presence of aflatoxins in peanuts. Aflatoxins are highly toxic mycotoxins, produced by *Aspergillus flavus*. The substance occurs naturally in crops grown in hot and humid conditions. Examples of physical hazards are small stones which may be present in dried currants, or bones in fish fillets.

When all hazards are known, Critical Control Points (CCPs) can be identified: points or steps in the production process at which control can be applied and a food safety hazard can be prevented, eliminated or reduced to an accepta- ble level. Following the identification of critical control points, preventive measures (or control measures) must be put into practice. Critical control points which have been identified must be monitored: checking that the pro- cessing or handling procedures at a CCP are under control. Corrective action must be taken when monitored values are above established critical limits. As with other quality systems, verification on a regular basis is required. A sche- me showing the principles of HACCP and a decision tree which can be used to identify CCPs, as developed by Codex Alimentarius, is shown in Figure 7.3.

Much experience with the development and implementation of HACCP systems has now been accumulated. It appears, however, that there are still some major problems associated with implementation, especially in small

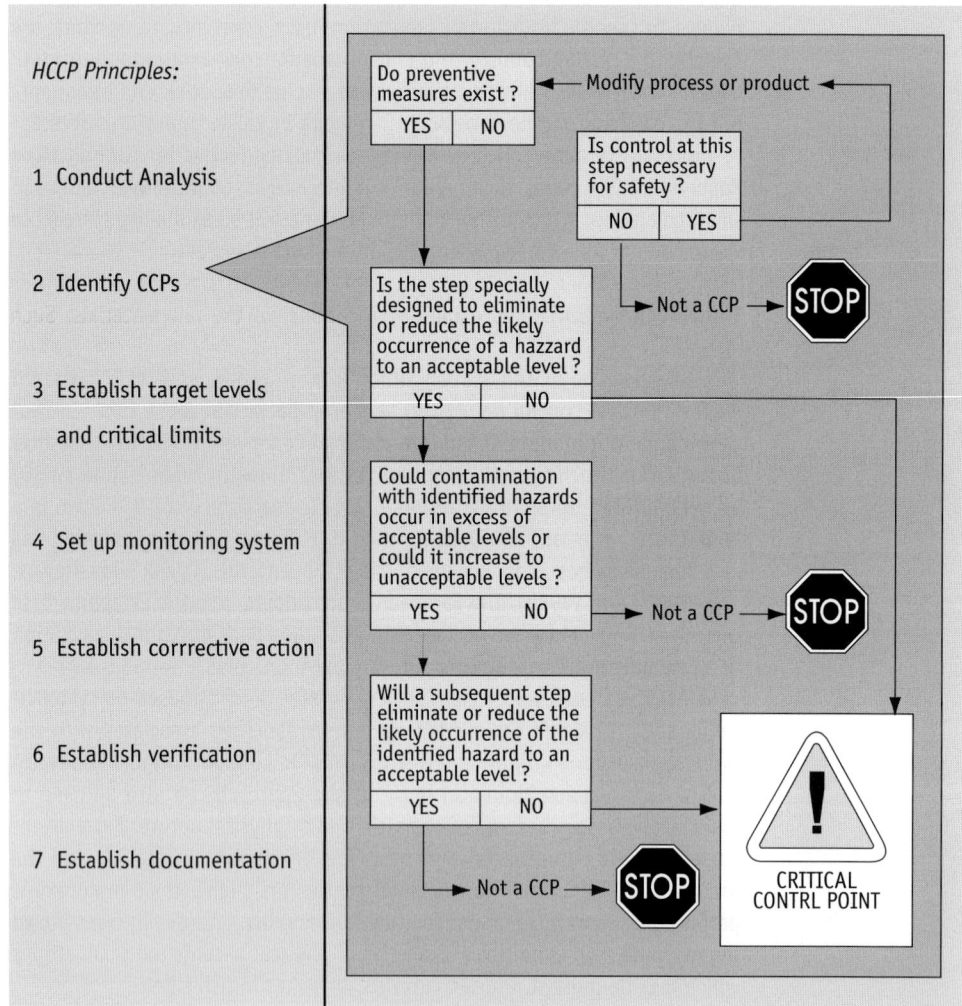

companies, where there is often not enough scientific knowledge available. There is also still debate in scientific circles concerning the extent to which the severity of risks must be estimated: most often it is a matter of setting priorities, since not all identified hazards can be eliminated in one operation. Priorities are often set on the basis of budgetary consideration rather than scientific knowledge about hazards.

Hygiene codes, when based on HACCP principles, can play an important role in the implementation of HACCP systems, especially for small businesses.

As with the implementation of GXP codes, in most cases some fine tuning with respect to specific conditions within the company will be necessary. It is appropriate to highlight the chemical hazards: in contrast to physical or microbiological hazards, a chemical hazard does not often lead to customer complaints. The risks associated with chemical hazards are often not of an acute toxicological nature but have to do with long-term exposure of consumers to low levels of unwanted substances. If a company is recording complaints, these records can often be used to estimate the occurrence of physical or microbiological hazards, but mostly there are insufficient data on chemical hazards.

Chemical hazards are often associated with raw materials, for instance in the case of the presence of contaminants in such commodities. Numerous countries have now introduced legislation setting maximum levels for a great number of contaminants. Contaminant levels often cannot be influenced during the production of food and not much knowledge on the fate of contaminants during processing is available. This means that these hazards often must be controlled using specifications for the raw materials. Such specifications must be realistic: there is no point in specifying zero tolerance (i.e. demand the complete absence of a contaminant) when it is clear that such a demand cannot be fulfilled by the supplier. It is expected that the development of production chain based HACCP systems will be an important topic in the near future (Whiting, 1995).

7.3.3 ISO-9000

The ISO 9000 family of standards and guidelines

In 1987, ISO (International Organization for Standardization) issued a series of standards, now known as the ISO-9000 family. In these standards, models for quality assurance and guidelines for selection and use of quality assurance standards are given. All ISO-standards are subject to periodical review and new standards may also be issued. Information with respect to available standards can be found in Table 7.1.

The essence of any ISO-based quality system can be summarized in a single sentence: **'Tell what you're doing, then do what you're telling and finally prove that you've done what you told'.** 'Tell what you're doing' means that procedures describing how work must be done are written down. During this

Number	Year of Publication	Title
		Table 7.1 The ISO-9000 family of standards and guidelines
8402	1994	Quality management and quality assurance - Vocabulary
9000-1	1994	Quality management and quality assurance standards - Part 1: Guidelines for selection and use
9000-2	1994	Quality management and quality assurance standards - Part 2: Generic guidelines for the application of ISO 9001, ISO 9002 and ISO 9003
9000-3	1994	Quality management and quality assurance standards - Part 3: Guidelines for the application of ISO 9001 to the development, supply and maintenance of software
9000-4	1994	Quality management and quality assurance standards - Part 4: guide to dependability programme management
9001	1994	Quality systems - Model for quality assurance in design/development, production, installation and servicing
9002	1994	Quality systems - Model for quality assurance in production, installation and servicing
9003	1994	Quality systems - Model for quality assurance in final inspection and test
9004-1	1994	Quality management and quality system elements - Part 1: Guidelines
9004-2	1992	Quality management and quality system elements - Part 2: Guidelines for services
9004-3	1994	Quality management and quality system elements - Part 3: Guidelines for processed materials
9004-4	1994	Quality management and quality system elements - Part 4: Guidelines for quality improvement
9004-8[1]	–	Quality management principles and guidelines for their application
10005	1995	Quality management: Guidelines for quality plans
10006[2]	–	Quality management: Guidelines to quality in project management
10007	1995	Quality management: Guidelines for configuration management
10011-1	1990	Guidelines for auditing quality systems - Part 1: Auditing
10011-2	1991	Guidelines for auditing quality systems - Part 2: Qualification criteria for quality systems auditors
10011-3	1991	Guidelines for auditing quality systems - Part 3: Management of audit programmes
10012-1	1992	Quality assurance requirements for measuring equipment - Part 1: Metrological confirmation system for measuring equipment
10012-2[2]	–	Quality assurance requirements for measuring equipment - Part 2: Guidelines for control of measurement processes
10013	1995	Guidelines for developing quality manuals
10014[2]	–	Guidelines for managing the economics of quality
10015[1]	–	Quality management and guidelines for training

[1] ISO/CD: Committee Draft: Standard is still under discussion; to be published
[2] ISO/DIS: Draft International Standard, to be published

process, it is often found that it is not clear how certain tasks should be performed; such findings can help in streamlining the production process. 'Do what you're telling' means that it is made sure that work is done according to the recorded procedures. 'Prove that you've done what you told' means keeping records, as well as performing audits. Building blocks to use in the development and implementation of a quality system are laid down in the ISO standards, summarized in Table 7.1. Which standards should be used in a specified situation depends on the nature of the company and the reasons why the company wants to obtain an ISO-certification. In ISO-9000-1 guidance is given for the use of the standards in the 9000-series. In general, two situations can be distinguished:

- Internal quality assurance: companies use ISO standards to improve efficiency, as well as the quality of products and services within the organization. The ISO 9004 standards are used as tools in Total Quality Management (TQM) systems;
- External quality assurance: customers ask for certification, some companies buy only from ISO-certified suppliers. Standards 9001, 9002 or 9003, dependent on the situation, may serve for this purpose;

Dependent on the main goal, defined by the management of the company, choices with respect to implementation of one or more of the standards can be made, as is shown in Figure 7.4. If the main goal of the company can be described as internal quality assurance, standards of the 9004-type are recommended. Guidance with respect to development and implementation of quality management is the most important topic in ISO 9004-1. Typical elements of quality systems are also described. It is important to notice that in ISO 9004-1 attention is given to economic aspects of quality assurance, for instance, making use of quality cost analysis.

If external quality assurance is the main purpose, a choice can be made between ISO 9001, 9002 or 9003. General information on the implementation of these standards can be found in ISO 9000-2. The main difference between these three standards is found in the scope: ISO 9003 gives a model for quality assurance in final inspection and test, whereas 9001 and 9002 are much broader: production, distribution/installation and servicing are also included. Moreover, in ISO 9001 design and development of products or services are also covered.

ISO 9001

The model for quality assurance, described in ISO 9001 will be discussed in more detail. The main purpose of 9001 (as well as 9002 and 9003) is external quality assurance: the supplier of products or services needs to prove to his customers that his quality assurance system is capable of giving a high degree of certainty that delivered products or services will meet the specifications. To make this possible, a number of matters must be addressed. In

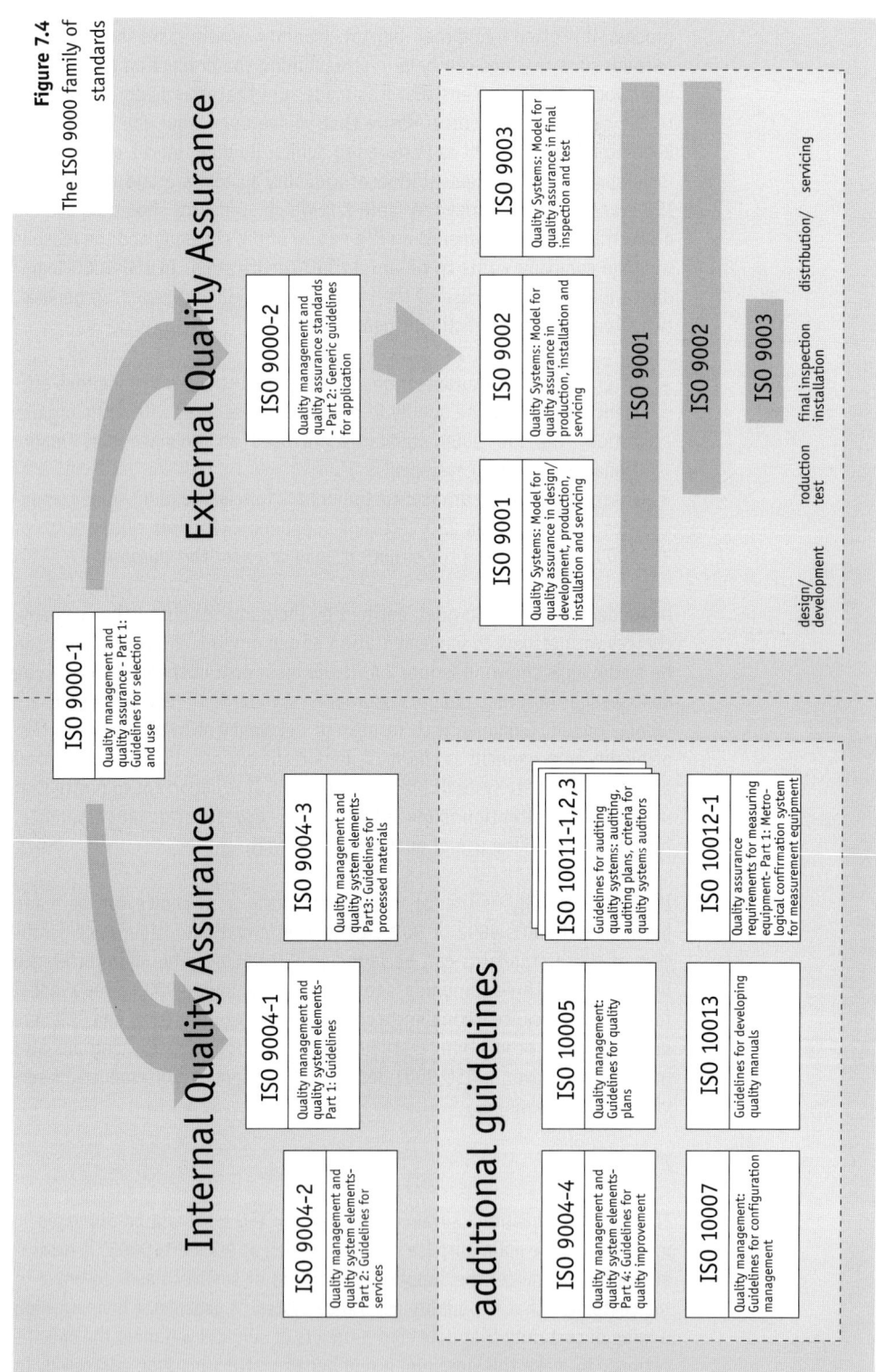

Figure 7.4
The ISO 9000 family of standards

External Quality Assurance

Internal Quality Assurance

ISO 9000-1
Quality management and quality assurance - Part 1: Guidelines for selection and use

ISO 9000-2
Quality management and quality assurance standards - Part 2: Generic guidelines for application

ISO 9001
Quality Systems: Model for quality assurance in design/development, production, installation and servicing

ISO 9002
Quality Systems: Model for quality assurance in production, installation and servicing

ISO 9003
Quality Systems: Model for quality assurance in final inspection and test

ISO 9001

ISO 9002

ISO 9003

design/
development

roduction
test

final inspection
installation

distribution/   servicing

ISO 9004-1
Quality management and quality system elements- Part 1: Guidelines

ISO 9004-3
Quality management and quality system elements- Part3: Guidelines for processed materials

ISO 9004-2
Quality management and quality system elements- Part 2: Guidelines for services

additional guidelines

ISO 9004-4
Quality management and quality system elements- Part 4: Guidelines for quality improvement

ISO 10005
Quality management: Guidelines for quality plans

ISO 10011-1, 2,3
Guidelines for auditing quality systems: auditing, auditing plans, criteria for quality systems auditors

ISO 10007
Quality management: Guidelines for configuration management

ISO 10013
Guidelines for developing quality manuals

ISO 10012-1
Quality assurance requirements for measuring equipment- Part 1: Metro- logical confirmation system for measurement equipment

Chapter 4 of ISO-9001, 20 different points which need attention are distinguished. Sadgrove (1995) showed that these points can be arranged in four fields, as is shown in Figure 7.5.

Figure 7.5
Arrangement of the clauses of Chapter 4 of ISO 9001 in four fields of attention: Work, People, System and Information (adapted from Sadgrove, 1995).

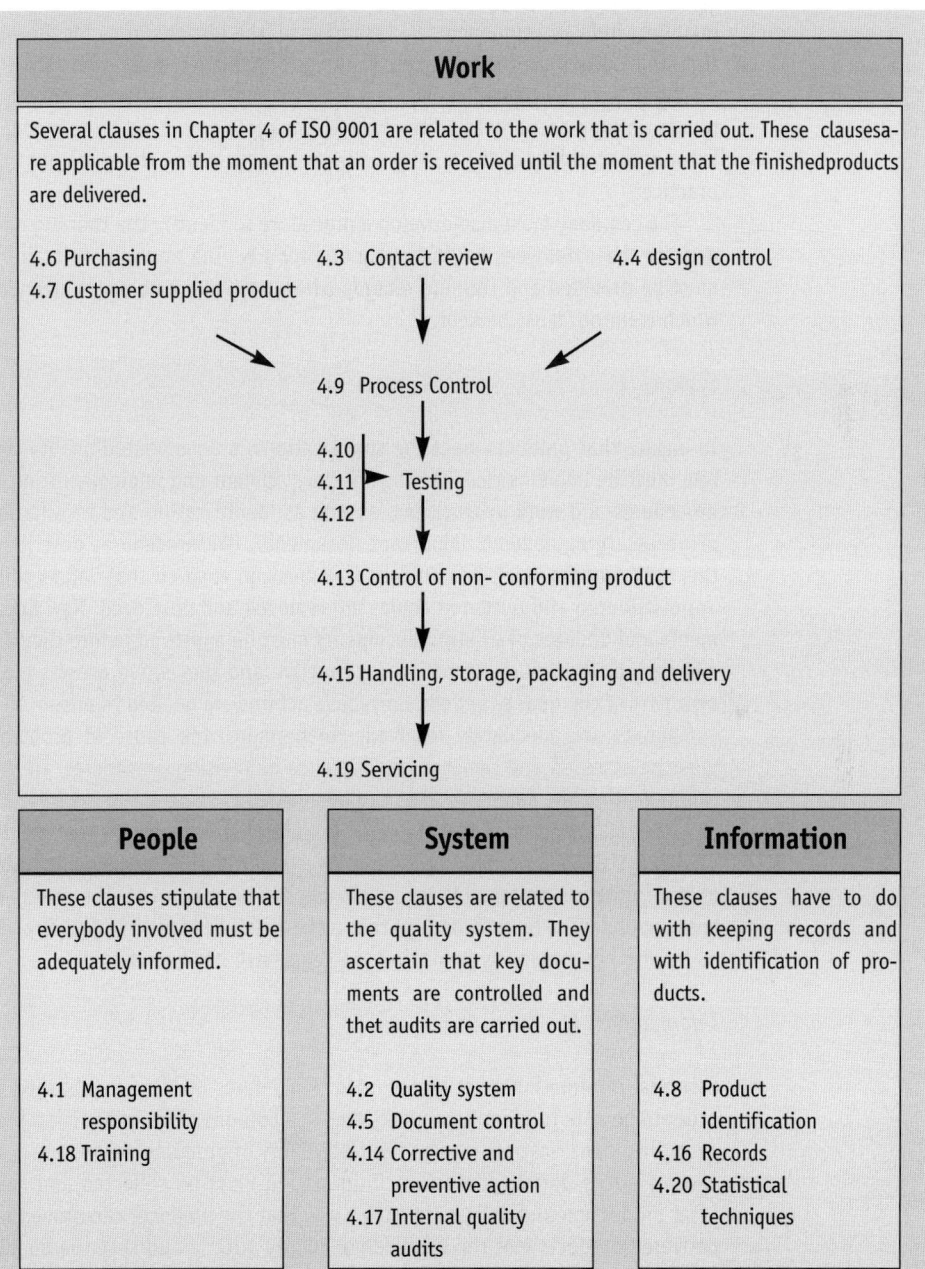

People

It is the responsibility of the management to formulate and maintain the company's quality policy. This policy must be communicated to the organization in such a way that it is understood at all levels in the organization. The employees whose work affects quality must be identified; an organization chart or job descriptions may serve this purpose. A quality manager must be appointed, responsible for development and maintenance of the quality system. This job includes, for instance, the responsibility for the writing and updating of procedures. The quality manager must report to the management. The management must check if the implemented quality system is working properly (quality review). If adjustments need to be made, it is the responsibility of the quality manager to ensure that these are put into practice.

The company must also develop a procedure to identify the training needed for the employees to do their jobs properly. The appropriate training must be provided and training records, showing which employees attended which training, must be kept.

System

To ensure that products meet the specifications, a documented quality system must be implemented. This means development and implementation of procedures and work instructions, as well as identification and installation of necessary equipment. Important documents, like procedures describing the work process, must be controlled: it must be ensured that valid copies are distributed and outdated copies are removed and destroyed. New documents and updates of existing documents must be approved before they are distributed. Procedures concerning corrective and preventive actions must be a part of the quality system. Corrective actions are needed to ensure that complaints are adequately resolved. Furthermore, the cause of problems must be assessed and removed, for instance by revising procedures. In this way repeating the same mistakes can be avoided.

Internal audits must be performed on a regular basis to ensure that the quality system is functioning properly. As a result of an internal audit, valuable information on possible improvements can be generated. The results of these audits must be recorded, so that a check can be made in a future audit as to whether previously identified problems have been corrected.

Information

Essential information must be recorded. Procedures must be established in order to be able to identify products during all stages of the production process. This identification ensures the traceability of products, for instance, in case of errors during production. Information must be collected and kept after production and delivery in such a way that the producer can prove that delivered products met the established quality criteria and that the quality system worked properly. Statistical techniques can be used to assess the quality of both products and production processes. If statistics are used, procedures must be available for the application of these techniques.

Work

Nine out of twenty clauses in Chapter 4 of ISO 9001 are related to management of the actual production process. At the beginning of the production process, the quality of purchased goods (e.g. raw materials) is of importance: this can be done by assessing the quality of suppliers. Furthermore, procedures must be developed to check that the design of the product is done in the way that was intended (this is not covered by ISO 9002). The resulting design must meet the established criteria. It is necessary to check that the designed product fulfils the customer's demands, as specified in the order.

Actual production starts with contract review: it must be ensured that supplier and customer are in agreement with respect to the content of the order and that the order actually can be fulfilled. The production process must be properly planned and carried out under controlled conditions. Controlled conditions means: suitable work environment and equipment and, if necessary, the presence of procedures describing the production process. Important aspects of the production process must be monitored and controlled. Inspection records must be kept. If a product fails inspection, procedures for preventing this product to be delivered to the customer must be present and it should be decided what must be done regarding the faulty product (re-work it to the right quality, repair it, re-grade for a different destination or destruction - after repairing or re-working a product it should be re-inspected). Procedures for putting right and preventing faults must be in place. These procedures include, for instance, how to deal with customer complaints and how to handle the elimination of potential problems. If action is taken, it is necessary to check that the measures give the desired results.

Regular, internal audits on the quality system must be performed by employees who have no direct connection to the work that is examined. These audits are used to show that the quality system is effective and that the procedures are actually followed. The results of internal audits must be reported and, if necessary, it should be checked to see whether effective corrective action has been taken.

7.3.4 Total Quality Management (TQM)

Total Quality Management (TQM) is a management concept which aims at continuous quality improvement, minimization of costs and customer satisfaction (Jablonski, 1991). Sometimes TQM is advertized as the next logical step after implementation of an ISO 9000 based quality system, as is shown in Figure 7.5. ISO standards of the 9004 type can be used as tools to establish a TQM system. According to Oakland 'reputation is built on the competitive elements of quality, reliability, delivery and price, of which quality has become strategically the most important. ... If quality is meeting the customer requirements, then this has wide implications. The requirements may include availability, delivery, reliability, maintainability and cost-effectiveness, among many other features'. The definition of TQM is not clear. In the literature, there is still continuing debate regarding the scope of the concept and how TQM must be implemented. It is however possible to give an indication of some important features of TQM; there appears to be a certain amount of agreement with respect to the following:

- Most important is customer satisfaction: to stay in business it is essential that the demands of customers are fulfilled. For customers, not only the intrinsic quality of products (taste, colour, freshness, safety, etc.) is important, but also a number of other criteria (extrinsic quality: how a product is actually produced, environmental issues, child labour, availability logistics, etc.). Therefore, a very broad definition of quality is used, as can be seen in the quote above;
- The quality of a product (intrinsic and extrinsic) only can be guaranteed if quality is accepted as a fundamental value in the company's philosophy or policy. This means that the company's management must be actively involved in the quality policy, thereby creating a culture in which all employees contribute to quality improvement;
- Suppliers should be full partners with respect to the quality policy of the company. If there is a close cooperation between a company and its suppliers, this will be very fruitful for both.

7.3.5 An integrated approach

An essential foundation of any activity involved in food manufacture, handling and catering is a thorough understanding of the appropriate requirements of GHP and GMP associated with the particular product or commodity area. The adherence to these good practices are the absolute minimum in any food business.

HACCP is now widely adopted as an essential approach to the systematic identification of hazards associated with manufacture, distribution and use of food products (Mortimore and Wallace, 1994). It provides a mechanism for defining preventive measures for hazard control. Whilst GMP and GHP address the generic requirements for manufacturing safe food, the benefit of HACCP is that it addresses specific determinants unique to a particular product and process.

Most food businesses have a quality system which addresses all aspects of quality control and assurance. There are many forms of such systems, perhaps the most widely utilised is that based on the ISO 9000 series of standards. Where such a system exists, HACCP is an integral part of the overall quality system (Webb and Marsden, 1995).

Figure 7.6
illustrates the
relationships
between the
commonly used food
safety tools

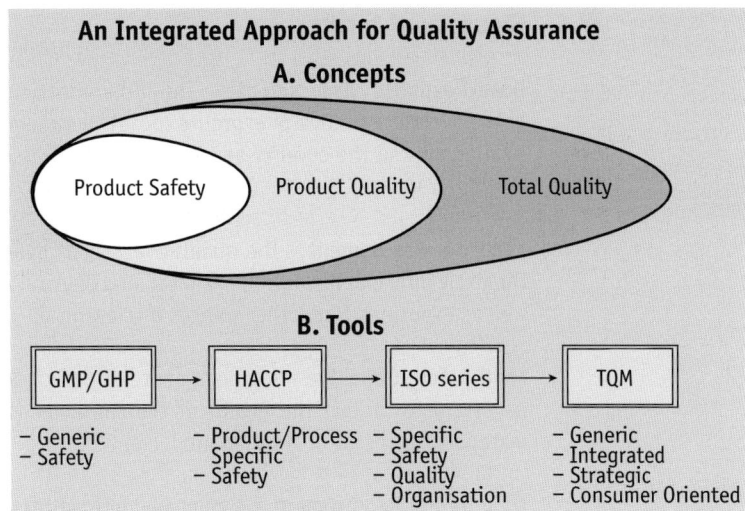

An Integrated Approach for Quality Assurance

A. Concepts

Product Safety   Product Quality   Total Quality

B. Tools

GMP/GHP → HACCP → ISO series → TQM

– Generic   – Product/Process   – Specific   – Generic
– Safety   Specific   – Safety   – Integrated
                 – Safety   – Quality   – Strategic
                                   – Organisation   – Consumer Oriented

From Figure 7.6 it can be appreciated that food safety management is an integral part of the overall quality management activity and a key component of the longer term managerial strategy to further enhance the safety and quality of products.

The tools for use in an integrated approach to the management of product quality are described. They comprise the use of those elements of Good Manufacturing Practice (GMP) that are specifically concerned with the general design and operation of hygienic premises and equipment, and the hygiene of personnel and their training; those GMP requirements associated with hygiene (often referred to as Good Hygienic Practice (GHP) requirements) form the basis for the operation of a hygienic food operation. The product quality requirements for the manufacture of a specific foodstuff, and the design and operation of the associated plant such that production of a safe food is assured, can only be established by applying HACCP; this is the second of the tools described. The importance of applying HACCP within a framework of GMP is emphasised, recognising the importance of both GMP/GHP and HACCP in assuring product safety. The third tool described is the use of a Quality Management System such as the ISO 9000 series as a means of effectively managing total product quality, recognising that the control procedures established in a HACCP plan fit well in such a management system and can be readily incorporated into it. The fourth and final tool described, Total Quality Management (TQM) embraces quality, productivity and safety at the operational and strategic level as a means for generating better commitment of all members of an organisation to achieving these aims, TQM will provide added confidence that products will conform to quality needs. It is of the greatest importance to understand that quality assurance is an indispensable part of the process of product innovation and that it helps in assuring that new products are safe and at the same time meet consumer demands.

7.4 Glossary of terms

Dose-Response Assessment - The determination of the relationship between the magnitude of exposure (dose) to a chemical, biological or physical agent and the severity and/or frequency of associated adverse health effects (response).

Exposure Assessment - The qualitative and/or quantitative evaluation of the likely intake of biological, chemical, and physical agents through food as well as exposures from other sources if relevant.

Food Safety Objective - A Government defined target which is considered necessary to protect the health of the consumer (this may apply to raw materials, a process or finished products).

Food Safety Requirement - A company defined target which is considered necessary in order to comply with a food safety objective.

Hazard - A biological, chemical or physical agent in, or condition of, food with the potential to cause an adverse health effect.

Hazard Characterisation - The qualitative and/or quantitative evaluation of the nature of the adverse health effects associated with biological, chemical and physical agents which may be present in food. For chemical agents, a dose-response assessment should be performed. For biological or physical agents, a dose-response assessment should be performed if the data are obtainable.

Hazard Identification - The identification of biological, chemical, and physical agents capable of causing adverse health effects and which may be present in a particular food or group of foods.

Quality - The totality of characteristics of an entity that bear on its ability to satisfy stated or implied needs.

Quality assurance - All the planned and systematic activities implemented within the quality system, and demonstrated as needed, to provide adequate confidence that an entity will fulfil requirements for quality.

Quality control - The operational techniques and activities that are used to fulfil requirements for quality.

Quality management - All activities of the overall management function that determine the quality policy, objectives and responsibilities and implement them by means such as quality planning, quality control, quality assurance and quality improvement within the quality system.

Total Quality Management - A management approach of an organisation, centred on quality based on the participation of all its members and aiming at long term success through customer satisfaction and benefits to the members of the organisation and to society.

References

Anon, 1993. Official Journal of the European Committees, No. L 175/1. Council Directive 93/43/EEC on the hygiene of foodstuffs.

Codex Alimentarius, 1985. Volume A: Recommended international code of practice; general principles of food hygiene. FAO/WHO, 2nd revision.

Codex Alimentarius Commission, n.d. Principles and application of the HACCP system. Alinorm 93/13.

Codex Alimentarius, 1995a. General Principles of Food Hygiene. Alinorm 97/13, Appendix II.

Codex Alimentarius, 1995b. Hazard Analysis Critical Control Point (HACCP) System and Guidelines for its Application. Alinorm 97/13, Annex to Appendix II.

Dillon, M. and C. Griffith, 1996. How to HACCP - An Illustrated Guide. 2nd ed. Grimsby: M.D. ISBN 1-900134-03-9. 120 pp.

FAO/WHO (Food and Agricultural Organisation. World Health Organisation), 1995. Application of Risk Analysis to Food Standard Issues. Report of a joint FAO/WHO expert consultation, WHO/FNU/FOS/95.3, Geneva.

International Dairy Federation, 1980. General code of hygienic practice for the dairy industry. Document 123.

Institute of Food Science and Technology of the U.K. (London), 1986. Food and Drink Manufacture - Good Manufacturing Practice: A Guide to its Responsible Management. Institute of Food Science and Technology of the UK. 58 pp.

Institute of Food Science and Technology of the U.K. (London), 1993. Listing of Codes of Practice Applicable to Foods. Institute of Food Science and Technology of the U.K. (London).

ISO (International Standardisation Organisation) (1994). *ISO 9000 Series of standards:*

ISO 9000 - Quality Management and Quality Assurance Standards - Part 1 - Guidelines for Selection and Use.

ISO 9001 - Quality Systems - Model for Quality Assurance in Design/Development, Production, Installation and Servicing.

ISO 9002 - Quality Systems - Model for Quality Assurance in Production and Installation.

ISO 9004 -1 - Quality Management and Quality System Elements - Part 1 - Guidelines.

ISO (International Standardisation Organisation), 1994. ISO 8402 Standard: Quality Management and Quality Assurance Standards - Guidelines for Selection and Use- Vocabulary.

Jablonski, J.R., 1991. TQM implementation, in Implementing Total Quality Management: an Overview. Pfeiffer and Co., San Diego, Cal.

Mortimore, S. and C. Wallace, 1994. HACCP: a practical approach. (Practical approaches to food control and food quality series No. 1), Chapman and Hall, London. 296 pp.

Notermans, S. and A. van der Giessen, 1993. Foodborne diseases in the 1980's and 1990's - The Dutch experience. Food Cont. **4:** 122 - 124.

Oakland, J.S., 1993. Total Quality Management - the route to improving performance. 2nd ed. Butterworth-Heinemann, Oxford. 463 pp.

Sadgrove, K., 1995. ISO 9000/BS5750 Made easy - A Practical Guide to Quality. Kogan Page Ltd., London, UK; ISBN 0 7494 1275 5

Sockett, P.N., 1991. Food poisoning outbreaks associated with manufactured foods in England and Wales: 1980 - 89. Communicable Diseases Report 1, Review No. 10, R 105-R 109.

Thatcher, F.S., D.S. Clark, J.H. Silliker, R.P. Elliot and A.A. Baird-Parket; International Association of Microbiological Societies (Toronto) International Commission on Microbiological Specifications for Foods (ICMSF), 1988. Micro-organisms in foods - Vol. 4: Application of the hazard analysis critical control point (HACCP) system to ensure microbiological safety and quality. ICMSF, London.

Webb, N.B. and J.L. Marsden, 1995. Relationship of the HACCP system to Total Quality Management, in: Pearson, A.M. and T.R. Dutson (Ed) - HACCP in meat, poultry and fish processing. (Advances in food research series, vol. 10), Blackie Academic and Professional, Chapman and Hall, London. 393 pp.

Whiting, R.C., 1995. Microbial Modelling in Foods. Critical Reviews in Food Science and Nutrition, **35,** (6), 467 - 494.

Further reading

Archer, D.L. and J.E. Kvenberg, 1985. Incidence and cost of foodborne diarrhoeal disease in the United States. *Journal of Food Protection* 48: 887 - 894.

Baird-Parker, A.C., 1994. Foods and microbiological risks. *Microbiology,* 140: 687 - 695.

Bryan, F.L., 1988. Risks of practice, procedures and processes that lead to outbreaks of foodborne diseases. *Journal of Food Protection.* 51: 663 - 673.

BS-EN-ISO 14001, 1996. Environmental management systems. Specification with guidance for use. BSI, Chiswick, London.

CAST (Council for Agricultural Science and Technology), 1994. Foodborne Pathogens: Risks and Consequences. Task Force Report No. 122, CAST, Ames, IA.

Davenport, T.H., 1993. Process innovation. Harvard Business School Press, Boston, Mass.

Mossel, D.A.A., 1988. Impact of foodborne pathogens on today's world and prospect for management. *Animal and Human Health. 1:* 13 - 23.

Roberts, T., H. Jensen and L. Unnevehr (Ed), 1996. Tracking Foodborne Pathogens from Farm to Table: Data Needs to Evaluate Control Options. Department of Agriculture, Economic Research Service, Food and Consumers Economic Division, Miscellaneous. Publication Number 1532, Washington D.C.

Todd, E.L.D., 1989. Preliminary estimate of cost of foodborne diseases in the United States. *Journal of Food Protection* 52: 595 - 601.

WHO (World Health Organisation) (1995). Report of WHO Consultation on Selected Emerging Foodborne Diseases, WHO/CDS/VPH95.142, Geneva

8 Regulatory aspects of food production systems

H. de Sitter

8.1 Introduction

Production and trade of food products involve a number of regulations and laws intended to protect consumer health and to prevent unfair competition. Both elements are of primary importance, and uniformity of regulations is necessary in order to promote the trade at a worldwide level. In addition, the food industry also has to deal with other regulations such as those concerning product liability, the environment, and standardization of sampling and measurement systems. Some examples concerning these regulations can be found in Middlekauf & Shubik (1989), Snijders (1987) and in the various regulations published by the European Union (EU). Generally regulation of production and trade of food product takes place at three levels.

1. The Codex Alimentarius is a complex of regulations and guidelines developed by the Food and Agricultural Organization (FAO) and the World Health Organization (WHO). These regulations and guidelines can be used by the participating countries for national regulations but there is no obligation to do so. Nevertheless the Codex has a large influence on national regulations.
2. The EU regulations and guidelines based on the Treaty of Rome have become increasingly important as they supersede national regulations. These are regulations that have direct legal power or have to be implemented into national law before a specific date. The details of EU regulations are explained in more detail below.
3. In addition there are also national regulations in the different member states of the EU.

With the constantly advancing integration of the European Union more and more matters are regulated from headquarters in Brussels. In addition to a large number of directives on aspects including food composition, labelling and food additives, the Council Directive 93/43/EEC on Food Hygiene (European Union, 1993) has led to a surge of activity in the food industry. The Food Hygiene Directive introduces the requirement of a food safety system based on the principles of Hazard Analysis Critical Control Point (HACCP, see Chapter 7). Food businesses will have to set up and implement the system. What the system should look like and how it should operate is explained in just five short sentences. Each individual food operation can give its own interpretation to these five sentences (see 8.4.1). The production of food in the Netherlands is in principle regulated in such a way that producers can produce and market whatever they like, unless it is forbidden. There is no system of prior approval, as there is for medicines for example. In the production of foodstuffs of animal origin, however, more direct control of production methods and production sites by the authroities has been common practice for many years. This control was introduced to protect the consumer, but in later years also to ensure healthy products for export as importing countries usually require certificates from veterinary officers.

Enforcement of the Council Directive 93/43/EEC will lead also to major changes in food control operations in the Netherlands. Dramatic changes during the last decade in food production, processing and distribution, as well as the rapid increase in international trade in food products, require an effective food safety control system. The HACCP principles can be a tool for effective control. Three limitations can be distinguished, however, in the traditional approach to regulation making :

- Terms in laws are frequently of a general nature, as they have to be applicable to different settings.
- These terms leave much to the discretion of inspectors, who may fail to distinguish   between important and relatively unimportant requirements. The latter is also due to the undifferentiated weighting of requirements in regulations.
- As modern technologies are introduced, they are often only partially covered by current legislation, and the official inspector may thus overlook factors which are critical to safety.
- Any official inspection is limited in time. Thus, the inspector's observations will relate only to parts of a particular process at a given point in time.

Normalization and certification are instruments that have not assumed enormous proportions in the food industry in the Netherlands. Those in favour of normalization and certification view the introduction of the concept of HACCP as a positive step. In addition to tangible standards, a system is now also required by law. The enforcement authorities will have to investigate how to make use of these instruments, bearing in mind that they will have to have an added value.

In the case of a food safety system set up by an individual food business, it will be the job of the enforcement officer to judge whether that system will indeed ensure safe food preparation. As long as the system of a food business does ensure safe food, and there are only differences of opinion on minor points, the job of the food inspector remains relatively uncomplicated. The problems start when a system is encountered, which does not convince the food inspector that food safety is ensured. The questions that then arise include what should be done with the business, what legal action should be taken against this business, and which legal clauses can be used successfully.

This chapter covers the regulatory aspects of processed foodstuffs in general and the enforcement of the regulations. Controls based on veterinary regulations, with respect to meat, fish and dairy products, fall outside the scope of this chapter.

8.2 Control of food and food production in the European Union

8.2.1 Introduction

This section gives an indication of the complexity of food control in the European Union. It is not an introduction to the different systems of food control in the EU member states. Food control is regarded as an important issue by all member countries, but each country has developed its controls as a result of its own cultural and historical background. The United Kingdom has its system of County Environmental Health Officers. They inspect and take samples in areas concerning hygiene, but these samples are then analyzed in separate official laboratories. Labelling of foodstuffs is checked by the Standards Officers. In the Netherlands all these activities are performed by one central governmental organization. In Germany the various states are responsible for food legislation and control. In most countries the Ministry of Health takes the lead, with considerable input from the Ministry of Agriculture. In France, however, the Ministry of Economic Affairs is also strongly involved in legislation and control.

Free movement of products is the main objective of harmonization. However, in recent years the protection of public health and adequate provision of information have also become very important considerations for the European Commission and the policy makers of the member states. Since the inception of the European Community in 1957 one of the main aims has been a common market for agricultural products. Meat, fish and dairy products belong to this group of products and as a result they have a longer history of harmonization. Strict regulations govern the export of these products to other member states, and these form the basis of the present harmonization.

8.2.2 Instruments used by the European Union

European Union legislation is a very complex matter, especially in terms of the various jurisidictions of the European Commission, the Council of Ministers and the European Parliament. Here we are only concerned with the instruments of legislation. It is important to note that all EU legislation still has to be incorporated to some extent by the member states into their own legislation. A time schedule is usually drawn up for this incorporation, which will depend on the complexity of the matter. Where a member state is late or does not want to implement a ruling, the Commission can start a procedure at the European Court of Justice. In such cases a Directive can also be declared binding for a member state by the Commission. This kind of action results in very complex cases coming before the European Court of Justice.

The European Union has four instruments at its disposal for drawing up European legislation:
1. *The regulation*
This is a ruling with direct legislative action. However, the penalty for breaking the regulation has to be laid down in the law of each member state.

2. The decision

These rulings also have direct legislative action, and likewise the penalty for transgressing the decision has to be laid down in the law of each member state.

The difference between regulations and decisions is that regulations are on general subjects and decisions concern specific subjects.

3. The directive

A directive indicates how national legislation has to be adapted. In rare cases (see above) the directive may have direct legislative power.

4. The communication

A communication is advice to the governments of member states.

These various rulings can be issued by the Council, the Commission, the European Parliament, or a combination of these. The rulings are developed in consultation with the European Parliament and standing committees composed of representatives from all member states. The procedure is time-consuming and Expert Committees are often consulted as well.

One example of an EU regulation concerning food production systems is the one dealing with product liability. On the basis of this guideline it has become much easier for the consumer to hold a producer responsible for damage suffered as a result of consumption of an unsafe product. The regulation is intended to protect private individuals in particular. Both producer and retailer can be held liable under this regulation.

Characteristics of the product liability regulation include:
- The regulation adds to the existing national regulations concerning product liability
- Only product damage and not transaction damage is included
- Only damage occurring during private use is included
- The description of the term 'unsafe product' is vague. The regulation is not meant to imply absolute safety but assumes 'reasonable safety'
- the producer must take all appropriate measures to limit the damage such as product recalls.
- the existing jurisprudence on product liability facilitates the transfer from the old situation to the new regulations.

Generally speaking, food producers and traders will still have to meet the standing requirements of the country in which the business is located.

8.2.3   Harmonization of the legislation

Since the first food directive on colouring matters was introduced in 1962, around 250 directives, regulations, decisions and communications have been issued concerning the harmonization of food and food control. These rulings can be divided in three areas: horizontal rulings (for all product groups), vertical rulings (for one specific product or group of products) and miscellaneous rulings (all others).

The present *horizontal rulings* cover the following groups:
- Labelling
- Pre-packaging
- Materials and articles in contact with foodstuffs
- Additives
- Processing aids
- Water for human consumption
- Pesticide residues
- Contaminants

The *vertical rulings* cover products including sugar, honey, natural mineral water, quick frozen foods, novel foods and novel food ingredients.

Miscellaneous rulings include:
- Sampling and analysis methods
- Official control of foodstuffs
- Free movement of foodstuffs
- Geographical indication and designation of origin
- Certificates of specific character
- Hygiene of foodstuffs

8.2.4 Harmonization of the control

Harmonization of the official control in the member states of the European Union is regulated by Council Directive 89/397/EEC (European Union 1989) on the official control on foodstuffs. This directive lays down how the European Union expects the observance of the rules and regulations concerning foodstuffs to be controlled. For example, the directive stipulates that the inspectors should have the authority needed to be able to perform their job. Directorate General III of the European Commission carries out checks in the member states. The directive also stipulates that member states should report on their controls to the Commission. This directive has introduced a coordinated control programme. Each year a number of topics is selected from proposals by member states for coordinated control actions in all member states.

The Commission has also started the Rapid Exchange of Information System for Foodstuffs. If a problem concerning foodstuffs arises, the other member states and the Commission must be informed about it through a list of contact points. In December 1996 it was decided that all control of foodstuffs (general and animal) would be moved from DG III and DG VI, and would fall under the auspices of Directorate General XXIV (Consumer Policy and Health Protection). A special inspection body is being created, based in Ireland. New standing committees will be formed to advise DG XXIV. A total of 260 EU inspectors will be appointed to work from Dublin.

8.3   Legislation and control in the Netherlands

8.3.1   Some history

The first official rules concerning food safety were introduced in medieval times, and were the initiative of municipal agencies. It was only in the second half of the 19th century that the municipalities of some large cities initiated supervision of foodstuffs by establishing special inspection services. The background to the formation of these services was the development of the sciences of chemistry and physics. The first official laboratory of this kind was established in 1893 by the Municipal Council of Rotterdam. The spectacular results of its activities stimulated other cities to take similar initiatives. Since then inspection, sample-taking and laboratory analysis have been subsumed within one organization.

In 1919 the first Food and Commodity Act and Meat Inspection Act were promulgated. The scope of the Food and Commodity Act was even broadened to include commodities other than food, in order to ensure fair trade practices for these other commodities as well.

The further history of food inspection systems in the Netherlands is to a large extent determined by the development of a number of disciplines including pharmacy, food chemistry, veterinary medicine, biology and law.

8.3.2   Legislation

The Netherlands has a number of laws intended to protect the health and safety of individuals in relation to foodstuffs. The most important of these is the Food and Commodity Act. This act dates from 1919, was modified in 1935 and completely restructured in 1988. The Food and Commodity Act supplies the authorities with a sound instrument to deal with all matters concerning people's health and safety, and it applies to all foodstuffs. Section 1 provides a definition of merchandise as meant in this act. Merchandise comprises foodstuffs, but also all other personal property intended for household purposes.

The Food and Commodity Act provides a framework, on the strength of which detailed executive regulations can be effected relatively quickly. In addition to the general and detailed regulations in the field of foodstuffs, a large number of regulations in the field of 'product safety' of non-food commodities have been introduced. Thus, commodities as diverse as packaging and utility goods, children's toys, children's beds and playpens, and also ladders have been legally regulated regarding the safety aspects of their design and construction. It is also possible to take action under the Food and Commodity Act itself, if upon inquiry, a product is found to be hazardous when used by people.

In addition to the Food Act, there are a number of other acts in the Netherlands which include requirements relating to people's health and safety. The Inspectorate for Health Protection, the Food and Commodity

Inspection Service (FCIS) has also been charged with the supervision of the observance of these acts. Generally speaking, legislation is aimed at protecting people's health and safety, making sure that the consumer is informed correctly, and stimulating manufacturers to act fairly with respect to each other and to the consumer.

A trend towards deregulation is noticeable. All existing rules and regulations concerning products will be reviewed. Two categories of rules and regulations will survive this operation:
- Those necessary for the protection of the health of consumer
- Those related to strong consumer expectations concerning the composition of a foodstuff

An increasing number of acts are being revoked, which in principle is a trend in the right direction. However, it is possible that deregulation will not succeed. Market forces play an important role in the process of deregulation. At present the consumer is the weak player in the field of consumer goods such as foodstuffs. Previously the Government has taken care of consumers, on the assumption that they cannot do this themselves. It is not clear, however, to what extent the Government can withdraw from this balance of power and still maintain public health at an acceptable level. Responsibility will devolve onto the shoulders of industry and trade, but the question remains as to whether they will accept this responsibility.

8.3.3 Supervision of the observance of statutory regulations

Supervision of the observance of statutory regulations in the Netherlands is carried out by the Inspectorate for Health Protection. This is a government agency of the Ministry of Public Health, Welfare and Sports and also part of the State Supervisory Agency for Public Health. For supervisory purposes the Netherlands is divided into thirteen areas, each with a regional inspectorate for health protection. Each regional inspectorate is charged with the inspection of production, distribution and sale of all food and commodity items in its district (1.0 to 1.2 million inhabitants).

At the beginning of 1998 it was decided to combine the Inspectorate for Health Protection with the Veterinary Inspectorate, also part of the State Supervisory Agency for Public Health, into one Inspectorate for Health Protection, Food and Commodities and Veterinary Affairs. A new regional structure will be introduced, with a limited number of regional offices. The opportunity will also be used to change the organization of field inspections in line with the changes in responsibilities and duties, and to strengthen the laboratories and development units of the present regional offices.

8.4   Food safety systems (HACCP)

8.4.1   The new requirements of the Hygiene Directive

Introduction
In recent years there have been two parallel discussions going on at international level with respect to food safety systems.
- the Codex Alimentarius Commission (referred to as Codex) as part of the General Principles for Food Hygiene
- the Hygiene Directive in the European Union (EU) to harmonize the hygiene requirements in the EU.

The results of the two discussions differ in some aspects. For the enforcement of the rules set by the EU, it does not matter if there is a divergence between the text of the EU and the Codex (Codex Alimentarius Commission, 1993). The enforcing authority will only refer to the rules laid down in the EU text. However, this situation is of course likely to create confusion, which makes the work of the inspector more complicated. For instance, people refer now to the 'HACCP rules', whereas what they actually mean is the EU directive. The main difference between the HACCP principles (see Figure 7.3) and the text of the EU directive (see below) is that the steps on verification and documentation are not included in the EU text. Some countries, including the Netherlands, require that documentation does take place when the EU directive is implemented. Mandatory documentation will remain a subject for discussion in the coming years for other countries as well as for the European Commission (FLEP 1996).

To complicate the situation further there are some limitations to the EU directive on Food Hygiene. It covers all stages after primary production. Harvesting, slaughter, milking and other primary stages are excluded. Furthermore, a number of vertical directives are in force in some animal product sectors including meat, fish, dairy, eggs and game. Although the legislators of these vertical directives form part of the same Directorate General in Brussels (DG VI), the level of HACCP differs considerably between the directives concerned. The Molitor report to the European Commission (European Commission 1995) describes this undesirable situation and makes a number of good proposals for improvements. The implementation of these propositions will take some time, however.

Commission Green Paper
The European Commission (referred to as the Commission) published 'The General Principles of Food Law in the European Union' (1997), better known as a Commission Green Paper. The aims of the Green Paper are :
- to examine the extent to which the legislation is meeting the need and expectations of   consumers, producers, manufacturers and traders.
- to asess measures for reinforcing the independence, objectivity, equivalence and effectiveness of the official control and inspection systems, and whether these meet their basic objectives of ensuring a safe and wholesome food supply and the protection of other consumer interests.

- to launch a public debate on food legislation, and thereby,
- to enable the Commission to propose appropriate measures for the future development of Community food law, where necessary.

Some consider this Green Paper the Commission's response to the Molitor report. The comprehensive document covers all matters concerning Food Law in the European Union. The six basic goals for the Community food law are:
- to ensure a high level of protection of public health, safety and the consumer;
- to ensure the free movement of goods within the internal market;
- to ensure that legislation is primarily based on scientific evidence and risk assessment;
- to ensure the competitiveness of European industry and enhance its export prospects;
- to place the primary responsibility for safe food on industry, producers and suppliers, using hazard analysis and critical control points (HACCP) type systems, which must be backed up by effective official control and enforcement
- to ensure the legislation is coherent, rational and user friendly.

In terms of the application of HACCP the following three points, currently under discussion within the European Union, are referred to:
- The relationship between the 11 vertical hygiene directives and the general directive on the hygiene of foodstuffs is mentioned. Work on simplification of the vertical directives has started. A large-scale consultation exercise on the interrelation between vertical hygiene rules applying to foodstuffs of animal origin has also started. A guide has been prepared by the services of the Commission, with the aim of drawing up a text based on certain common principles, such as HACCP, to be extended to cover all directives. The aim is also to eliminate unnecessarily detailed provisions and contradictions in the text. Priority should be given to ensuring that there is a coherent and consistent body of legislation relating to food hygiene. It is reiterated that this can be achieved best by applying HACCP principles and limiting detailed prescriptive provisions to cases where they are considered essential.

- In the hygiene directive the HACCP principles on verification and documentation are not deemed necessary. The conclusion of the Commission on this subject: 'Each food business is left with the flexibility to decide what requirements are necessary, subject to the supervision of the competence authority.' This leaves room for a variety of interpretations.

- A third issue is the exclusion of primary production in the general directive on the hygiene of foodstuffs. There is no general EU legislation covering the hygiene of products of non-animal origin at the primary agricultural production stage. For foodstuffs of animal origin the primary production stage is covered by the veterinary hygiene rules. It is not clear whether the existing rules to ensure the safety and hygiene of primary products of non-animal origin, such as those concerning pesticides and contaminants, are sufficient. This is a matter to be discussed further.

The Commission Green Paper presents the following, very broad definition for consideration: 'Foodstuff means any substance or product, whether processed, partially processed or unprocessed, intended to be ingested by humans, with the exception of tobacco as defined by Directive 89/662/EEC, medical products as defined by Directive 65/65/EEC, and narcotic or psychotropic substances controlled by Member States pursuant the relevant international conventions.'

As an analysis of the present situation and an outline for the future this Commission Green Paper can be regarded as a valuable contribution to the discussion. Proposals for solutions to the many problems are, however, thin on the ground.

The requirements for a food safety system
The requirements, according the EU Directive 93/43/EEC, (article 3, point 2) are:
'Food business operators shall identify any step in their activities which is critical to ensuring food safety and ensure that adequate safety procedures are identified, implemented, maintained and reviewed on the basis of the following principles, used to develop the system of HACCP (Hazard Analysis and Critical control Points):
- analyzing the potential food hazards in a food business operation,
- identifying the points in those operations where food hazards may occur,
- deciding which of the points identified are critical to food safety - the 'critical points',
- identifying and implementing effective control and monitoring procedures at those critical points; and
- reviewing the analysis of food hazards, the critical control points and the control and monitoring procedures periodically and whenever the food business operations change.'

The Commission realised that small and medium-sized businesses would find it difficult or impossible to comply with the above-mentioned requirements. As a result the 'Guides for good hygiene practices' were included in Article 5 of the directive. These guides can be developed by food business sectors and representatives of other interested parties (e.g. appropriate authorities or consumer groups), and assessed by the member states to determine the extent to which they may be presumed to comply with Article 3 of the directive. The Guides, which need official approval, will become the handbook for food safety for the appropriate sector and replace the individual food safety plan of a business. These Guides should not be confused with GMP (Good manufacturing Practice) or GHP (Good Hygiene Practice). These latter are non-official documents which can be used voluntarily.

8.4.2   Implementation of the new requirements

The different countries in the European Union will find their own solutions to the problems of this new legislation. In the United Kingdom industry has been familiar with food safety systems such as HACCP since the introduction of with the Food Safety Act in 1990. This act introduced the 'Due Diligence Defence'. This defence is designed to balance proper protection of the consumer against defective food and the right of traders not to be convicted of an offence they have taken all reasonable care to avoid committing. The result should be to encourage all concerned to take proper responsibility for their products. This defence enables someone to be acquitted of an offence if they can prove that they took all reasonable precaution and exercised all due diligence to avoid committing that offence. Although the burden of proof lies with the defendant, the case does not need to be established beyond reasonable doubt. The court only needs to be persuaded that the case is made out on the balance of probabilities. In the United Kingdom the application of the HACCP system, as developed by Codex, quickly became accepted as the major form of proof of 'due diligence'. The food ndustry in particular was therefore quick to adopt HACCP for this reason.

Sweden also made the setting up of an in-house food control programme mandatory in 1990. In other European countries, however, control of food safety systems by the authorities will be introduced with the implementation of the Hygiene Directive. All countries have their own problems with the implementation. In France, for instance, the Directive is implemented through two interministerial orders: the first deals with the distribution of foodstuffs; the second is directed at businesses that process and package foodstuffs other than meat. The order regarding distribution applies in particular to small business operations such as butcher shops, bakers and confectioner shops, as well as non-sedentary vendors at open-air markets. In Germany, a federal state, food legislation is the responsibility of the various states. The Hygiene Directive has been implemented however by the national government through the 'Verordnung über Lebensmittelhygiene' (LMHV). Finding solutions to the problems that arose took some time, and the legislation was only accepted in July 1997, and came into force six months after that date.

All countries have developed the Guides for good hygiene practices, but in divergent ways. It is not clear how these developments should be pursued. In some countries the Standardisation Associations are involved, and in others these associations play only a minor role. Only the Netherlands has notified the Commission of a substantial number of Guides (20), more than the number of notifications from all other member states put together. The next section is devoted to a more detailed description of the problems surrounding implementation and enforcement in one country, the Netherlands.

8.5 Implementation of HACCP, with special reference to the Netherlands: A case study

8.5.1 Preparing for the inspection of Food Safety systems

The start
Even before the publication of the EU Directive 93/43 the Inspectorate for Health Protection in the Netherlands realised the impact this directive would have. A senior position was made available for a new staff member whose job would include both the introduction of food technology and implementation of HACCP in the industrial sector. It soon became clear that the implementation of HACCP was practically a full time job. A working group was formed, and the first step in developing the inspection of food safety systems was to gain knowledge about the system. A group of seven experts (including a biochemist, senior inspectors and a microbiologist) was sent to Campden & Chorleywood Food Research Association (UK) for an extended HACCP-workshop. On the basis of this workshop, and with the aid of Wageningen Agricultural University, a short course was developed for a further group of 13 food inspectors. In cooperation with representatives of industry, 7 factories with a high level of quality awareness were requested to undergo the first inspections. The inspectors were required to make a thorough study of the process of the company, and a theoretical HACCP plan was prepared for each company. When the actual HACCP-plans were studied, it became apparent that the inspectorate applied HACCP far more thoroughly than the factories. The businesses concerned learned a lot from this operation. The inspectorate learned that it was on the wrong track, but it also gained experience in audit techniques.

Building up knowledge and experience
After these first experiences the inspectorate continued to examine the internal organization of the inspection of food safety systems. In the meantime, however, a further five inspections were planned. The idea of first setting up an inspectorate plan was discarded, and the position of the inspectorate also became more clear: a food business should set up its own food safety plan and then be obliged to follow it. Only in a case where the inspector is convinced that the plan and its execution would not ensure food safety and the inspector can substantiate that (in court), would the inspectorate be able to propose further legal action. At this stage it also became clear that checking a large number of operations using checklists would not be an appropriate way to carry out inspection, especially not for the larger operations. It might be possible at a later stage to use checklists for checking on the starting condition, e.g. GMP, and elements of the HACCP plan. Checking the hazard analyses and selection of critical control points can never be done with simple checklists.

Just before the directive came into force the inspectorate performed a 'quick scan' at about 20 % of the larger factories (De Sitter & Feenstra 1996). Of the

300 factories scanned, 7 % said they were prepared for the requirements of the directive. Only a rough check was performed, and in general the inspector only partly agreed with the factories' own opinions. Two-thirds of the total number had started drawing up a food safety plan and made some progress with it. One-third had not done anything. Another important observation was that most factories did not use the hazard analyses. In most plans the selection of critical control points was done using already existing standards. Existing standards were evaluated and some became a CCP. However, such a system has no added value as it does not provide a way of enhancing food safety.

The transition phase
The results of the quick scan and the fact that most of the small and medium sized businesses were still busy developing the Guides of good hygiene practice made everybody realise that enforcement of the directive was not yet appropriate. In consultation with the representatives of interested parties it was decided that 1996 would be the year of transition. All businesses were expected to start or continue setting up their food safety system, and sector representatives in small and medium sized businesses also gained time to finish their Guides of good hygiene practice.

Meanwhile the inspectorate had time to address the problem of developing the system correctly, in particular the appropriate use of the risk analyses. In 1996 a limited number of thorough inspections was performed to test and improve the revised procedure. Improvements were made to the reporting of the inspection results and, for each of the 'Guides of good hygiene practice' issued, a project team of food inspectors was formed to develop the enforcement of the directive for that sector.

8.5.2 Practical approach

Large companies
At the end of 1996 the inspectorate performed another quick scan at 300 companies (De Sitter, 1997). The results indicated an improvement compared to the previous year, but still only 25 % said they were prepared. Most of the companies (85 %), however, were at least busy with HACCP, especially the larger businesses. There were also a number of companies which had not done anything. These companies would be subjected to the first enforcement action in 1997. It became apparent that the small industrial businesses would be the most difficult group. They require extra attention, but the inspectorate could not develop the system specially for them. Other ways to organise support for them have to be developed.

In 1997 the inspectorate started a project in the industrial sector. Each company is visited with the purpose of establishing whether that company is engaged in the process of developing a food safety system as required by the directive. As soon as imputable negligence concerning the requirement can be established, official action will follow. Progress will be recorded and the intention is to inspect all companies within a year. During these inspection visits, which take about half a day, attention is paid to the general hygiene conditions and the risk analyses, the first steps of the system. Only at later stages will inspectors look into the next steps of the system. In this way the inspectorate will increase the depth of the inspections. The inspectorate will also continue with thorough inspections on a regular basis. Some factories, which believe they are ready with the system, have already offered to undergo an inspection.

Small businesses
Most small food operators just want clear regulations, so they can put their energy into making and selling their product. Most businesses lack the capacity and knowledge to perform their own HACCP study. Although HACCP is a system, to get the best results, it has to be executed by the individual enterprise. The inspectorate is a strong supporter of the guides for good hygiene practice for small and medium sized businesses, and this system of guides has been used for nearly 10 years in the Netherlands. The existing guides have been adapted to include the requirements of the directive. There are now about 20 guides for good hygiene practice which are officially approved by the Ministry of Health.

These developments will be built upon by visiting all small and medium sized businesses to assess the application of the guides in each sector. Here, the first point of interest will be the use of the guide by the individual business. In the first place this involves acquiring the guide and making a start with it. In due course the depth of the inspections will increase and more rules and regulations of the guides will be enforced. The advantage of this approach is that the pace of the increment in depth will be adapted to the sector. It is expected that the organised representatives of the sector will play a role in providing instruction and information to the sector.

8.5.3 Hazard anlysis

The inspectorate found the level of application of hazard anlysis in the food safety plans by industry was generally low. Industry will have to be encouraged to use the instrument. The HACCP system (see Chapter 7) is directed towards food operators and is built up around the production of a product. In addition to the HACCP system the Codex Commission discusses the protocols for the system of 'risk analysis'. Risk analysis is built up around a particular risk and consists of the following steps: risk assessment (hazard identification, exposure assessment, hazard characterisation and risk characterisation), risk management and risk communication. The system of risk analysis is meant for all sectors, but especially to help governments to develop standards (Notermans et al. 1996). The term Food Safety Objectives is used in this respect. The results of the various risk analyses should be used by industry in their hazard analysis, and also by government to set the safety objectives for industry.

The discussion of the risk analysis system in the Codex Committee on Food Hygiene is directed towards the theoretical aspects of building up the system and is interesting for scientists but not for food business operators. The latter want to know what is safe, so in the mean time there should be practical assistance for the industry. Existing scientific knowledge should be translated into workable guidelines for industry. For that purpose the inspectorate has sought contact with the organised Food Industry of the Netherlands. A discussion platform on this subject will be created. It is not yet clear what direction this will take, but it is the intention of the inspectorate that all relevant matters can be discussed in that platform. Matters which are certain will be laid down and followed; matters which are still subject to discussion will be established. In this second case the platform will have to find ways of finding solutions to the problems: practical solutions for the short term and solid solutions for the long term. In this way fundamental discussion on the practical problems of hazard anlysis can be brought to an appropriate level. It is important to avoid repeating these discussions each time in the different production locations. A senior staff member has also been appointed to coordinate the work on risk analysis.

8.5.4 Certification

At the beginning of 1995 the first HACCP Certificate was granted to a company in the Netherlands by an accredited (ISO 9000) firm. There were, however, no agreements on the criteria. All firms were allowed to use their own criteria, which meant that certification had no value for the enforcement authority. Together with the Accreditation Council (Raad voor Accreditatie) in the Netherlands, an effort was made to come to prior harmonization of the criteria. Harmonization in retrospect, which is pursued in the Netherlands for the ISO-9000, is a laborious and difficult process. After more than year of many meetings, uniform criteria (CCvD, 1996) were issued, and all seven certification companies with authorisation for the food industry sector in the Netherlands, agreed to follow the certification scheme established by the 'Central Committee of Experts'.

One certification firm is now accredited for HACCP certification. More will follow soon. The enforcement authority hopes that harmonized criteria will lead to the issue of valuable and, above all, comparable certificates, which may be useful in the execution of their work. It remains to be seen whether the effort put into setting up the system has been worthwhile.

8.5.5 Conclusions

Hazard analysis is considered the most valuable part of the whole HACCP operation. When the food industry is capable of applying hazard analysis appropriately, we will have arrived at a situation where we can speak of increased food safety. However, the road will be long. Experts have not yet reached agreement about how to apply the system of risk analysis or how to use the results for hazard analysis of individual companies. The results of risk analyses are also important to governments, as they form the basis for the formulation of food safety objectives. The enforcement authority will play an important role in this process.

- If rules are enforced too strictly, resistance will be encountered, which could result in an attitude of non-cooperation, making the whole process even more difficult. In the darkest scenario the directive could become an empty ruling.
- If, however, the directive is not enforced strictly enough, businesses will not get the push they may need to make that difficult step forwards. HACCP is a difficult process, with a lot of consequences for operations within the business. Most businesses will need the external incentive to start with HACCP.

The enforcement authority has to apply the correct pressure on the market. At present the number of cases of food poisoning and food intoxication in the Netherlands is estimated at between 2 and 4 million per annum. Pro-active food safety systems for food businesses, like HACCP, will reduce this number. This will be partly due to lower infection levels in raw materials, partly due to less cross-contamination in the kitchen and partly due to the fact that the products consumed will have lower levels of infection and that fewer infected products will be consumed. In my opinion, procedures like those being adopted by the Netherlands Inspectorate for Health Protection will lead to the best results and will ensure that the EU Directive on the hygiene of foodstuffs indeed increases food safety in the Netherlands.

References

CCvD, 1996. Criteria for the assay of an operational HACCP system (in Dutch; English version in preparation). Centraal College van Deskundigen, c/o VAI, The Hague, the Netherlands.

Codex Alimentarius Commission, 1993. Guidelines for the Application of the Hazard Analysis Critical Control Point System. CAC/GL 18-1993 Supplement One to Volume One, General Requirements Second Edition, Section 7.5, 95-103.

European Commission, 1995. Report of the Group of Independent Experts on Legislative and Administrative Simplification. Com(95) 288/2 final, Catalogue number CB-CO-95-334-EN-C, Office for Official Publications of the European Communities, Luxembourg.

European Commission, 1997. The General Principles of Food Law in the European Union. Commission Green Paper Com (97) 176.

European Union Council Directive 93/43/EEC, 1993. The Hygiene of Foodstuffs. Official Journal of the European Communities, 36 L 175 (19 July 1993), 1-11.

European Union Council Directive 89/397/EEC, 1989. The Official Control of Foodstuffs. Official Journal of the European Communities 32 L 186 (30 June 1989), 23-26.

De Sitter, H. & Y. Feenstra, 1996. Seven percent of businesses have an operational HACCP plan. Voedingsmiddelentechnologie 6, 16-18 (in Dutch).

De Sitter, H., 1997. A quarter of all factories claim to be ready. Voedingsmiddelentechnologie 9, 11-13 (in Dutch).

FLEP, 1996. FLEP Bulletin on the HACCP Symposium, October, 26-27 1995. Food Law Enforcement Practitioners, Rijswijk, the Netherlands.

Middlekauf, R.D. & Ph. Shubik, 1989. International Food Regulations Handbook; Policy, Science, Law. 562 p. Marcel Dekker, New York.

Notermans, S., G.C. Mead & J.L. Jouve, 1996. Food products and consumer protection: a conceptual approach and a glossary of terms. International Journal of Food Microbiology, 30, 175-185.

Snijders, G.M.F., 1987. Produktveiligheid en aansprakelijkheid. Deventer, the Netherlands. 323 p.

9 Summary and future prospects

W.M.F. Jongen and M.T.G. Meulenberg

The many changes in the market for new food products call for a repositioning of existing food production systems and raise the question whether the concepts currently used can survive the challenges of the future. What we see is that apart from market saturation, a number of other developments have a large influence on market conditions. Generally consumers are becoming better educated and more demanding. They are also becoming less predictable in their purchase behaviour, eat more outside the home and are more conscious about health-related aspects. As a result there is a continuous need for new products and a more differentiated food product assortment. Related to this development product life cycles become shorter, and efficiency and flexibility of food production systems become even more important.

In this book many aspects relevant to innovation in food production systems are addressed. Each contribution to the book draws a clear picture of the current situation and future developments in its own domain. However, for successful planning and implementation of product and process innovation it is no longer sufficient to base this on a collection of individual elements. The complexity of the issue of product innovation and product acceptance requires an integrated approach. In fact, as may have become obvious from the previous chapters, there is a need for new concepts in which the various disciplinary approaches are combined into one integrated, techno-managerial approach. Technological inventions, such as those in the field of biotechnology, have to be translated into products which are attractive to consumers. Conversely, changing consumer values and habits will stimulate innovation in food production technologies which will in turn lead to the production of new products. This interdependency between consumers' wants and needs on the one hand and technologies and research on the other has been recognised by many food companies, but is not yet systematically implemented. The interrelationship between technology and consumer behaviour should receive more attention in the modelling of food product innovation.

An additional point which we stress in this book is that there is a need for a chain-oriented approach to product innovation which considers the whole food supply chain from breeders, through processing up to the consumer in one integrating concept. Traditionally, food supply chains have been characterised by two distinct features: 1. the one-way communication along the chain from producers of raw materials to the users of end products (the consumers) and 2. the poor understanding of the concept of product quality. Quality was and in a number of cases still is, predominantly based on technical criteria and producers have tended to focus in particular on costs and productivity. Actors in the food supply chain have this approach to quality in common. In addition, each actor in a food supply chain will use specific quality criteria such as homogeneity and storability of raw materials at industrial level and ease of handling at the retail level. Sometimes these specific criteria can conflict with end product quality. As a result there is a need for a unified concept of product quality and acceptance throughout the production chain. It requires a chain reversal in which the consumer has become the focal point. Food production systems of the future can no longer be solely production driven but should be characterised as primarily consumer driven.

The contributions to the book also underline the importance of the relationship between the food production system and its environment. This is not only the case with respect to the food consumer, the focal point of the environment of every food production system, but also to the political and legal environment, the facilitating services and new technologies becoming available to a food production system. This environment deserves continuous monitoring by food production systems, if they are to play a leading role in product innovation.

The content of the book suggests that progress in the research of food product innovation should be made not only by further elaborating the topics covered in the various chapters but also by modelling the interdependency between technology and managerial (including marketing) elements of food product innovation. Consumer perception and preferences are the starting point for such a model of food product innovation. How are changes in consumer preferences and market economics translated into the necessary technological developments? A series of studies on future consumer issues has recently been carried out for the Dutch National Agricultural Research Council (NRLO). Meulenberg (1996) has analysed the socio-economic developments in the food market and translated them into consumer categories. Jongen et al. (1997) have used these categories and developed a model for translation of consumer preferences and perceptions into desired technological developments. The model is based on a systems analysis which uses the consumer as the focal point. A stepwise approach is followed in which seven successive steps are distinguished. These steps seem to form a useful framework for an integral model of product innovation in food production systems, and can be summarized as follows:

I. *Thorough analysis of the socio-economic developments in specified markets*

II. *Translation of consumer preferences and perceptions into consumer categories*

III. *Translation of consumer categories into product assortments*

IV. *Grouping of product assortments in product groups at different stages of the food supply chain*

V. *Identification of processing technologies relevant for specified product groups*

VI. *Analysis of state of the art in relevant processing technologies*

VII. *Matching specified state-of-the-art processing technologies with future needs*

Following this model the study showed that successful linking of Research & Development programmes within companies to market dynamics requires a number of new technological developments to be implemented. In connection with this model we also offer some conclusions and suggestions:

1. *The increased competitiveness in the market and the observed changes in purchase behaviour of the consumer require 'dedicated' production systems which follow market dynamics more closely.*

    There must be a breakthrough in thinking from craft to 'design for manufacture', making use of information technology and computer management systems.

    Biotechnology must be developed further, to modify and/or add desired properties to raw materials and ingredients.

    More fundamental research must be done on structure-function relations with respect to product design technology and fabricated foods.

2. *The increased complexity of the issue of product quality and acceptance, and the costs associated with product innovation necessitate structured approaches and integration of marketing and R&D for efficient use of knowledge and labour.*

    Systems such as Quality Function Deployment (QFD) and Effective Consumer Response (ECR) will be of great importance and should be developed and evaluated so that they are more suitable for use in food product innovation

    The relation between Food and Health with a focus on the so-called non-nutritive components must requires further research.

3. *Integration of knowledge from different research areas such as sensor technology and materials technology will be necessary in order to be able to meet future consumer demands for product quality.*

    Developments in material sciences and in the field of (bio)sensors should be explored for application in food production systems, e.g. in new packaging concepts.

It is obvious that our knowledge about the relationships between market changes, consumer behaviour, food products and processing technologies is still by and large insufficient. Nevertheless the proposed stepwise approach seems promising and deserves further attention in order to transform it into a useful approach to strategic investment in product innovation, in particular in future technologies and R&D programmes.

References:

Jongen, W.M.F., A.R. Linnemann, G. Meerdink & R. Verkerk (1997). Consumentgestuurde Technologie-ontwikkeling; Van wenselijkheid naar haalbaarheid en doeltreffendheid bij productie van levensmiddelen. NRLO-rapport no. 97/22, September 1997, Nationale Raad voor Landbouwkundig Onderzoek, Den Haag, 40 pp.

Meulenberg, M.T.G. (1996). De levensmiddelenconsument van de toekomst. In: NRLO-Rapport, no. 96/4, November 1996, Nationale Raad voor Landbouwkundig Onderzoek, Den Haag, pp. 1 - 31.

Key-words

Key-words